Wakefield Press

Where Shadows Have Fallen

Adrian Mitchell, formerly at the University of Sydney, has since then busied himself in writing a number of books all published through Wakefield Press. These have an Australian reference, and they are all based in historical fact. They are all engaging stories of people and events that should be better known than they are. His *Plein Airs and Graces: the life and times of George Collingridge* was short-listed for the Prime Minister's Literary Award.

Also by Adrian Mitchell

Drawing the Crow

Dampier's Monkey

Plein Airs and Graces

The Prohlot

From Corner to Corner

The Beachcomber's Wife

Peat Island

Where Shadows Have Fallen

The descent of Henry Kendall

ADRIAN MITCHELL

Wakefield Press
16 Rose Street
Mile End
South Australia 5031
www.wakefieldpress.com.au

First published 2020

Cover designed by Stacey Zass
Edited by Penelope Curtin
Typeset by Michael Deves, Wakefield Press

ISBN 978 1 74305 748 3

A catalogue record for this book is available from the National Library of Australia

Wakefield Press thanks Coriole Vineyards for continued support

'My past will not bear analysis and I always dread its being raked up.'

Henry Kendall
(to Henry Halloran, 2 October 1878)

Contents

Prologue		1
Chapter 1	Double Dealings	10
Chapter 2	The Sins of the Fathers	26
Chapter 3	Very Much Given to Indulge in Spirits	49
Chapter 4	Thirty Pieces of Silver	64
Chapter 5	There Goes Mad Harry	81
Chapter 6	The Twofold Life	98
Chapter 7	The Encircling Gloom	119
Chapter 8	Not in his Right Mind	139
Chapter 9	A Sign of Bad Blood	152
Chapter 10	A Terrible Agent for Evil	168
Chapter 11	The After Life	190
Notes		204
Index		221

Prologue

When Henry Kendall, the leading Australian poet of his day, died in Sydney in 1882, obituaries appeared in papers and journals so promptly that they must have been prepared well in advance of that unhappy event. Not all of them though. Those that appeared a day or two later may be assumed to have been freshly composed, even though Kendall's final illness had been widely known. These articles expressed the universal regret, with genuine compassion.

One of the most extensive obituaries appeared in the *Freeman's Journal*, a journal to which Kendall had often sent his material and where he preferred to publish. Francis Donohue, who wrote the piece, identified succinctly the problem he and all others faced: 'It is pleasanter to review our poet's works than his life', he wrote.[1] Like so many reviewers called upon to sum up Kendall's achievement, however, Donohue felt he could not wholly avoid a few remarks on the life of 'our first of singers'. Candour was called for at this moment; posterity should know it all.

Yet, like everyone else, he also felt called upon to be circumspect. Common decency required no less. Kendall would have wanted honesty, but his life had presented an unedifying spectacle; and, while the obituaries did not exactly evade that fact, Donohue for one had no wish to tear down the poet's character. The poetry was what mattered, more than the man. Besides, so the memorialists said, everyone knew the essential facts of Kendall's delinquencies and it was unseemly to lay them out again.

In the modern era, his story is not so well known, or only in the broadest terms, with little detail of the delinquencies hidden away in his correspondence, and in occasional newspaper reports from those years.

Likewise, the offences committed by his grandfathers, his father and mother, and his identical twin brother. He was not proud of his personal and family history, and quite understandably concealed as much of it as he could. Besides, he was by temperament a private man – yet he hinted to a close friend that he had good reason to be guarded about himself and his connections.

While it is true that Kendall's significance for us rests on the poetry he wrote, we have quite properly an interest in the man who wrote the poems, and the kinds of experience that informed them, an interest in what is now sometimes called the 'back story'. We are no longer as well acquainted with Kendall's history as his contemporaries were. These days too we like to check whether the portrait that has percolated down through the years is altogether accurate. As will be seen in what follows, much that has been said of Kendall has been actually misleading. Which is not to denigrate the poems.

Early versions of Kendall's life emphasised that he was essentially a child of nature. He was said to have learned the ways of the forests and mountain creeks at an early age and continued to commune with what he felt was the spirit of Australia. From the outset of his poetic career, he was proud that he was native-born – this at a time when the majority of the population still spoke with English and Scottish and Irish accents. He signed his early poems 'Henry Kendall, N.A.P.', Native Australian Poet. And he believed in Australia's future, though he was not very clear about just what that should be. He had not so much an actual vision as the *idea* of a vision – of Australia, of nature, of himself as the agent for the poetic vision.

In this, he was less an apprentice to, say, William Wordsworth, and more of the transcendentalist school of Ralph Waldo Emerson – neither of them being particularly Australian. He had clearly read and absorbed Emerson's essay 'The poet', in which case it was no modest ambition to see himself in that role, the poet as seer, the one who discovers and comprehends the deep meaning of nature, the relation between form and soul, and through which 'the visible becomes everlastingly new – everlastingly suggestive', as he wrote in a letter in 1865.[2]

But almost immediately a deep and abiding question pushes itself forward. How did Kendall know what he knew? How, given that he had almost no formal schooling, and, given that his parents were not at all wealthy and that their domestic arrangements were unstable, how did he access the range of books and the range of writers suggested throughout his poetry? Where did his extensive vocabulary come from? For he was far more articulate than say either Lawson or Paterson.

We are told persistently (including by Kendall himself) that he was educated by his scholarly father; and prompted to poetry by his mother, who may or may not have published a small volume of poems. If that were so, such a work has never surfaced; and if that is a story, we are not sure whose story it was. But Matilda Kendall – her baptismal name was Melinda, although within the family she was known as Matilda – was a dab hand at colouring the truth. Or gilding the lily, whichever metaphor is preferable.

Throughout the generations the Kendalls were linked to schoolteaching. Henry's grandfather, Thomas, had been both a tutor and a teacher in England, and his role in the mission settlement at New Zealand's Bay of Islands was to teach English to the Maori children there, as well as to establish a Maori grammar by which subsequent waves of missionaries and settlers were enabled to understand and communicate with the local people. Yet Thomas Kendall was not himself an educated man. On the contrary, one prominent reviewer of Judith Binney's account of him (*Legacy of Guilt*, 1968) summed him up quite bluntly as ignorant and ill-read.[3]

Henry's father, Basil, was educated by Thomas, and that would imply that his schooling cannot have been particularly extensive. Basil, in his turn, was from time to time a teacher, whenever he was not attending to sheep; and even Henry Kendall himself is said at the end of his life to have taught a class on the mid-North Coast of New South Wales, at Camden Haven. They all seem to have had enough confidence in themselves, but whatever they accomplished as schoolmasters could have been at no very advanced level.

By report, Matilda Kendall had more self-confidence than most, as well as more opportunity than the others, and she too ran a little school in her home in Sydney's Newtown, and then St Peters, and down in the Illawarra. None of this is evidence of scholarship, however, or deep learning. Rather, it testifies to necessity. This was no more than a way to make a bare living.

On the evidence of his acquaintance and fellow poet P.J. Holdsworth, Henry Kendall was an omnivorous reader as a boy, though how and where he managed to lay his hands on books remains a mystery.[4] Neither he nor his family could move about with boxes and boxes of books – their circumstances were too straitened for that. When Basil died, impoverished, whatever he owned was sold up. Henry was so poor in Melbourne that anything of that kind would have been sold or pawned; likewise, when he was left behind in Newcastle, he had no possessions with him. He had a few favoured books at Camden Haven,[5] but he was not a bookish man. In the short interval when he had access to Lionel Michael's library in Grafton, he read as much as he could, even while walking along the street. He was hungry for words.

He seems to have had a good memory for whatever he read, sometimes too much so. He acknowledged that himself, in the Prefatory Sonnets to his second volume, *Leaves from Australian Forests* (1869), when he admitted that in his poems he sometimes unwittingly echoed the lines of others,

> … *notes that unto other lyres belong:*
> *Stray echoes from the elder sons of Song.*

He acknowledged that he was haunted by the words and music of the great poets of the past, and carried the wonder of their verses with him, just as the scents of the forest are carried with one and on one. That was an image he particularly liked – he had used it on another occasion in a letter to Charles Harpur, in which he paid tribute to his mentor and conceded he may have echoed him somewhat: 'For we cannot leave a cedar grove without carrying away some of the fragrance [from] the perfume-scattering leaves of those beautiful trees'.[6]

And sometimes, like Robert Schumann, he unwittingly echoed himself. His head was filled with poetry, and in particular the sound of it, the lilt, the flow of the verse. That is what he remembered. His particular strength was in poetry as song, lyric ('our first of singers'), and not so much in poetic meaning or insight. As it turns out, that was also his weakness. He delighted in the effects he could generate through double rhymes and internal rhymes, he was given to 'obtrusive, meaningless and inexorable alliteration, and trite and flabby epithets', to too much ornamentation.[7] He lacked discipline and economy, and let his lines run on, so that his original inspiration was dissipated in a welter of words.[8] On the other hand, he sometimes found dazzling images, and those are what we read him for.

Vivian Smith very astutely remarked that Kendall lacked self-confidence, and it was this that made him over-prolific. 'He seems to have been of a depressive temperament, given to self-doubts and deep inner uncertainties.'[9] He rarely held on to a composed set of verses. He published as soon as possible, which suggests little in the way of carefully considered reflection – an approach consistent with his way of inspiration, the discovered view of some poetic landscape, some inviting view up along a creek, some contained vista, some inveigling promise of a further and more glorious precinct, 'a beauty out of sight'. In particular, he saw the hint of that promise in terms of a patch of dazzling light within or beyond the shade, virtually a halo. That signified to him vestiges of the spiritually uplifting.

By way of contrast, there is at the same time a constant refrain in his poetry of the vision lost, or alienated, or inaccessible, because it was by its very nature beyond this world; or, subsequent to the deep unhappiness of his years in Melbourne, and the shadow upon his soul which followed – the Shadow of 1872 as he termed it – he convinced himself of his unworthiness to approach any such transcendent, that is, visionary, realm. That is what Vivian Smith meant by Kendall's depressive temperament. He was a despondent poet: in some sense he had always been drawn to the mournful and melancholy. His vocabulary lent itself to the expression of moaning and wailing, the weeping and failing. Even such a nominally bright and enticing poem as his well-known 'Bell Birds' ends with a remembrance of 'the pain of my losses'. He could never forget that – it was ingrained in him.

While the details of his family history, and more particularly his own, give very real grounds for Kendall's despondency, the orientation towards complaint is nevertheless of long standing in the poetic tradition. The troubadour's complaint to the woman he would woo, the shepherd's complaint to a less elevated Phyllis or whomever, the customary lamentation of the poet who has not been regarded, and whom the world will never discover ... these are all variants of that same convention of sadness, the sadness of humanity, which is said always to be an element of the beautiful. That too was an aspect of Kendall's brief. It was part and parcel of what he understood to be poetic. In his case, though, it became persistent to the point of unrelenting. Certainly, habitual.

The actual story of Kendall, and the Kendalls, was initially established by the scholarly researches of Bishop T.T. Reed. His DLitt thesis 'The Life and Poetical Works of Henry Kendall' (Adelaide, 1953) is the basis for the critical commentary that has followed. I am indebted to that work, just as is everyone else who writes about Kendall. Reed did not have the benefit, nor the burden, of Judith Binney's *The Legacy of Guilt* (1968), her conscientious study of Henry Kendall's grandfather, the Rev. Thomas Kendall, with its central proposition of the moral dilemma of a man of Calvinist principles seeking to find his way, but losing it by that very effort. Her book is a ready source of information about Henry's paternal grandfather.

Reed had a more complete training in religious history and theology than most and was professionally well placed to comment on Henry Kendall's religious views. He remarked, apropos those poems which are specifically about religious matters:

> Kendall's Biblical narrative poetry is dull. It lacks an appreciation of religious truths as well as sharing in the defects of his Australian narrative verse ... [They] appear rather poetical exercises than the outbursts of deep religious fervour, informed with an understanding of the doctrines and truths which underlie the stories and themes involved.[10]

In his judgement – and he had the particular qualifications to make that judgement – Kendall had no more than a loosely held faith. Nor should that be surprising. The Kendall family were conventional in their religious attachment, mostly to the Church of England, although some were stalwart members of a Wesleyan chapel or a Baptist tabernacle. The main point is that they were steady, loyal and self-effacing adherents to whichever denomination they chose.

Yet, because of Judith Binney's argument about the intrinsic Calvinist dilemma in which Thomas Kendall found himself, and lost himself, subsequent critics and scholars have taken up those terms to read a corresponding guilt and obsession into the temperament of the grandson – not least, the next most important commentator on Henry Kendall, Michael Ackland (*Henry Kendall: The Man and the Myths*, 1995). Ackland's is a comprehensive survey of everything to do with Henry Kendall, and a conscientious application of Binney's analysis to his poetic career.

When Binney's work was republished posthumously in 2005, it was re-reviewed, and much less kindly than the first time round. Experts in the field found that, not only was her writing stodgy, but her understanding of Maori culture was limited. They pointed out how seriously limited

Thomas Kendall's understanding was too, grotesquely so. The application of Calvinist doctrines to his situation was not exactly beside the point, but it left much of what happened in the Bay of Islands mission settlement uninspected, and misunderstood.

Ackland lacked the benefit of these revised views, but what he might have considered is the way by which Henry Kendall alone, of all his siblings and indeed all his father's generation too, and their children, his cousins, inherited this Calvinist guilt. Indeed, Ackland might have considered whether Calvinism is something that can be inherited, as though a set of beliefs is genetic. Kendall's disposition to gloom came from somewhere, but as the pages that follow show, there were any number of experiences to contribute to this, quite independent of his grandfather's religious convictions. And if the grandfather contributed in some dominant way to the making of Henry Kendall, then where on earth did Kendall's self-effacement come from? For the Rev. Thomas Kendall was no shrinking violet.

I have therefore taken a different line from Ackland to examine who Henry Kendall was, and what tempered his verse, though I acknowledge here the very great benefit I have derived from the extent of Ackland's work, and the much that I learned from it. The remaining work to be acknowledged is Michael Wilding's *Wild Bleak Bohemia: Marcus Clark, Adam Lindsay Gordon and Henry Kendall. A documentary* (2014), which assembles virtually all the reliable evidence about Henry Kendall, most particularly of his time in those all-important years in Melbourne. Wilding's is a resource I have turned to whenever I could not set my hands on the original material. If there are errors in the material quoted from either of them, and indeed from Reed as well, then those are faults of my own transcription. Should the text should be fault-free, at least insofar as transcribing passages is concerned, then that will be because of the sharp scrutiny of my ever-reliable copy editor, Penelope Curtin.

If Kendall were not a poet of some standing, there would be little point in gathering together a reading of his character and his temperament. His life did matter after all, though in his darker moments he must have had his doubts. The other remarkable figure in his story is his wife Charlotte, steady, admirable, reassuring, and forgiving. Some of his most moving poems acknowledge her loyalty, poems (apart from the Dedication to her of his second volume, *Leaves from Australian Forests*, a poem which movingly presents her, 'my bright, best friend', with a gift sustained by love, and in which more poignantly he acknowledges *her* dedication) written towards the end of his life, especially the poem 'Araluen' (1879). There he reaches out to her in a heartfelt gesture of reconciliation, remembering together the loss of their first-born child:

> *You that sit and sob beside me – you, upon whose golden head*
> *Many rains of many sorrows have from day to day been shed;*
>
> ...
>
> *Let me feel that you are near me, lay your hand within mine own;*
> *You are all I have to live for, now that we are left alone.*

That had been the most distressing experience of his life. He had spent the previous 10 years accusing himself, and tormenting himself, and evading it too, in the bottom of a bottle. For this poem, he did not have to analyse the circumstances all over again; he had only to meet the emotion of it, an emotion he spent all his career articulating, of loss, and the need for forgiveness, a way to forgive himself.

'Araluen' is not profound, but it is profoundly moving. Its emotional register derives entirely from the honesty of a simple gesture. In reaching out to Charlotte, he had made his peace with her again, reconciled himself to her, and acknowledged her steady loyalty to him through all the grief he had brought upon them, not just at that time but in the years subsequent to the Shadow of 1872, and their separation. He wrote at the very end of his life to Henry Parkes, acknowledging her utter worthiness:

> It will please you to know that in helping me you have brought the beautiful light of happiness to a face of one of the noblest women that ever lived. My wife will hold your name in reverence; and the reverence of a spirit that has been tested by fire and not found wanting is worth having.[11]

There could be no resolution. His grief, their grieving, was ongoing. What Kendall mastered was a poetry of resignation, of the acceptance of limitations. A poetry, so to speak, of modified rapture – quietly brave, without maudlin sentiment or false bravado. A poetry we can admire in its place:

I never can reach you, to hear the sweet voice
So full with the music of fountains!
Oh! when will you meet with that soul of your choice,
Who will lead you down here from the mountains?
A lyre-bird lit on a shimmering space;
It dazzled mine eyes and I turned from the place,
And wept in the dark for a glorious face,
And a hand with the Harp of Australia!

* * *

I have had help and assistance from many quarters. The special collections librarians in the National Library of Australia, the State Library of New South Wales, the Fisher Library of the University of Sydney, the Barr Smith Library at the University of Adelaide, and of the local studies collections at Ku-ring-gai Library, Hornsby Library, Gosford Library, Ulladulla Library, Milton Library, Port Macquarie Library, Laurieton Library and Grafton (Sir Earle Page) Library all demystified the arcana of their diverse shelving systems. The volunteers at Henry Kendall Cottage, Gosford, were likewise readily helpful.

I have both enjoyed conversations with Neville Adams about his personal recollections of Fairy Meadow and appreciated his directions to the special attractions of its environs. I especially thank my colleague Geraldine Barnes for reading the draft chapters as they spilled out, and for her elegantly expressed misgivings wherever those were called for. Likewise, to my wife Maureen, who started me out on this project, took photographs of everything, accompanied me through cemeteries and forests to the north and south of Sydney, and not least delivered buttered hot cross buns in and out of season.

Rob Browne, an indirect descendant of the Kendalls, has been the worried recipient of many snippets about his confusing forebears. I hope his anxieties are allayed when he brings himself to read these pages.

1

Double Dealings

Henry Kendall's immediate forebears came from what, in social terms, might well be called poles apart. One of his progenitors was a disgraced Irish-born soldier, court-martialled for desertion just as the war between America and Canada was declared. The actual dereliction of duty took place before the ratification of all that skirmishing that had been taking place on Lake Ontario, in the forests of Quebec, and in upstate New York. The British had been every bit as provocative as the Americans. They had forcibly boarded American ships in search of sailors who had absconded from the Royal Navy – they needed to replenish their manpower for their ongoing sea battles with Napoleon.

The other progenitor was a former Lincolnshire schoolteacher who had heeded the call and answered Samuel Marsden's ambition to bring the gospel to the famously cannibalistic savages of New Zealand.

These two incongruent branches of Henry Kendall's ancestry converged in Sydney in 1814, only to diverge almost immediately. No sooner was Patrick McNally brought out of the holds of the *Surrey* than he was on his way to Pitt Town, one of the five recently established Macquarie towns, and close to the immediate supervision of the truculent Samuel Marsden, Senior Chaplain of New South Wales, no lover of convicts and not of the Catholic Irish either. Whereas Thomas Kendall, having made himself known to Marsden, his immediate superior, was almost immediately sent on to reconnoitre a suitable base for missionary operations in New Zealand's Bay of Islands.

Patrick McNally was aged 17 when he tired of the soggy windswept fields of Roscommon, and the drudgery of tenant farming. There were other worlds in which to make a life. The natural beauty of his county was not in question, but the substantial grand houses that were being built on overwhelmingly large estates were an aggravating reminder to the impoverished labouring classes – the peat cutters, the fence menders, the potato pickers and the wagon drivers – of the Penal Laws, which for two hundred years had entrenched the privileges of the Protestant ascendancy. The McNallys were amongst those who were never going to make much of themselves.

Not that Patrick McNally, nor County Roscommon for that matter, was especially restive. This was a precinct of Ireland well beyond the pale, and Cromwell had left it alone in the seventeenth century. It was not wealthy enough to be of interest to Old Ironsides; and being for the most part a quiet county and out of the way, Catholics had found comparative security there. At the same time, it was more loyal to William III than a good many other counties. That was consistent with the intricate political shifts and balances of the times. A statue of King Billy with a suitably respectful inscription had long stood in a park at Boyle. When Patrick eventually had children, the first two were named William and Mary.

On the other hand, the main events of the United Irishmen Rebellion of 1798, just previous to Patrick McNally's enlisting, had taken place a little to the north of County Roscommon, and various uprisings continued all about it. It would have been extraordinary if the heady sentiments of liberty had not touched the community at large, especially after the ruthless suppression of that incautious breach of the peace.

When the famine came, when the potato crops rotted in their raised 'lazy beds' in the boggy fields, Roscommon lost disproportionately more of its population than anywhere else. For those who survived, widespread unemployment and dispossession followed, and the general sentiment changed; but Patrick McNally was long gone by then.

With many other young men in much the same circumstances as himself, he enlisted in an Irish regiment, the Prince Regent's County of Dublin Regiment of Foot, raised in 1804 and one constituent of what was more widely known as the 100th. While that regiment was established because of the growing menace posed by Napoleon, it suited the interests of the British to remove potential troublemakers from the areas of need; it also suited its requirements for an increased military presence in their territories in the New World. This was just 10 years after the British parliament had reversed a prohibition against the Irish serving in the armed forces, a different matter entirely from forbidding them to own a rifle.

It was also a better strategy to have relatively untested troops in America rather than in Europe, where Napoleon was making significant threats towards Britain, bringing together a vast army with the undisguised intention of crossing the Channel.

In next to no time at all, Patrick McNally was off across the Atlantic, to join other British forces in defending the Canadas against increasingly serious incursions, initially border raids, by troops both regular and irregular from the headstrong ambitious young nation to their south – and incidentally, the sponsor, along with France, of the political ideals that had given rise to the uprising of the Society of United Irishmen.

Just exactly when McNally enlisted and just when he embarked, is not known. The initial contingent from his regiment went to Nova Scotia, Canada, in October 1805, at the very time of Nelson's victory at Trafalgar. If Patrick McNally were among those, then he would have had a hard time of it. They sailed into early winter storms, and one-half of them drowned off the coast of Newfoundland when their transport ship was wrecked. Perhaps he was a survivor, or perhaps he was one of those who travelled later, and more safely. Henry Kendall's early biographer, however, Mrs Agnes Hamilton-Grey – more a hagiographer than a biographer – romanticised that McNally had seen service in the Peninsular War and was present at the death of Sir John Moore.[1] Not only that, he had turned the sod to bury his General. This on the ramparts at the dead of night, according to Charles Wolfe's famous poem, digging out the clods with his bayonet ('We buried him darkly at dead of night …').

There are complications with that claim to fame. For according to Kendall family lore, Patrick McNally's first child Mary was born in Canada in 1807. That is where the McNallys were, not in Spain but on the opposite side of the Atlantic. Sir John was buried in January 1809. If Patrick McNally did join the fighting in the Peninsular War, it could not have been before the commencement of hostilities in 1807; and Sir John did not take up his command there until 1808. Private McNally could not have been in two theatres of war at the same time. Nor could his wife have been on both sides of the Atlantic while she was giving birth. Either Mrs Hamilton-Grey was wrong in her account – and critics have discerned that she was in error about many matters of detail, and lacked critical judgement – or the family record was astray. It is of course possible that both are at fault.

The story grows murkier. Patrick is said to have married his wife Judith, née Kilfroy, or McDermott, or Kilfroy McDermott, in Canada in 1808; that is, after Mary was born, and when he had just attained his majority (which detail may have been a determining factor in their domestic arrangements). Their son William was born, likewise in Canada, in 1810, which is when Patrick deserted his post. If Patrick had married before he left Ireland, for Kilfroy was a name known in Roscommon, then Judith would have had to follow him to perhaps the Iberian Peninsula (unlikely, given the military situation there, but not impossible), and then to Canada. If they were not married at the time, it would have been that much more difficult for her to accompany him to his various postings. Difficult to establish herself as separate from those other unattached women, the camp followers who went along with the licentious soldiery. Womenfolk did follow their soldiers, along with the general baggage. In some engagements they might carry water out into the field of battle. In the garrison they did the laundry, and there are even records of their making the soldiers' beds and sweeping out their tents, as well as tending the wounded. Florence Nightingale was far from being the only woman present at Crimea 40 years later.

Whatever the case, there is no disputing the military evidence recorded at a General Court Martial held at Chambly, Quebec, 21 October 1812. Private Patrick McNally was found guilty of having deserted his regiment on or about the month of February 1810; that is, at the time of the birth of his son. And he had been lying low for the intervening two years, keeping out of the way of the authorities.

The British units were the hard core of the Canadian defences. The 100th served initially as the garrison for Quebec City; they were later used as marines in an attack on Sackets Harbour on Lake Ontario. They were scheduled to transfer to Halifax, but with a heightening of hostilities, McNally's regiment was assigned instead to Fort Chambly, on the main route along the Richelieu River, the waterway south from the St Lawrence and into upstate New York. The commander of the British forces, General Brock, thought highly of the 100th. He reported them to be robust, active and very handsome – but he also seemed to think they were mainly from Northern Ireland, and Protestant.[2] If that were the case, then why would the regiment be renamed in 1813 the Prince Regent's County of Dublin Regiment?

One might imagine that the fort itself was a safe enough place, but it would have been another matter altogether to be patrolling the heavy forests, where at any moment they might stumble across an American raiding party led by Indian guides. James Fenimore Cooper, an almost exact contemporary of Patrick McNally, wrote again and again in his Leatherstocking novels of these dangerous buckskin warriors gliding silently between the trees, much less visible than the redcoats with their clumsy long rifles.

Not that the Americans had an exclusive tactical advantage in this respect. The British used Indian scouts too, and their ally the formidable Shawnee chief Tecumseh is still remembered for his part in the successful attack on Detroit, leading 600 warriors and terrifying the American defenders, to the extent that they surrendered without a fight. The warhawks in Washington had seriously underestimated the resistance the Canadians would offer, as they had likewise forgotten that a significant population had left America at the time of the War of Independence and relocated in the Maritime provinces and the Canadas. These were known as the United Empire Loyalists, although that did not necessarily translate into a deep attachment to the British. They had chosen to remove themselves from the zone of conflict, or so they had thought. They were not likely to rise up to join the republicans, as was presumed. It was much the same mistake as had been made by Wolfe Tone in Ireland, in 1798. Not everyone was a radical at heart.

For a young spalpeen from the fields of Roscommon, military glory was less an attraction than his sweetheart Judith Kilfroy, perhaps by now his wife, undoubtedly the mother of his two children. He had more immediately pressing responsibilities than defending the realm. This was not a good time to be brought to account though, as the military antagonism between the two sides had become more and more intense. The Canadians – with the 100th right in the thick of the fighting – captured two United States ships which had sailed across the border and up the Richelieu River. The fact that those had been trespassing did not seem to have embarrassed Washington; they were infuriated at having lost their vessels to the Canadians and that is what gave rise to President Madison's declaration. It was now an actual war.

McNally was fortunate. British resolve had hardened with the death of their hero, General Brock, at Queenston Heights, near Niagara Falls, shot by a marksman (and according to legend, a Kentucky sharpshooter, a very Davy Crockett). That calamity took place just one week before McNally's court martial, and the military was in no mood for clemency. One soldier who was arraigned for desertion at the same trial was sentenced to 800 lashes 'inflicted in the usual manner'. He would not have been much use to anybody after that.

For his part – or rather, his absence from it – Patrick McNally was sentenced to be transported as a felon for life, together with a fellow deserter. He was returned to Quebec, the most securely fortified town in Canada at that time, a precaution perhaps, given that the war with the Americans still had to run its course, and held there until he could be sent on to England. It was not uncommon to brand deserters with the letter D.[3]

In fairly short order he was transferred on to England, and there awaited a convict transport ship. His wife and children followed him back across the stormy Atlantic, and they too waited on the outcome. There, in the following months, and in such meagre circumstances as they could manage, Judith gave birth to her third child, Eliza, a child also conceived in Canada.

McNally's young family were permitted to travel to Australia at the same time as he was, though in a separate vessel. He was kept below deck on the *Surrey*,[4] while she and the children were given free passage aboard the *Broxbornebury* (sometimes spelled Broxbournebury).

Judith travelled in estimable company despite being unlikely to have interacted with the likes of Sir John Jamison and Judge Jeffrey Hart Bent. She would have been a little likelier to make the acquaintance of Mary Greenway and her three sons, who were on their way to join Mary's husband Francis, the convict architect.

Also aboard were 120 female convicts, some 40 of whom had been rescued from the Cape Verde islands, where they had been stranded for about a year, left there by an American privateer who had seized their original transport ship and taken it to New York as a prize of war.

When they were rescued, the women were reported to have been all but naked, and starving. They were carried back to Portsmouth Harbour and transferred to a hulk until the *Broxbornebury* was ready to take them to their original destination. As convicted felons, they were not permitted to set foot on British soil, which in turn suggests that Patrick McNally would have been subject to the same harsh practice – held on a hulk until the *Surrey* was fully provisioned.

The ships sailed in a convoy of 13, an inauspicious number, on 22 February 1814. Quite early in the voyage, in a heavy gale, the *Broxbornebury* separated from the fleet. Months later she caught up with the *Surrey* again, off the New South Wales coast, where the larger convict transport was found drifting, its sails flapping idly, 'in disorder' and flying distress signals.[5] Typhus had broken out. Some 40 convicts had died, as had several soldiers and crew, and the chief officer; the captain was dying, and so was the surgeon. With only one junior officer fit enough for duty and most of the crew disabled by their suffering, the *Surrey* required assistance to sail the short distance up the coast and into Sydney Harbour. The two ships dropped anchor there on 28 July, but because of the dread of contagion the *Surrey* was directed to the north shore and quarantined there for a month, the first ship for which such a precaution was imposed by the Sydney authorities.

Judith must have been apprehensive, observing from the decks of the *Broxbornebury* the hapless *Surrey* wallowing about, and learning that typhus had broken out among the convicts held below, her husband among them. Curiously, this mischance had taken place off the coast from Shoalhaven, where in the future the McNallys would hold property; and where Thomas Kendall's last effects would wash up on shore.

Equally whimsical, the *Surrey*'s figurehead was Minerva,[6] among other things the goddess of poetry. Her powers were not called upon just yet.

While hazel-eyed Patrick languished in quarantine, his wife and children were safely landed. She would have had to find accommodation, and then set about making arrangements. As she was a free woman and married, she could apply to have her husband assigned to her; she could also apply for a grant of land. Patrick was landed ahead of the full month of quarantine, for he was listed to be sent to Liverpool for distribution.

That being the case, she must have set about matters very

expeditiously, to retrieve him from the coils of the system. The 1814 General Muster[7] shows him to have been granted a ticket of leave, assigned as a labourer, and 'off stores'. He had to earn his own keep, and hers. In the following year their fourth child, Melinda, was born, out on the then-frontier at Pitt Town, where the McNallys had taken up residence, in all likelihood as share farmers, the common procedure in those times for people in their circumstances.

Six months later again, on 14 April 1816,[8] the new baby was baptised at St Matthew's Anglican Church, Windsor. That was not the Greenway church which now graces the township, nor its unfortunate predecessor, built by Henry Kitchen – the one at which Governor Macquarie placed a holey dollar under the cornerstone, only for it to be stolen that very night. He replaced the coin and re-laid the sandstone block, whereupon the same thing happened again. Patently, the Lord helps them that helps themselves.

When after that inaugural mischance Francis Greenway inspected the building, he claimed the bricks were below standard and the workmanship inferior, and had the entire building pulled down. He would rather build it himself. As the rejected bricks were put to use elsewhere and withstood the subsequent assaults of flood and time, that raises doubts about the real reason for his action.

The original St Matthew's, precursor to both of the above, was replaced in 1817, the year following Melinda's christening. Remarkably, another St Matthew's, but this time a Catholic church, was built in Windsor in 1840. As though the first one did not signify. As though there were not enough saints to go round.

About the time of Melinda's christening – a somewhat fanciful name, nothing like the more run-of-the-mill William and Mary and Eliza – Judith had been granted land at Castlereagh, further up the river, dated 10 September 1818. Patrick, too, had been issued with a certificate of exemption; that is, exemption from government works, and it was renewed year after year.

That suggests what Patrick and Judith may have been at in Canada, working a small parcel of land somewhere out of sight of the militia, with a little hut perhaps and where they could enjoy their very young family. It was a distinct advantage in the new colony of New South Wales to have had some farming experience. Such settlers were favoured with grants of land, emancipists too. The colony was in need of their produce. Judith, who 'came free', as she is identified in the Lands registry, was distinctly eligible. And again in 1819, after her Castlereagh grant, she was favoured with a further 50 acres in the Hunter Valley,[9] the newly opened lands that were so exciting to the Cornstalks (as the new generation of Australian-born were coming to be known) along the Hawkesbury. Not that the McNallys took active advantage of this second grant; they appear to have let it go. They were settling down and starting to make a life for themselves. Another two children were born, Sarah in 1820 and John in 1821.

Everything seemed to be working out for the McNallys at last. Patrick had won enough favour to be appointed overseer of a working party to clear land for one of the early settlers in the district, a John Harris at South Creek – where Samuel Marsden also held property, building his handsome Georgian house Mamre,[10] and experimenting with raising sheep. That was on [illegible] August 1822. Three weeks later Patrick McNally and his work gang were occupied in constructing fencing around the Rev. Henry Fulton's property. What happened thereafter is not entirely clear. There was a dispute over the fencing contract, there was an accusation of pig stealing, possibly as many as five little pigs, and Patrick – somewhat like Tom the piper's son – appears to have run away from the clearing party.

He was arrested and imprisoned for a while but then released with the charge not proven, but according to the 1823 Muster[11] he and his family removed themselves from harm's way, or possibly temptation, to Sydney town, taking up residence in Kent Street.

That side of the township was signally *déclassé*. That was where the licentious soldiery had been quartered ('Barrack Street') and led down to all the promiscuous activity along Cockle Bay. It was a place of works and factories, and boarding houses and rented cottages. It was where labourers, free or freed or ticket of leave, took up residence with their families.

By this time Melinda had become identified as Matilda, both within the family and in official records, for she had been so named in the muster of the previous year, 1822.[12] In that same record Patrick is identified as a Government Servant to his wife, and Judith is the householder. It is not impossible that Patrick's brush with the law had made it impossible for them to continue down on the farm. It is also not impossible that the McNallys, like too many of their compatriots, ticket-of-leave men and emancipists, found themselves handing over their titles or their grants to a local publican. Purely speculative, but then Matilda, Tilly, as she was called inside the home, acquired a taste for alcohol from somewhere, and at an early enough age.

In amongst all this, Bishop Reed in his pioneering study, *The Life and Poetical Works of Henry Kendall*, laid down as an established fact that Patrick McNally had been an Irish policeman. It is difficult to see how this could be so, how McNally could have fitted that into his curriculum vitae too, especially as he was specifically exempted from government assignments in consequence of being assigned to his wife. The source of this misapprehension is discoverable in the November 1828 General Muster, where a Patrick McNally is listed as a constable in Liverpool. But that one was aged just 30, 10 years younger, and had come out to Sydney on the *Martha*.[13]

The McNallys' brief moment in the sun was over; they were soon having a difficult time of it again. Melinda, as Matilda, went into the household of the Rev. Richard Hill, in Castlereagh Street, the opposite side of town, across the social divide marked by the Tank Stream. According to the General Muster of 1823, she was there as a 'servant with Rev. Hill', though she let it be known subsequently that she went there as a governess.[14] That is patently a nonsense. The Hills had no children. And this putative governess would have been at the time all of eight years old when she went there, and aged nine in the muster. It is an extension of her habit of reinventing herself, beginning with the name change, an early indication of her instability. Her famous son would follow that disposition.

From time to time she was even known by her employers' name, as Matilda Hill.[15] Certainly she was known as Matilda, as that is her given name in the 1828 census, when she was still with the Hills. Henry Kendall grew up believing that his mother's name was Matilda, and provided that detail for his marriage certificate in 1868. It is one of many fabrications deriving from her.

Other confusions were grafted on to this early adjustment of the record. According to Marjorie Kendall, the family historian:

> When Judith McNally died in Campbelltown, Mrs Hill, who had known Judith in Ireland, took Melinda and her sister Sara into the household of her husband, Rev. Richard Hill at Castlereagh St, Sydney. Melinda and Sara were well educated in the Hills' household, writing pleasant verses and doing fine needlework.[16]

That creates difficulty, however, for there is uncertainty about the precise date of Judith McNally's death. Some think that she may not have died until 1840. The fact that Patrick's pardon came in 1843 could have been in consequence of her passing away, as the renewal of his ticket of leave had all those years been conditional upon his living with her.

In any case, Judith and Patrick are listed in the 1823 General Muster as residents of Kent Street, so that it was not a case of the Hills taking in a motherless child, or children. Melinda, or Matilda, or Tillie, however she was to be known, was not sent out to work because her mother had died.

Additionally, there is the question of how Mrs Hill might have been acquainted with Judith in Ireland. The Rev. Richard Hill was the son of a London schoolmaster and there is nothing to suggest he was acquainted with Ireland. His wife's maiden name was Kerrison, a Suffolk name. (Mrs Hamilton-Grey, Kendall's adoring hagiographer, was confident that Mrs Hill's maiden name was McDermott,[17] but that is her mistake, not a mystery. McDermott was the maiden name of Patrick McNally's wife.) The Hills married in 1808; he was not ordained until 1813, after which he served in several curacies until their departure for New South Wales. Their link with Ireland prior to 1808 is very tenuous. It seems to rest on no better source than that they shipped out to Australia on the *Hibernia*.

Setting aside Marjorie Kendall's conjectures, it is highly likely that Matilda benefited from her time with the Hills, for they were instrumental in advancing the cause of early childhood education. Indeed, the reverend gentleman had quite advanced ideas about infant schools and free public schools. He also had a very considerable library, renowned in the community. But, as it was disproportionately weighted towards theology, it would have been unlikely to entice a youthful reader. This is where Matilda might have been led to *The Pilgrim's Progress*, and tales from the classics. If she had been taught the art of fine needlework, that would not have been out of the ordinary for a young girl fortunate enough to find herself in a quiet, genteel home.

The Rev. Hill was respected by his clerical brethren. Samuel Marsden thought well of him, for his conscientious attention to his religious duties, for his evangelism if not for his tolerance. Although Hill had not the benefit of a classical education, he had nevertheless been ordained by the Bishop of London; and he was associated with Marylebone parish, where Charles Wesley lived and worked and was buried. For Marsden, that would have signalled a likely commitment to religious zeal.

Hill would have done his reputation no harm in the estimation of the Senior Chaplain by storming unannounced into the governor's office when he first landed in Sydney, having hastened ahead from Hobart to denounce the behaviour of the surgeon aboard the transport ship on which he and his wife had taken passage. Subsequent enquiry revealed that the surgeon had indeed mistreated the convicts in his care. Marsden liked Hill's style, even if he himself might not have thought to complain about the misfortunes of those who were experiencing the painful consequences of their sentences. Macquarie, of course, warmed to Hill's active concern for the welfare of the prisoners.

In the annual musters at this time, Matilda is identified as a Protestant, living in a Protestant household. She had been baptised into the Church of England. But in 1827, when she was aged 12, her father arranged for her to be baptised into the Roman Catholic faith, in a secret ceremony in Dempsey's house in Kent Street, well known in Catholic circles as a meeting place. Patrick's name alone is recorded as present on that occasion, not his wife's. While it is open to speculation as to why that should be so, there is no basis to suppose that Judith may have died, for his ticket of leave in this year continued to require that he reside with his wife.

But it does open the door to conjecture. Judith had been content for her children to be baptised as Protestants. Patrick is the one who insisted on reclaiming his daughter, literally taking her over to the other side. Given Sydney's early history, Irishness and Catholicism were all but interchangeable terms. The Irishness, rather than the Catholicism, would play a part in his grandson's upbringing.

Through her relocation to the care of the Hills, Tilly was in a position to make something of a new life for herself. More than that, though, one surmises, on the basis of her future behaviour, to a considerable extent she reinvented herself. She found the freedom to make herself into something she had not been. Not that the Hills were the guilty party here. Her own father must have been the conduit by which stories of and from Ireland were relayed to her and her siblings. That is confirmed by his action in having her baptised again. And it has to be from him that one of the persistent stories – myths, in Ackland's sense – derives, for how else would it have been known? McNally would have been in a position to quash it if he had wished.

The family persisted with the claim that they were descended from a famous McNally, Leonard McNally, defending lawyer for the leading figures in the Irish uprising of 1798, these being Wolfe Tone, Lord Edward Fitzgerald and the revered Robert Emmet, the revolutionary Irish patriot, who was brought to trial in 1803. Yet A.G. Stephens, for one, was unsure about the connection:

> His father is supposed to have been Leonard McNally, historically prominent as a Dublin lawyer, litterateur and 'Castle tool', at the epoch of Irish [illegible] This attribution rests on the testimony of his reputed granddaughter, Kendall's mother, the pretty and witty Tilly McNally.[18]

Evidently, he did not think Tilly was an entirely reliable source, and he had his misgivings. At much the same time, though, Bertram Stevens had no such doubt. He affirmed as a plain matter of fact that she was the 'granddaughter of Leonard McNally, a Dublin notable of his day'.[19] After all, that was what Henry Kendall's son Frederick had affirmed in 1903.[20] But Alexander Sutherland had already tempered his admiration for this putative ancestor:

> The good nature of his broad and rosy face, the singular wisdom and luminousness of his conversation, his shrewd wit, and his unvarying kindness, had to atone for a dirty slovenliness of person and a certain shiftiness of principle which was a serious set-off to his finer qualities.[21]

The radical lawyer Leonard McNally was credited with being a loyal member of the republican Society of United Irishmen. He was one of the earliest functionaries in that aspirational bid for Irish independence, a founding member, and served as its chief legal counsel. He had been deeply involved in developing the plans for a general uprising, shepherded by

Wolfe Tone. These came to very little, however, as they failed to win the promised assistance of forces from France.

McNally had taken steps to establish himself in the better circles. He had begun life as the son of a grocer, and was one himself, until he went to London to study law. He could not have done that if he had stayed a professing Catholic; it was more acceptable to be a member of the Church of Ireland, to which he converted. While he published a pamphlet supporting the Irish cause, he also earned something of a social reputation writing songs, comic operas and plays. One of his songs, 'Sweet lass of Richmond Hill', was the toast of the season in 1789 and a favourite of George III after it had been performed at Vauxhall Gardens. There were already the makings of a double aspect to his persona.

The various uprisings in Ireland were unsuccessful in different ways, and the leadership was all brought to trial. McNally was their lawyer from first to last, yet none of them managed a successful defence. That was not thought to be McNally's failing, though; it was instead the inevitable outcome from a judicial system inherently biased against the sentiments and just claims of the Irish. They wanted their own independence. The court was unlikely to give it to them.

McNally's great moment was in his connection with the trial of Robert Emmet for high treason. Emmet's defiant and inspirational address from the dock at the closing of the proceedings echoed around the world:

> Let no man write my epitaph; for as no man who knows my motives dare now vindicate them, let not prejudice or ignorance asperse them. Let them rest in obscurity and peace, my memory be left in oblivion, and my tomb remain uninscribed, until other times and other men can do justice to my character. When my country takes her place among the nations of the earth, then, and not till then, let my epitaph be written. I have done.[22]

It was a powerful speech, though it did not persuade the judge to relent. Irish patriots both at home and abroad, especially in America, applauded the sentiments and the bravery. Emmet was elevated by it, his name revered. And their man McNally was by his side. When in the fullness of time the lawyer passed away, at the age of 68, McNally was given a patriot's funeral. That was in 1820.

Then matters became complicated. McNally was reported to have died in February, but in fact that was his son, and lawyer-like he sought damages from a Dublin newspaper that had circulated the misinformation, an early instance of fake news. However, he tidied up the matter by dying himself four months later, leaving behind a daughter. Presumably she, or her agent, was instrumental in the next startling revelation, exposed by an enquiry into whether his pension was to be continued. For it turned out that Leonard McNally, far from being the public patriot, had been acting as a secret agent for the British government. An alternative reading is that the Lord-Lieutenant himself demanded to know why a government pension had been paid to such an ardent nationalist.

Either way, the truth about Leonard McNally began to unravel. Apprehensive of being arrested for his activities back in the days of clandestine meetings with the incipient Society of United Irishmen, he had agreed to keep the authorities informed and himself safe. He reported on who attended those meetings and, so it transpired, he was the one who betrayed Sir Edward Fitzgerald. When matters came to court, he let it be known in advance what the defence of each of his clients would be; he let it be known that Robert Emmet would not be calling witnesses, and that he would not cross-examine the Crown's witnesses, unless they lied. He all but ensured that the defendants would be found guilty. And for this, he received payment, as well as a pension. As well as his clients' fee, presumably.

As a final twist, although he had identified himself as a Protestant for most of his adult life, he asked for a priest, and absolution, on his death bed. It makes his famous image of the lass from Richmond Hill all the more poignant – a rose without a thorn.

In light of which, it is difficult to determine what, if anything, there was to boast about by the connection. Halfway across the world, the McNallys would have been entirely unaware of this exposure. By the time of Sinn Fein, a century and a half later, McNally was marked as 'undoubtedly one of the most treacherous informers of Irish history'.[23]

With no son surviving Leonard, it is a puzzle to know how Patrick McNally could be a descendant, unless illegitimate – and if that were the case (and it formed no part of the family legend), how he could have claimed that surname unless he had been in some way acknowledged by his father, his existence in some way admitted.

It is of course feasible that Patrick and Leonard were related, if not all that closely.

What is very clear is that the McNally assertion of a connection to the man they believed a great patriot was an assertion of their Irishness. They may have been very proud of it; but their assumed legacy was blemished and unreliable. A good story, though.

2

The Sins of the Fathers

Like Patrick McNally, so too Thomas Kendall, Henry Kendall's other forebear and namesake, came from a quiet rural county, out of the way and long if sparsely settled.

Apart from invasions by Romans and Vikings and threats of invasion by Napoleon and Hitler, Lincolnshire has enjoyed or endured a fairly placid history, an uneventful round of good harvests and poor harvests, as the seasons determined. Farming has been the common vocation, by sterling yeoman stock for the most part. Not everyone in Lincolnshire was a poacher, however celebrated those were in song.[1] Swagmen in Australia achieved much the same extravagant notoriety.

As with Roscommon, so too with Lincolnshire – this was not a county given to radical change. The northeastern region of it was mainly agricultural country. Thomas Kendall was born there, of elderly parents, and spent his earliest years on the family farm. The countryside about North Thoresby is flat and open, improved by massive drainage works over the preceding centuries, although still with extensive saltmarshes towards the coast, and beyond which grey seals might sometimes be seen lolloping in the shallows.

The Kendalls' was a small farm, and his father at 66 years of age was unlikely to have laboured as long and hard in his remaining years as he had earlier, for he survived until the grand old age of 93.[2] An elder brother, Edward, Thomas's senior by nine years, would have borne the brunt of their father's expectations about the property. With five girls in the family as well, it was always a struggle to improve their standing in what little community there was. Improve in the things of this world, that is – his mother was a devout woman.

At the age of 14 Thomas Kendall left home to live at a solicitor's, where, as he subsequently wrote, 'there was no religion'.[3] A year later he went to teach as a monitor – essentially, a senior student helping with the instruction of the juniors – at a larger village school on the other side of Grimsby; and a year later again he was invited by a former teacher and clergyman from his original village to be an assistant at yet another small school, at North Somercotes,[4] close to where the grey seals still come ashore to bask along the sands.

That is to say, from his early teenage years he had separated himself from his family. He was intent on improving himself in the secular sense, by working with and for educated men, though Charles Dickens had yet to expose in *Nicholas Nickleby* (1838–39) how demeaning schoolmastering could be. Given the clerical background of his employers, Thomas's spiritual improvement was supervised too. He was introduced to a range of religious tracts, the salutary lives of saints and bishops and books of faith. Yet at this time he purchased a little farm of 15 acres near the village. He had learned that much from his father, to hold close to the land. That was a different kind of security, a practice he would adhere to.

After two years more of study and agriculture and teaching in his own right, he changed pasture once again, taking up an appointment as a children's tutor near what was almost a hamlet, Kirmington, not at all distant from his original billet at the solicitor's. In that neighbourhood he met Jane Quickfall, married her and returned to North Thoresby, setting up as a draper and grocer.

He did not prosper. The times, or the seasons, were not propitious. With a young family to support, for two daughters were born early into the marriage, his resources were strained. In hope of improving his circumstances, he bought a load of hops and took it to London 'on spec'; and it was there that at the age of 27 he changed his course in life.

In November 1805, with Nelson's body still immersed in a barrel of brandy and the *Victory* limping back to England, Kendall happened to walk past Bentinck Chapel in Marylebone, not at that time the most salubrious quarter of London. As he passed by, the chapel doors chanced to open and he heard the congregation singing. He was uplifted by the joyfulness of it. That evening, he attended and heard the singing of psalms; and he heard the Rev. Basil Woodd preach.

Evening preaching was an unorthodox innovation at the time and had not been readily accepted by the Church of England at large. Woodd had originally been appointed as a morning preacher (1785). But he was energetic, enthusiastic in the cause, and he revelled in the pulpit; and he was moved to expand his activity to include evening services. He also turned his hand to hymn writing, much like Charles Wesley, who had lived and worked nearby, and who had been a communicant at the new St Marylebone church just up the road from Bentinck Chapel. Wesley had played the organ there, and in due course was buried there. Woodd fell far short of Wesley's six thousand hymns, of course, but it is clear that hymn singing was well entertained in his chapel. And there could never be enough of preaching. Undoubtedly, he shared Wesley's evangelicalism. Thomas Kendall was swept up in the enthusiasm.

It is in this connection that a passing detail might be elaborated. Thomas Kendall had come up to London to make a sale of his load of hops. That might seem something of a handicap, given his religious awakening. But not necessarily. Charles Wesley was not against beer – given the state of London's water supply, beer was much safer to drink. He drank ale himself, while his brother John in Bristol was not teetotal either and once described wine as 'one of the noblest cordials in creation'.[5] However, they both disapproved of the consumption of spirits, and they both denounced intemperance and inebriety. These failings were to be the Kendall family's persistent weakness.

In one of those tantalising convergences which thread throughout the Kendall story, St Marylebone is where Richard Hill, the minister with whom Matilda McNally would be placed in Sydney, was married. That was in 1808, by which time the Kendalls had just moved into the area. In his ministry in Sydney, Hill was connected with the Church Missionary Society, and Kendall was to become its servant. Hill went on to serve as assistant secretary to the Society's Australian auxiliary. His earnest social conscience and his zeal, undoubtedly encouraged by the connection with St Marylebone, coloured Matilda McNally's younger years.

Bentinck Chapel had been built by and for the Portland family, about 15 years previously; subsequently the Dukes of Portland committed themselves to the renovation of St Marylebone, resulting in the larger and somewhat ostentatious church that survives today. It had an intriguing history. In the early eighteenth century it was well on the way to falling to its knees, although not in supplication. That prior church had a reputation as a convenient place for clandestine marriages, which was what led Hogarth to use it in his *The Rake's Progress* series, and apparently with very little imaginative modification – it was fit for Hogarth's purpose just as it was.[6]

As that part of the town gentrified, and with the investment of the Portland family who were seeking an appropriate crypt, St Marylebone was wholly rebuilt, leaving Bentinck Chapel without a specific parish purpose. This then became identified as a chapel of ease (a chapel for the convenience of those who lived at a distance from the parish church), and later as a proprietary chapel (a private chapel made available to the public), which Woodd purchased without difficulty in 1793; over the years he built up a large following there. Such chapels were where the more progressively evangelical preachers were likely to find a pulpit. Woodd was one of the leaders of that wing of the Church of England at that time and also of the Church Missionary Society. These days we might think of him as a revivalist.

Thomas Kendall returned to North Thoresby, reclaimed his family, sold up his possessions and moved to London, his second daughter only one month old. For seven years Thomas Kendall attended and worshipped at Bentinck Chapel, and taught at the Sunday School, a seven-year interval wholly in keeping with Old Testament predispositions. In that time he heard Woodd preach that the soul of the heathen could be saved, and he began to envisage himself as an agent for their salvation.

In that time too, three sons were born, the second of them Basil, father of the poet Henry. Thomas filled in his weekdays as a teacher. Given that later he readily acknowledged that he had a temper, it might be imagined that his teaching practice was more *Nicholas Nickleby* than benign Oliver Goldsmith. Spare the rod and spoil the child.

In subsequent correspondence with Woodd and with Rev. Josiah Pratt, the secretary of the Church Missionary Society, he wrote of the suddenness of his 'conversion', very much in the manner of the dissenters from the age of Bunyan onwards. Judith Binney, in her authoritative study of Thomas Kendall, reads this steady stream of correspondence with his superiors as articulating his tormented Calvinism, and so it might well appear. But it has always to be kept in mind that he had a particular purpose in these letters. He wished to impress his local pastor, who would be the one to recommend him as suitable for the missionary effort; and the secretary, who would be pivotal in determining that acceptability.

In other words, he had a vested interest in presenting himself as an exemplary case. When we test the evidence, however, we see a distance between what he turned out to be and what he should have been (argued cleverly by Binney as the requisite fall in the Calvinist schema) and on the other hand by affirmations made by and about him without any perceptible warrant.

For example, the London Missionary Society learned harsh lessons by early failings and defections by converts and proselytisers alike when it attempted to bring Christianity and civilisation to Tahiti – not least the all-too-cautionary circumstances following 'King' Pomare's conversion, when he set about testing the benefit of the new god in inter-tribal battle,[7] an almost exact forerunner of what would happen in New Zealand. The Church Missionary Society, a separate missionary group, determined on a variant approach, of bringing civilisation (meaning trade) first and then introducing the theology.

That, certainly, was the intended strategy of Samuel Marsden, who had come to England from Australia at this juncture precisely to encourage the formation of the Church Missionary Society. It meant that missionaries should in the first instance have serviceable skills, such as twine spinning, shoemaking, carpentry and the like. Matters were delayed while the committee debated Thomas Kendall's suitability. Marsden proposed that Kendall might be taught something practical like ironwork. Kendall proposed instead the benefit of his farming experience. In the end, they settled that he would be useful as a teacher. He had experience in that.

Woodd recommended Kendall's skill in acquiring languages. There is no ready evidence of any such gift, other than Woodd's say-so. Kendall seems not to have had any other European language, and he certainly had no classical education.[8] That was a double disadvantage. Without a classical education, he could not be ordained. More specifically, as would become apparent, he had no sense of grammatical structure, yet he was commissioned to establish a Maori grammar – more exactly, a New Zealand grammar, for the word 'Maori' had not been written before 1843, although it had been used in speech well before then. All the assistance he had was a Polynesian word list already established in Tahiti, and a book *Some Account of New Zealand; particularly of the Bay of Islands, and Surrounding Country; with a Description of the Religion and Government, Language, Arts, Manufactures, Manners, and Customs of the Natives, &c &c* (London, 1807), written by an improbably named John Savage. He had not read Captain Cook's journal of his voyages to New Zealand. Which rather left Kendall to blaze his own trail, untrained and underprepared.

Arrangements were at length made for him and his wife to take free passage to Sydney, together with their five children, and in addition he was provided with a land grant, although in return the Kendalls would be required to teach in New South Wales for three years. He was intent on establishing that security for himself. He had inherited that resolution from his father, if not much else.

They sailed on the *Earl Spencer*, a convict transport. Kendall was shocked by the rough language of the sailors, always likely to be colourful if not profane; and even more so by the convicts who were 'singing obscene, lewd songs'.[9] One, though, Richard Stockwell, had been recommended by clergymen in Bristol, a decent young man who had found himself on the wrong side of the law. Kendall sought him out and had him released from his chains to become their servant, which role Stockwell was required to perform for the next three years. With a salary, and a servant, and an entitlement to land, the Kendalls appeared to be getting along in the world.

They arrived in Sydney in October 1813, where Marsden was waiting, together with two other would-be missionaries from England, William Hall and John King.[10] These two had sailed out with Marsden several years earlier, while Kendall's appointment was being determined. They had been prevented from proceeding with the intended mission, however, because of ongoing hostilities with the Maori, by which is meant slaughter of visiting crew, massacres in reprisal and reciprocal killings for perceived insult, plunder, treachery, kidnap, pillage, the whole unhappy history of early contact. Patently, it was not the best of times to launch a mission. On the other hand, as this was not so different from the behaviour between tribes most of the time, a sceptic might think that would have been no special reason for the delay.

Hall and Marsden had clashed on their voyage to Australia. They were both stubborn men, and convinced of their own opinion. King and Hall resented working for Marsden while they awaited Kendall's arrival. In their view, they were to work for the Church Missionary Society. Worse, while they were working on and off for Marsden or indeed for themselves, their missionary salary was suspended.

Kendall arrived to an awkward situation. Naturally, he wished to present himself well to Marsden, which to the other two was tantamount to siding with the enemy. He had his own reservations about Marsden, of course, especially about what seemed to him unnecessary dilatoriness. But patently, Marsden's chief difficulty had been in acquiring a ship and a captain prepared to encounter the formidable Maoris.

The plan of settlement was first to send across an exploratory voyage to the Bay of Islands. The chosen vessel was the *Active*, and its mission was to open up trade with the natives. Kendall and Hall sailed in March 1814 by way of Van Diemen's Land, arriving at the Bay of Islands in June, to meet up with a chieftain Marsden had fortuitously met on his previous recruiting drive in England, bringing him back both to health and his native land, together with a bag of grain to sow. The unhappy conscript had been working on a whaler between New Zealand and Norfolk Island, and unwittingly ended up at the furthest side of the world.

Given the uncertainty of their likely reception, it was brave of Thomas Kendall to go ashore to sleep among the Maori just one week after the *Active* dropped anchor. While he was keen to get on with the process of conversion, he was also eager to make close contact in order to begin his other commission, the compiling of a vocabulary of the local tongue. This was going to be a fraught undertaking in any case, but it was rendered more questionable at least to begin with by Kendall's own accent.

Thomas Kendall spoke the dialect of the Wesleys, of Sir Joseph Banks, Matthew Flinders, George Bass and Sir John Franklin, Flinders's nephew by marriage. Given his rural origins, Kendall's dialect was undoubtedly more pronounced than theirs. His more illustrious countrymen, having spent their formative years at university, in the manse or in the Royal Navy, would have polished their grammar, if not their diction. Here is a cautionary reminder, that how Kendall spoke modified what he heard, and his record of Maori vocabulary must in some manner of speaking have been affected by his pronunciation.

The two missionaries struck up a friendly relationship with the New Zealanders. Kendall saw the advantage for him of carrying two or three of their senior people back to Sydney, to assist him in acquiring fluency in their language. One chief in particular, Hongi Hika, seemed in his turn particularly interested in finding out more about the *pakeha*, and the ways of the white men. Especially, as it turned out, their firearms. Kendall was concerned that they should be treated with respect on board the *Active*, but the captain had somewhat more prejudiced ideas. With Kendall insisting on his way, and the captain sure that it was his ship and that he commanded what happened on it, the two became more and more truculent, ending with the captain threatening and then attempting to shoot the missionary.[11] It is not known what Hongi, his fellow chiefs and their entourage made of this heated confrontation, but it cannot have made for an easy and harmonious crossing. It is, however, an early and revealing hint about Kendall's temperament.

Kendall and Hall reported favourably on their visit but not on the captain they had engaged. In November of that year Marsden, the three missionaries with their families and servants, a gentleman volunteer, 10 Maoris with their accumulated gifts from the governor and other well-wishers – and a new captain with his wife and child – all boarded the *Active* and set sail once more for New Zealand. Kendall's two daughters remained behind at the Female Orphan School in Sydney[12]; the boys accompanied their parents.

The Tasman Sea misbehaved as it customarily does, and both Marsden and Kendall were severely seasick. Kendall was no sailor, or not at this time. He had been a farmer, and then a teacher. He was a landlubber. He found himself in an unhappy place, when it is impossible to maintain one's dignity. The gentleman passenger, one John Lidiard Nicholas, described Kendall as so ill that he was made to:

> forget for the moment that he had a wig upon his head; which falling off, in his endeavours to relieve his stomach, dropped overboard, and left him under the necessity of tying a red handkerchief around his temples, which, with the death-like paleness of his face and the grim languor of his eyes, made him appear so complete a spectre, that he forcibly reminded me of Banquo's ghost.[13]

En route they stopped by to enquire into the massacre of the crew of the *Boyd* (1809) and the subsequent retaliation by whalers; at which time Marsden sought to establish the innocence of his former friend, a chief named Te Pahi. Then they continued to the northern end of the Bay of Islands, to a place called Oihi, in Rangihoua Bay, where Marsden had determined the mission was to be set up under the protection of another chief, Ruatara, on a steep and broken site, all rock and clay and scrub, which made it impracticable for the newcomers to establish anything like self-sufficiency.

Kendall, possibly still sporting his red handkerchief, preferred the gentler country further to the south, at a place that in following years would become famous in New Zealand history, Waitangi. He remembered enough about farming to appreciate the possibilities of the rolling country there, though it was much darker than Lincoln green. The closest reminder of his native land were the large numbers of fur seals in the bay. He was tempted.

Marsden would have none of that. They had either to agree to his decision or return back across the Tasman. They had to settle where they were under the protection of a friendly chief; and close to where the Maori whom they were to convert all lived. But the site Marsden insisted upon would not be able to support the little community. That meant they would be reliant on his sending provisions from Sydney; either that, or they would have to trade with the local people.

The Europeans remained aboard the *Active* while the Maori built them a flax hut. They would have to live communally as the natives did to begin with, an antipodean version of 'when in Rome, do as the Romans'. In the meanwhile, on Christmas Day, Marsden preached the first sermon in New Zealand, at a specially constructed pulpit down on the shore, and with people from two local tribes in attendance, their chiefs wearing uniforms given to them by Governor Macquarie at the time of their recent visit, and maintaining exact discipline (following the lead of the Europeans, as standing, sitting, responding, staying silent, bowing their heads). Marsden was much gratified. By the end of February he considered that sufficient accommodation had been provided for those who were to be left behind. He formally purchased a plot of land for the mission settlement, approximately 200 acres, and sailed away, leaving a gift of muskets and powder, and the wherewithal to acquire more from the sale of the land. That set an unfortunate precedent.

At which point matters began to unravel. Chief Ruatara, who was meant to be the missionaries' protector, but whose involvement was more like toleration of them, died of tuberculosis almost immediately. They were on their own now. The three families, together with the family of the captain of the *Active*, the Hansens, found the enforced intimacies of living in the long hut intolerable, with nothing but a mud floor – no windows, no chimney, and ready access for wind and rain – and cooking outside in all weathers. The builder among them, Hall, agreed with Kendall that they would do better to relocate to Waitangi; he made the move, but Kendall changed his mind and stayed put, leaving Hall isolated and exposed to attacks from less accommodating natives. That did not predispose Hall to think kindly of him.

Neither Hall nor King welcomed Kendall's appointment by Governor Macquarie as magistrate in the Bay of Islands and throughout New Zealand. That commission seemed to formalise what was already implicit, his assumption of authority over the other two. They would not be advised by him, however, for he was, in their view, no better than them. He, on his part, appeared only too ready to give them the benefit of his advice. They resented too his assumption on the basis of his office that he had the right, if not the responsibility, to meet visiting ships – they suspected that gave him an advantage in buying goods with which to trade to the Maori.

Jealousies began to emerge, heightened by the compression of their all living together. The two manual workers resented what they thought the easiness of Kendall's role as schoolteacher. While they toiled at clearing and building, he was writing his lists of words and constructing lessons in the local language. He published the results of this preliminary reconnaissance in Sydney in 1815, *A Korao no New Zealand; or, the New Zealander's First Book: being an attempt to compose some lessons for the instruction of the natives.*[14] They also began to resent the toll on the common supply of food, for the one way Kendall could encourage the Maori children to come to his school was by feeding them. When Hall began building permanent accommodation, he built for his own family first, and was not expeditious in setting about cottages for the others.

Yet another pattern began to emerge. Kendall would join with the incoming captains and avail himself of their hospitality:

> he goes on board ships that comes [sic] in, and gives us a bad name to the Captain in short he does all he can to abease us and to exalt himself … I do not approve of his getting intoxicated.[15]

The necessity of commencing trade with the local community for their sustenance was one thing; his drinking was another. When after a year or so the Kendalls did move into their own cottage, that meant that he sometimes left his wife and children in the care of their manservant, Richard Stockwell. The young man had, after all, held that role when Kendall first voyaged to the Bay of Islands, an interval of just over five months.

That is how it must have happened. Kendall's wife and their servant would not have chanced assignations out in the bush and the shrubbery where the local people went foraging and hunting; and there could have been no inappropriate intimacy in the long communal dwelling. In the year 1815 Stockwell and Jane Kendall, now in her 30s, began a liaison, which became exposed when she was delivered of a child; and given that her son Samuel was born in June of 1816, it seems that he must have been the cuckoo in the nest.

This child looked nothing like her other children, William Hall testified later, relishing the disgrace of it. Jane was forced to confess her adultery,[16] and Kendall and his wife became estranged. It is very tempting to think of Jane, with her maiden name Quickfall, as a figure from the pages of Restoration comedy or picaresque novels, where the moral calibre of characters is signposted for the reader.

The child was named Samuel, presumably for Kendall to ingratiate himself with Marsden (who was surprisingly measured when he learned of his protégé's domestic unhappiness), just as his preceding son had been named in honour of the Rev. Basil Woodd. If, on the other hand, the name was after the biblical Samuel, then there is a cautionary hint, in that, after Samuel's early summons but not by the prophet Eli as three times he imagined, it is written: 'Samuel did not yet know the Lord, neither was the word of the Lord revealed unto him'.[17] Jane's child was not an outcast, for he was taken into the family. It may even be that Thomas performed the baptism – whether he did so, or one of the others, none was ordained to do so. But in such a committed community, with deeply held convictions, the child's soul would have been seen as in a parlous state.

As for Stockwell, he was obliged to complete his three-year term of servitude, and that must have made the remaining two years an embarrassment – apparently the meter had been reset when he came to New Zealand. He was then sent back to New South Wales. Kendall declined to take him back into his household.

This was not an ideal time for Thomas Kendall to commence his school (it failed within two years). Besides the domestic and communal strife, there were disruptions in the relations between the assigned help and the Maori. Drunkenness and fornication were common. One such disturbance resulted in a convict who had been assigned as a blacksmith attempting to shoot Kendall. Kendall, intemperate, attacked him with a chisel. It would not appear to matter very much in just what order these two events took place.

Tensions between the three missionaries reached a peak at about this time, exacerbated by the shortage of provisions, the crowding together, and the necessity of finding a basis for trade. The Maori were not interested in the usual frivolities of colonial encounters – mirrors and beads and the like. They wanted iron, and they wanted good-quality iron. They were very astute. But above all, they wanted muskets. They had learned the advantage of those. They would not trade their pork or potatoes for anything less; and if the missionaries were unwilling, then the ships, especially the sealers and whalers with their notoriously dissolute crews, coming into the bay in increasing numbers, were happy to oblige them.

Which resulted in two outcomes. On the opposite shore of the bay, an unruly haven began to emerge. Kororareka, later known as Russell, soon won a reputation as the hellhole of the Pacific. And as the tribes accumulated modern weaponry, so the basis for New Zealand's musket wars began to consolidate. Neither upshot represented a signal triumph for the Church Missionary Society.

Potato-growing began to replace the kumara and taro patches around the Maori *pas*, and they gathered flax. They knew what the whaling ships wanted; they traded for muskets and good iron. Their rapidly increasing armouries meant that they had ready to hand the means of defending themselves against raids by neighbouring tribes. And they had the resources to avenge past defeats – Hongi in particular. He was intent upon acquiring the power to overwhelm any other tribe, but one in particular, the hated Ngatiwhatua. In time he would bring back huge numbers of captives from the Hauraki Gulf country, as many as two thousand, to clear more land and to work the enlarged potato fields, and to grow flax, anything to encourage trade with visiting ships.

What Kendall thought of this practice of slavery, in the age of Wilberforce, is not recorded.

Supplies from Sydney were dilatory. There was no avoiding the issue. Step by step the missionaries became involved in trading in guns. They were not comfortable with that, but needs must when the Devil drives. Kendall, with his readier access to incoming ships, was suspected of using his advantage, as intermediary between the Maori and the ships (and rewarded by both), and acting on his own behalf.

News of this inevitably went back to Marsden. He returned to New Zealand in mid-1819, together with a new superintendent of the mission, Rev. Butler, an ordained minister who, like Kendall, and indeed like Marsden, had a violent temper. They all seemed to carry their convictions to the point of intransigence. In the course of this visit, Marsden negotiated with Hongi for a large grant of land, some 13,000 acres, to develop a second mission at Kerikeri. The transfer was agreed for 48 felling axes, useful given the great stands of trees thereabouts; useful too, subsequently, for more nefarious deeds.

The arrival of Butler failed to re-establish order, let alone harmony. Kendall resented losing his leadership; the newcomer was determined to impose his authority. Ructions between them, and between Butler and the other settlers, commenced almost at once. Marsden returned a third time in mid-February 1820, and immediately convened a formal inquiry into Kendall's activities as a gunrunner. He had reprimanded all of them on the previous visit; they had agreed to stop it, but then resumed their trade in bartering for muskets. Kendall's reaction was only to be expected.

The investigation ran on for two days. Butler's journal records how Kendall raged and stamped and stormed about, and refused to answer[18]; and then – predictably in such circumstances – he took to airing his many grievances. Bubbling away in the background was another issue altogether. Kendall was making arrangements to return to England, taking with him not only his draft of his little treatise 'A study of the New Zealand Language', but also chief Hongi, and young chief Waikato. He had sent an early version to the Missionary Society, who in turn had passed it on to a Cambridge professor of linguistics, Professor Lee, who had found it insufficient. That provoked Kendall; he would elaborate it further, and he would go to England himself to explain his work. He had been beavering away at a Hebrew grammar, borrowed from the invidious Butler. It is not immediately apparent, from the outside, just how much use that might have been to him.

He refused to heed Marsden's displeasure, and he dismissed Butler's anxiety that without Hongi's protection the mission at Kerikeri would be overrun. Indeed, he was sufficiently confident about his connection with the Maori that he was prepared to leave his wife, now reconciled, and children for however long his visit would take. Besides, Stockwell was well out of the way.

Kendall left just two weeks after Marsden's arrival. A day or two later, when the ship on which Marsden had taken passage was being further unloaded, a barrel marked 'Leather' and consigned to Kendall was hoisted out of the hold. It was opened on deck, and inside was discovered a small consignment of muskets. But Kendall had gone. So too had Hongi, who would have welcomed them very much indeed.

There were all sorts of reasons for Kendall's defiance of Marsden, and his intemperate departure. One was that he feared his work on the Maori vocabulary might be superseded by work being undertaken at Cambridge University. Much more important though was his determination to be ordained, to put himself on an even footing with Butler and so to make himself independent of him. That was his nature, he would truckle to no one.

The travellers went straight to Cambridge, where it immediately became clear to Professor Lee, an oriental linguist and protégé of the Church Missionary Society, that Kendall had almost no sense of grammatical organisation. The professor also put paid to Kendall's belief that Maori were descended from the ancient Egyptians. He acknowledged that Kendall had assembled a useful word list, and demonstrably he could speak with his two associates in their own tongue. What is more, though Kendall was not especially conscious of its importance at this stage, he had the beginnings of an understanding of their culture. This would become the basis for his future work, and his increasing confidence in it. With the Maori chiefs assisting, Kendall and Professor Lee were able to assemble in just two months a publishable work, *A Grammar and*

Vocabulary of the Language of New Zealand.[19] Kendall had fulfilled the Missionary Society's directive.

The committee was not so welcoming of Kendall's ambition for ordination, however. They were aware of his conflict with Butler, and his insubordination. They thought that he should return and learn humility; but they changed their tune when Professor Lee wrote in support of Kendall's wishes, and of the benefit which might follow from that. The Bishop of Norwich was prepared to ordain him even without the requisite knowledge of Latin and Greek, because the society guaranteed that Kendall would not return to England, or not as a practising minister.[20] The condition of his ordination was that he preached exclusively in New Zealand.

Kendall would conveniently forget that proviso in seven years time, another unfortunate reminder of those biblical covenants.

Meanwhile, Hongi's interest in the long voyage was also being met. From mid-October he and Waikato were taken up by the fashionable world as models of the Noble Savage. Lords and ladies, dukes and duchesses, royalty, parliamentary leaders, chancellors and vice-chancellors, bishops all swarmed to titillate themselves by inspecting these exotic beings and their extraordinary tattoos. Their portrait, together with Kendall, was painted. They were presented to George IV, who gave them engraved guns, and a coat of chain mail for Hongi and a helmet for Waikato. They were taken to the Tower of London and to the arsenal in Woolwich, which left Hongi astounded and ecstatic. He had arrived at a place beyond all fantasy.

Hongi noted too that the king had either never heard of Samuel Marsden or had forgotten about him; and that he had not banned powder and muskets for the New Zealanders. He was well pleased by the royal reception.

He was not so pleased with his reception by the Church Missionary Society. The gifts presented to them were rejected with disgust as too meagre. The two Maori knew exactly what gifts had been given to two previous visiting chiefs, gifts both large and numerous. It would be seen as shaming for Hongi to return with anything less than they had received. The churchmen had much yet to learn about diplomacy.

The following May, some 14 months after they had set out, Kendall, Hongi and Waikato returned to Sydney. Kendall and Marsden had words, of course, about Kendall's defiance and about how relations with the

Maori were to proceed thereafter. They agreed to disagree. Hongi exchanged all his presents, excepting the coat of mail, for muskets and powder. His mission was all but accomplished. His contempt for Marsden as a man of low worth, instigated by the king's failure to remember him, was compounded by Marsden's refusal to give him gifts he would have liked, such as a horse or a length of scarlet cloth, offering instead a quantity of nails.

Kendall was busy in Sydney too. In Britain he had been given goods and presents by a French nobleman[21] who fancied himself as forming a comprehensive colony in New Zealand, only a little less ambitious than Marsden himself had been, or William Wentworth would be in the next generation. According to the Frenchman, writing years after the event, Kendall sold these for quite a considerable amount, and used some of those funds to purchase guns, both for himself and for Hongi.

When he arrived back in the Bay of Islands, Kendall thanked those local people who had looked after his family in his absence, for 16 months in all. He dispersed more than 20 muskets, and two pistols – in particular, three rifles to the elderly Rakau and his wife, and one to their son, for they had kept the closest watch over Jane Kendall and their now six boys. Two babies had been born in a reconciliation of sorts just before Thomas went away. Now it was time to resume his pastoral and domestic duties.

But he also returned to the troubling trade in guns. He defended this activity as customary. If a Maori wanted a musket for his produce, he would not be put off with hoes and fish-hooks. It was no secret that such items of trade as hatchets and axes, items endorsed by the society, were acquired for use as weapons of war.

They were all in on it; even Jane Kendall had, during Thomas's absence, 'been singled out for accusations of trading with muskets to purchase pigs'. Kendall was attacked for this on his return.[22] William Hall, always one for scandal, let the Church Missionary Society know as a matter of interest that Kendall had returned with muskets and barrels of powder, and that Kendall was buying up all the available local food to sell it on to passing ships for further quantities of firearms. As Marsden was not doing anything about it, perhaps the society would.

Hongi had his own plans. In fewer than two months, with as many as a thousand muskets available to his warriors, the Ngapuhi chief, invulnerable in his chain mail armour, led an astonishingly destructive attack well to the south, against the people of the Auckland-Coromandel country; and returned with yet a further two thousand slaves. Nine of these were eaten on their return, and two of the heads were impaled on a fence close to the mission house.[23] Kendall chose to understand this as insolence directed specifically towards his personal nemesis, Butler, not as a threat towards the settlement as a whole. Hongi's disdain for Christianity was becoming more and more evident. Christianity was 'a religion possibly fit for slaves but irrelevant for warriors'.[24]

Hongi's own warrior code was leading to disruption. In his pursuit of vengeance, *utu*, to reclaim and then assert tribal pride, Hongi was distorting the customary Maori balance of power, decimating whole tribes, forcing some to flee to other lands, uprooting them from their traditional lands. His warriors were invincible, and his was now the dominant force in the north. The effect of this was much worse than either Marsden or the Missionary Society had envisaged.

About this time, a new trade, the trade in preserved heads, began to evolve – not that there is any indication that Kendall ever acted as go-between in such an arrangement. Joseph Banks had traded for a preserved head, *toi moko*, when Captain Cook arrived in the vicinity in 1769. He had offered a pair of linen drawers in exchange; the old man with whom he was negotiating accepted the undergarment but then refused to relinquish the head. Banks resorted to presenting a musket, in the military sense, not as a gift.

Others followed suit:

> Gradually … contact with European whalers and sealers led to more trading in preserved heads and … as the desire for guns spread among the Maori in the early nineteenth century, the trade escalated. Soon specialist agents were being sent from Australia to pick out the best heads, and the Sydney Customs House began to list these imports under the heading 'Baked Heads'. Over the course of the fifty years following Cook's first visit, trade in human heads reached such intensity, and inter-tribal warfare escalated so ferociously, that many believed the Maori would be completely annihilated.
>
> It was the intricate facial tattoos worn by Maori chiefs that made their heads particularly attractive to Europeans … So great was the demand

> for tattooed heads that by the early nineteenth century, Maori chiefs were forcibly tattooing their slaves before killing them to sell their heads for a profit … The Maori tattoo, once an elaborate work of art developed over a lifetime and testament to a man's courage, honour and social status, had become a decoration designed only to please …[25]

The heads were smoked in order to preserve them. And Hongi had captured any number of tattooed warriors to supply the market.

In terms of cultural exchange, the Maori showed themselves to be much more astute than the Europeans and their missionaries. Back in London, the Church Missionary Society was increasingly alarmed by news of Hongi's horrendous activities, and – courtesy of William Hall – of Kendall's reprehensible backsliding. In the mid-year, over a series of meetings, the committee resolved that Kendall must be stood down; but their letter of dismissal did not reach him until a year later. By which time, he had become involved in an even more serious breach of discipline.

Tungaroa,[26] the comely daughter of the old *tohunga* (a respected wise man, or priest) Rakau, who had protected Jane and her boys during Kendall's absence, had been installed in the household as a servant in that interval. She had previously been a student at Kendall's short-lived school, with its intriguing barrel organ; now, at the very interesting age of 17 or thereabouts, she provided Thomas with direct access to the Maori way of things. Jane was in her late 40s, and pregnant again. These two, in a household full of males. From what Thomas had estimated for his school records, Tungaroa had been born at just about the very time he underwent his change of course at Bentinck Chapel. Now he was about to change course once more.

In December, at the beginning of the heady weather of summer, and when the Bay of Islands is at its most beautiful, the newly ordained Thomas Kendall began an affair with his charge. Rumours about this highly irregular domestic arrangement began to circulate amongst the tittle-tattle community, that he slept with the girl in his own house, and then in her *pa*, sometimes after divine service. Outrage upon outrage. Towards the end of January, a plunder party seeking compensation – for she had been pledged, so the Maori said – raided Kendall's house at Rangihoua, helping themselves to his fowl house and to two asses. In the next month another larger party broke into Kendall's house, seized various items, and one warrior swung a hatchet at him. Waikato, the minor chief who had accompanied him to England, intervened; but matters within the household were not to be resolved quite so readily.

The news spread from Rangihoua to Kerikeri, the second mission settlement; and with it came an increase in tensions between the missionaries. There must have been ongoing domestic tension too. For in March, when Kendall felt obliged to confess his sin, he was continuing to live with Tungaroa. He went away with her, taking several boxes of possessions with him, to live in another *pa*, well out of the way of everyone. There they stayed for about a month, to mid-April, nearing the end of summer. Then he fled, leaving everything and everyone behind him – first to Whangaroa, further north up the coast; and soon after across country to the west coast, to Hokianga river, when the weather rolling in from the Tasman Sea must have corresponded more completely with his mind, if not his feelings.

In Hokianga he stayed aboard Captain James Herd's *Providence* until late in August, acting as translator and go-between, while the Maori cut spars from the nearby forest for trade. He may have found some little comfort, if temporary, in that, and he preached in the blustery weather both to the Maori and such seamen as would listen to him. He made one significant penitent gesture – he tramped back through the dripping interior to baptise his son. But the contempt of the other settlers, and their contempt for his wife too, drove him to return to the wilder coast.

For one reason or another, this child would be the last of their progeny. That might have been a function of Jane's age, or of her outrage. Either way, it says something about that side of their future relationship.

Thomas earned himself no respect with his various attempted defences. Binney argues the antinomianism of his thinking, that he needed to fall so that he could be saved; and that like Conrad's Kurtz (in *Heart of Darkness*), he had succumbed to the 'fascination of the abomination'.

But there is a rather weaker side to his various intemperate self-justifications. And in showing this he demeaned himself. He let it be known that he had been thinking of his wife's previous betrayal of him, as though a little tit-for-tat was grounds for such a serious breach of his marriage oath and of his clerical standing. He stooped so low as to claim that he was driven to it by his wife's heavy drinking while he was absent in England.[27] The other settlers had all remarked on his own heavy drinking, over many years. He attempted to exonerate himself by arguing that he had to become as the Maori to understand their culture. He pointed out that he had taken steps to separate himself from temptation, by leaving the mission – but as a number remarked, while the girl remained in his house then he could not really claim to have broken with the cause of his moral failure. When eventually that did happen, for the Maori at least there was no longer any reason to call for punishment.

In none of this is there any acknowledgement of affection for the young woman in question. She almost does not signify. Thomas's eldest son, Thomas Surfleet Kendall, wrote in his diary on 12 October 1822, 'The last of the native females quitted the house this week by the disire [sic] of the Revd. Thos. Kendall'.[28] Binney reads that as quaint phrasing, touchingly formal. It could just as well be read as icy disgust.

The settlement continued in an uproar. In February 1823, having reconciled himself with Jane and his family, he shifted them and all their possessions to a Maori village, Matauwhi, just around the corner from Kororareka (Russell). He had possibly been unnerved by those recent assaults. He would be safe under the protection of a different chief, who was antagonistic to Hongi (so perhaps giving Kendall some distance from the control Hongi held over him), though his justification to the Church Missionary Society was more ingratiating. He was changing his native associates.[29] Kendall said many things at many different times.

Marsden was swift and to the point in his correspondence, of course; and he followed it up with an explosive visit in the middle of the year, braving the turbulent weather of the Tasman Sea. He brought with him a letter from the society: they had found Kendall's trading in muskets unacceptable. They did not yet know it, but there was now this even more inflammatory cause of outrage, his adultery. Kendall must leave New Zealand. Marsden was adamant. Never tactful, he embittered Kendall by bluntly reminding him of the biblical injunction that the sins of the fathers would be visited upon the children. So much for a religion of compassion. There was ill will between both of them.

On 7 September 1823 Marsden and the Kendalls and some others boarded the *Brampton* to sail to Sydney. But in a rising gale the ship was wrecked on a shoal, which would thereafter be known as Brampton reef. Marsden was prompt to make his way to shore. He was the first to be rescued by the mission boat; whereas Kendall and his family were left aboard the crippled vessel for three days while the little mission boat shuttled uneasily back and forth with distressed passengers, and their goods and chattels. It took a full week to rescue everyone and everything. Eventually the Kendalls made their way back to their former home – that is, well away from the mission settlements but rather close to whatever was giving rise to its subsequent character as a cesspit of reprobates, rakehells and bullyboys.

The Maori noted slyly that this misadventure had happened on a Sunday. Perhaps the *pakeha* God was upset that they had been breaking the Sabbath? Which just went to show that they had in fact been listening.

For Kendall, however, it was a sign, a divine intervention. He had been saved again. And that convinced him that he had more work to do in New Zealand. There they stayed for a further two years, in which time his sense of conviction had adjusted somewhat to the realities of his circumstance.

In January 1825, on the Firth of Thames, Kendall encountered Captain Richard Florance of the *St Patrick*; Thomas's son Joseph had sailed there from the Bay of Islands with the captain. There Kendall learned of the growing British merchant colony at Valparaiso, the thriving deep-water harbour in newly independent Chile, and of their need of a clergyman. Kendall was still intent on returning to the mission community from which he had been excluded, and besides the Maori community had shown they were unwilling to let him go. They gained by his presence. He translated for them, he negotiated arrangements with visiting captains. When they learned that he was now seriously considering leaving, they gathered at his place, threatened him, and broke his windows. They were already in a belligerent mood, for they were about to attack a neighbouring tribe.

Yet this is not quite the way the family told the story subsequently. The Kendalls, like the McNallys, were prone to amend, if not reconstruct their family narrative. Many years later, when one of Thomas's younger sons was himself an elderly man, he used to give a somewhat adjusted version of why they all left New Zealand, and how:

> Although he left New Zealand at the early age of 7 years, he had a wonderfully clear recollection of many incidents that took place while he

> was there. His father, about the year 1823, wished to leave New Zealand in order to educate his family, and embarked aboard the *Brampton*, but was wrecked at the entrance of the Bay, and had to return to land ... The Kendall family ultimately left New Zealand for Valparaiso when John was 7 years old. They had great difficulty in getting away, as the Maories [sic] objected to their going, and they had to slip away when the latter were at war.[30]

Nothing there whatsoever of the stormy arguments, the domestic unhappiness, of crisis upon crisis, the discipline enjoined upon Thomas Kendall and his defiance of that. Their removal was their father's enlightened choice, to do the best by his children.

When the warriors went off about their particular business a day or two later, Jane saw their chance. She grasped at the opportunity to leave a situation that must have been intolerable for her.[31] The Kendalls sailed on the *St Patrick* with Captain Florance for Valparaiso, Chile, in no little part so that the children could mature in European company. There could be no going back now.

Yet the terms of his appointment in Valparaiso were somewhat chancy. His was an unofficial role; on which grounds he may have reconciled himself to trespassing over the bounds of his ordination. Or he was prepared to ignore them. For undoubtedly the English and American community there would have expected to hear sermons regularly. His living was supported by subscriptions gathered from the British colonists, he readily consecrated a burial ground and conducted funeral services there, he performed weddings and baptisms. But he did not preach in a church, for there was none.

It began to dawn upon him that the terms and conditions of his appointment were not quite satisfactory. His quondam parishioners were constantly coming and going. He found the climate disagreeable, and he endured a severe attack of dysentery. All about the little town were either tidal marshlands or steep hillsides, trapping the frequent fogs that came in off the sea. Even so, it rarely rained there, unlike the variable weather in the Bay of Islands. And those steep hills were only lightly timbered. There was none of the greenness he had been accustomed to in New Zealand, none of the heavy hanging clouds.

The wife of the British consul, whose children he had been tutoring, decided to go back to England, taking the children and that part of his income with her.[32] This consul was not, as some commentators propose, Christopher Nugent, who as consul-general resided in Santiago, but Henry William Rouse, the vice-consul, and rumoured to be the illegitimate son of George IV 'and an oriental lady'.

The colony began to moderate its enthusiasm for supporting the reverend gentleman and his family and the subscription system was wound up, but not before the presentation of a final gift to assist the Kendalls to migrate back to Sydney.

As they made their passage across the Pacific to New South Wales, their daughter Susanna (sometimes spelled Susannah) was being married in St James' Church, by special licence, Rev. Richard Hill officiating.[33] This was just a matter of a fortnight or so before her parents' ship docked. The timing is curious.[34] Hill also subsequently performed the marriage of her younger sister, Elizabeth, to Thomas Florance, one of the many sons of Captain Florance.[35] Curiously, Thomas Florance (born 1783) was just older than Elizabeth's mother, Jane; and only a few years younger than her father. It was almost a mirror image of Thomas's disagreeable connection with Tungaroa, the same age as the Kendall girls.

And the awkward child, Samuel, Jane's shame, died shortly after their return, after a very brief illness. He would feature no more in the revised family history. The given name 'Samuel' is thereafter discretely but conspicuously absent from subsequent generations of Kendalls.[36]

3

Very Much Given to Indulge in Spirits

Before the family set sail for Valparaiso, Thomas Kendall's eldest son, Thomas Surfleet Kendall, had stood firm against his father's proposal to leave their home in Matauwhi and move to Kerikeri, to the shelter and protection of chief Hongi. He remonstrated with his father about that plan, because that would ensure their separation from the mission community. Shortly after, in 1824 (though not necessarily in consequence), he was sent back to England to be apprenticed as a carpenter.[1]

Just as his father's health had failed when he moved to another climate, so Thomas Surfleet sickened in the land of his forebears; and he grasped at the opportunity, when it was offered, to join an expedition by the New Zealand Company, whose intention was to establish a settlement at Hokianga in the timber country on the west coast, opposite the Bay of Islands. He readily accepted an invitation to act as their interpreter, for like his father and no doubt with instruction by his father he too had become fluent in Maori.

Here again is to be found an adjusted version of the actual events. When, many years later, Thomas Surfleet Kendall died – he lived to turn 76 – his obituary circulated a story for which he alone must have been responsible. Either that, or the reporter managed to muddle the facts expediently. According to the *Kiama Independent* (9 November 1883), the family had resided in the Bay of Islands for 11 years, 'at the expiration of which time they returned to England by the whaler *Mary*, Captain Renwick, arriving there via Cape Horn after a six months passage'. That may have been Thomas Surfleet's voyage; it most certainly was not Thomas Kendall's, nor that of his family. And it sidesteps the terms on which Rev. Thomas Kendall's employment by the Church Missionary Society was terminated. Which was not an aspect of their past that any of the Kendalls wished to revive.

Thomas Surfleet had been in England for the best part of two years when he chanced to come across Captain Herd, an old friend of his father's, and former owner of the *Providence* aboard which Thomas Kendall had found refuge when he fled from the consequences of his liaison with Tungaroa. Herd was on the point of bringing 30 settlers out for the New Zealand Company. According to the *Kiama Independent*, Thomas Surfleet sailed with them and served as interpreter for about two years (the arithmetic is decidedly a tight fit):

> and during that period [he] was the means of saving two vessels and their crews from destruction by the natives; and an incident occurred during the same period which, had it not been for Mr Kendall's sagacity and prompt action, would have resulted in the whole of the party being killed.[2]

Just what that incident was is not recorded, but the young man evidently possessed readiness of mind and common sense. He was mature for his age, and his father would vest his confidence in him.

The proposed New Zealand settlement was not a success,[3] and whereas the gentlemen investors resumed their activities back on the other side of the world, Thomas Surfleet Kendall returned to Sydney, arriving there in 1827 like the rest of his family, but considerably ahead of them, as early as February. He seemed to have little knowledge of their movements. For example, he does not appear to have had much connection with his sister's marriage. As for the others, he recounted that he was surprised at breakfast one morning when, after residing for some six months with Mr John Powell at Parramatta, his father arrived unexpectedly from Valparaiso. That was the story he liked to recount; on that basis, he was hardly *au fait* with their movements either.

Thomas Surfleet's accommodating host was in all likelihood John Vittoria Powell, son of the John Powell who had been one of the mission workers in the Bay of Islands. Powell was considered too sympathetic to Thomas Kendall and was, accordingly, aboard the ill-fated *Brampton* when Marsden attempted to reimpose his own sense of order and control upon that unruly settlement.[4]

Kendall Sr, now returned from South America, was without an income. His urgent need was to redeem the land he had been promised all those years ago, when he first came out to New South Wales. He wrote to the Lands Board in late October 1827 and received the welcome response that he should proceed to make a selection of 1280 acres forthwith – that is, two square miles.

Although he had no gainful employment, he was hardly on his uppers. On his application it was noted that he held capital of £1354/9/5.[5] Evidently his dubious trading operations in the Bay of Islands had had their compensations.

His address in Sydney for the time being was c/- Thomas Barker, newly established as a flour miller. Barker had been a fellow passenger on board the *Earl Spencer* when they had come out from Britain some 14 years previously, though their acquaintance was unlikely to have been close. He was less than half the age of Thomas Kendall; Kendall was travelling with his wife and five children. Nevertheless, some kind of bond of recognition had been struck, and endured.

Barker had been a precocious 14-year-old with an aptitude for mechanical engineering and had been accompanied by his guardian, likewise a gifted engineer and manufacturer. Within a few years Barker started out on his own, and built a windmill in Macquarie Street; on the success of that he bought a dilapidated steam mill and renovated it himself, and was just on the point of starting up a large steam-driven flour mill down near Cockle Bay, at the corner of Sussex Street and Bathurst Street – close to where the McNallys lived.

Thomas Surfleet Kendall took up accommodation at this time in Pitt Street, Sydney, where he worked for two years as a carpenter and joiner[6]; his brother Joseph joined him there. That became the Kendalls' town address. Basil had not yet returned from Valparaiso, Susanna was married, and Samuel had died. Apart from Elizabeth, the elder Kendalls now had only the rump end of their family to provide for.

The indications are that in his quest for suitable country Thomas Kendall was much obliged to recommendations by the assistant surveyor of the South Coast district, beyond the Illawarra. This was none other than Thomas Florance, son of the captain who had taken the Kendalls to Valparaiso, and indeed who had pointed them to South America in the first place. Thomas Florance had only just completed his survey of that part of the New South Wales coast and its hinterland; in May of 1828 he had charted Ulladulla harbour, past Mollymook and Narrawallee, and explored the creek for four miles inland. There he came across large stands of cedar, an unusual and potentially profitable discovery, as this was as far south as cedar grew.

It is telling how promptly Kendall made his way there. He knew about timber. He had seen the beginnings of that industry in New Zealand, the felling, the cutting, the shipping of it. And he had already taken matters into his own hands, apparently, for he had acquired a boatload of cedar from down on the Illawarra, and was discovered clandestinely transferring that prized cargo to another vessel in Port Jackson, on 13 December 1827. He had not long been in the colony – long enough to familiarise himself with a cunning stratagem, but not long enough (by his own communication with the customs officers who had seized his cutter) to have familiarised himself with the requirement to pay duty ahead of such actions. Besides, he begged to advise them, it had been his intention to sell the timber back to its original owner. That is not an immediately convincing defence.[7]

Thomas Mitchell, the newly appointed Surveyor-General, was subsequently critical of Florance's part in the Kendall selection, and administered an official reprimand[8] when Florance's connection with the Kendalls became public by his marriage to Elizabeth Kendall (May 1829).

Thomas Florance, Elizabeth's senior by 20 years, had spent some time in Canada, almost in echo of Patrick McNally, though under quite different circumstances. He was several years older than McNally, and went to Canada first as a surveyor, then served for two-and-a-half years as a military engineer in the War of 1812, and in much the same region as McNally. Like McNally, he returned to England (in this case voluntarily), only to leave again as soon as he could arrange passage to Australia. He had not found the weather agreeable in Canada, nor in England.

Although how he came to encounter the Kendalls in Sydney is unknown, it is reasonable to assume that his father's previous acquaintance with the ex-missionary and his family had something to do with it. Whatever the case, Florance decided that Miss Elizabeth's company was congenial, and he began to pay his addresses to her; and likewise to her father.

Which prompted appropriate outcomes. In mid-1828, that is, in the winter months, Thomas Kendall went sailing down the coast in his own small boat, together with his 10-year-old son John and with two pairs of sawyers. He was not wasting any time. Clearly, he anticipated putting his men to work. Guided by an Indigenous man they had taken aboard somewhere near Jervis Bay, they made their way further south and into a 'budgeree harbor more further on',[9] called Nulladolla (Ulladulla).

Here is another modification of actuality. It had been claimed for the family history that, 'as far as is known, [they were] the first white men to enter the port'.[10] Yet they cannot have been the first Europeans to enter it, because Thomas Florance for one had already been there. But that does not make quite such a good story, it does not fit the pioneering legend so splendidly.

They camped in the little harbour overnight, uneasily sharing the foreshore with a large party of natives, then sailed back up the coast five miles to a creek about which, Thomas Mitchell suspected, Florance had tipped off his prospective father-in-law. The timber thereabouts looked very promising. Kendall and his party cleared a place for a house, built bush huts for the sawyers and opened a way through the thick brush, a muddy track back to the boat harbour. He had found his selection; here was a superlative stand of red cedar. The sawyers set to work almost at once, felling trees, digging their sawpits down on the banks of the creek, cutting the massive trunks into great planks. Red gold, the cedar was called. There was ironbark too, and turpentine, mahogany, blackbutt, coachwood, all of it desirable. White cedar as well.

Not long afterwards, Thomas Kendall returned with a load of provisions, and attempted to take his boat up the Narrawallee creek. John's recollection of that found its way into his obituary:

> They experienced great difficulty in getting the vessel in the entrance, but succeeded by fastening a rope to a tree and every time a wave lifted the vessel the party gave the rope a pull, thus getting her over the bar.[11]

Once they were over, it was relatively easy to work the boat up the creek; but clearly that would be no way to manage it out again with a cargo of hundreds of cedar planks.

Shortly after Kendall's claim was gazetted, Thomas Florance took up an adjacent holding, likewise of 1280 acres, and likewise cedar country, granted in recognition of his services to the Surveyor-General's department – for he and the department had gone their separate ways after the Surveyor-General formally criticised Florance's surveying work in the Hunter River district, together with his 'unbecoming and insulting manner'.[12]

As the timber on Kendall's property was felled, bullocks hauled the logs out to the creek, where they were squared and sawn and cut to a length, and floated down to the sea on the ebb tide, over the difficult bar at the creek's mouth and out to the waiting boat; and Kendall skippered it back to Sydney. He was confident enough of his sailing skills to do this at quite regular intervals – by the reports of the shipping news, almost on a monthly basis.

He invested some of his returns in improving his property, as was required – clearing, fencing, developing a farm, erecting sheds. This in time became known as Kendall Dale, and the landholding there became a kind of Kendall compound. The family lived there, his wife Jane and the younger children. But some of his income he turned towards further investment, and in 1831 he took over an existing grant of 500 acres at Kiama. He settled his son Thomas Surfleet Kendall, recently married (young John Powell was one of the witnesses), on this property, and named it Retreat Farm.

That is where his son's carpentering skills were put to good use – here, in his 24th year, Thomas Surfleet built with his own hands a farm house, which he called Happy Villa (not, as is sometimes written, Happy Valley, the literary associations of which would suggest a much more conflicted person). He built a dairy, a kitchen, he built farm buildings, he built fences around the paddocks and soon had healthy crops of wheat and corn.

Not content with that allocation, he petitioned for (as was allowed) a marriage portion for his wife, née Caroline Rutter. She was granted 100 acres, adjoining her father-in-law's property, and named Orange Grove. The Kendall domains were being expanded. Thomas Surfleet likewise petitioned for himself, though he had to wait some years before he too was conceded a further allocation, 320 acres, down in the same part of the country and called Darling Forest. Collectively, the Kendalls had become substantial landholders.

It was not always plain sailing, going up and down the coast in a smallish boat; but that was at first the only means of transport. Conditions were rudimentary, at best. An old-timer recalled arriving in Ulladulla harbour in 1857 and being lowered in a bag to a waiting boat, to be taken ashore. The only harbour facility was a mooring chain.[13] Kendall had grown to trust himself up and down that precarious coast, however, and with each trip he became more experienced in the ways of the challenging winds. Besides, he had already survived a calamity at sea, and believed that to signify a divine purpose. He was destined for some greater work. Perhaps that confidence sustained him on a second occasion.

Though at this distance, it is a question whether his belief was altogether separate from his self-belief.

Late in 1830 he was coming back from the South Coast, meaning he had a cargo aboard. Those coastal waters can turn freakish very quickly. The press reported what happened:

> The Rev. Mr. Kendall and his boat's crew had a miraculous escape, on Tuesday night, from a watery grave. They were sailing, with a stiff breeze, from Illawarra to Sydney: about 10 o'clock a sudden gust blew the boat completely over, and being eight miles from land, the unfortunate passengers gave themselves up for lost; the men contrived to get upon the keel, but Mr. K. was entangled in the boat, and could only just keep his head out of the water. After remaining in this perilous position for some time, inevitable death staring them in the face, the boat suddenly righted, and all hands were providentially saved.[14]

Providential indeed; and so it was for the boat, for it remained in use. The Lord looking after his own. The headlines identified the event as miraculous. That would only have served to inflate Kendall's sense of himself as intended for some greater work.

Thomas Kendall built a property for himself out from Ulladulla, although he did not spend his time there. He still yearned to publish a revised version of his Maori grammar, not least because Marsden was opposed to it, and ridiculed it. But it was also the original condition of his employment by the Church Missionary Society, and an improved reissue might be the means to return from his disgrace and to retrieve their favour.

Marsden had made up his mind early, at the time of Kendall's eviction from the Bay of Islands, that his subordinate's representation of the Maori tongue was 'incomprehensible'. Twice Kendall attempted to have a revised version go to press, but Marsden had bustled about Sydney, intimidating printers to prevent Kendall publishing his *Grammar*, apparently from sheer spite. Particularly he scoffed at Kendall's insistence on contriving diagraphs to represent Maori speech. How was anyone meant to pronounce 'ng', Marsden blustered. The New Zealanders should learn to pronounce words in the English manner. Now Kendall wanted to introduce another, 'wh'. Marsden would have none of it, and certainly not while there was any residual connection with the activities of the Church Missionary Society.

Kendall's enthusiasm had been renewed on his way back from Valparaiso, when his ship had called in to Tahiti and he met a like-minded missionary who had successfully published a grammar for the natives there. Now Kendall set about trying to raise the costs of an amended publication through subscription. The Rev. Thomas could be just as stubborn as Marsden. But that meant he had to spend a good deal of his time up in Sydney, presenting himself to potential subscribers, talking up the worthiness of his project, showing himself to have continued his interest in the Maori. He published a long letter in the *Sydney Gazette* (8 January 1831) under the pseudonym 'Solicitus',[15] on the 'origin, language and religion of the New Zealanders', in which (Professor Lee notwithstanding) he again pressed the notion that the Maori were of Middle Eastern origin, and were alluded to in several biblical references. These were a commendable people, he declared, now that they had been enlightened by the activities of the missionaries. And they could be seen walking about the streets of Sydney. They were no longer remote, and insignificant.

One of those who subscribed, and the only one of his sons, was Basil. The others were not bookish types, it seems. So did his friend of many years, Thomas Barker; and Robert Cooper ('Robert the Large', who had already built Juniper Hall in Paddington), William Wentworth, and to give him his due, Samuel Marsden. Kendall must have continued as a vexation to Marsden, for he was commonly conceded the title 'reverend', even though by the terms of his licence his pastoral activity was confined to New Zealand. Kendall did not claim it for himself in, for example, advertisements when he was in quest of bullock drivers to work down on his properties.[16] Yet he had from the first declared his intention of performing clerical duties in the neighbourhood of his land grant.[17] That was why he had requested an allocation where no other clergyman resided. And Ulladulla was far enough out of Marsden's line of sight to be of no consequence to the Colonial Chaplain.[18]

Basil, the second son, had at long last also returned from Valparaiso, where he had been at sea – not in the moral sense but quite literally. For, as Thomas reported in a letter to the Church Missionary Society in 1827, at the commencement of the return of the rest of the Kendalls to Sydney, Basil 'was situated with Commodore Wooster'.[19] In his years at the Bay of Islands he had undertaken some boat building and house building, he had learned to sail, and he had learned to navigate. His younger brother Joseph had enjoyed much the same set of experiences, and in time would become a certificated captain. Basil does not appear to have acquired any specified rank in his time at Valparaiso, but was evidently satisfied, at least as a young man, with the romance of the sea. What else could he have done with his time in Chile?

Despite this, his son Henry subsequently claimed that 'He [Basil] was an officer in the Navy – a lieutenant in the Anglo-Chilean Service'.[20] Judith Binney, however, was confident that 'there are no records of Basil Kendall amongst the foreigners enlisted as officers; indeed, the need for foreign officers no longer existed as most of the [Chilean] fleet had been transferred to the Buenos Aires government ...'[21] Henry had to be wrong. And that would not be the only time.

It would have been a more enthralling story of the Hamilton-Grey kind if Basil had in fact (as she maintained) sailed with the colourful and dashing Lord Cochrane, Commander-in-Chief of the Chilean navy in the heady years when it was fighting to establish Chile's independence from Spain. Bertram Stevens for one believed it: 'While in South America he [Basil] saw service under Lord Cochrane, the famous tenth Earl of Dundonald'. Cochrane was renowned for his extraordinary and bold manoeuvres against the French, to the extent that Napoleon nicknamed him *le loup des mers* (the Sea Wolf). Frederick Marryat sailed under him as a midshipman and based his novels on those experiences; Forester's Horatio Hornblower is likewise based on Cochrane, and so too is Patrick O'Brian's Jack Aubrey (*Master and Commander*, for example). He even appears in two Flashman novels. But Cochrane had left Valparaiso before the Kendalls set out from New Zealand, and all that Basil Kendall would have encountered is the legend he, Cochrane, left behind him.

He left behind Captain Charles Whiting Wooster, who had been involved in raising the blockade of Valparaiso in 1818. This was in a ship named the *Lautaro*, none other in fact than the former East Indiaman *Windham*, escort to the fleet of convict transports, including the *Surry* and the *Broxbornebury*, which had brought the McNallys out to Australia. The Chilean agent in London arranged the purchase of the *Windham*; it sailed to Valparaiso, was fitted out with 44 guns and its new name,[22] and after a fierce and successful engagement against the great Spanish frigate *Esmeralda*, drove her off. The *Lautaro*'s original captain was killed in the engagement, and Charles Wooster took his place. He had formerly been the captain of an American whaler; and had fought the British during the War of 1812. That might lend some weight to what happened next.

For when Cochrane was given the command of the Chilean navy, the portly Wooster ('the Prince of Whales') resigned. When Cochrane departed, Wooster resumed the command of his old ship, but that did not turn out well. His crew mutinied against him. By 1824 the *Lautaro* was moored at Valparaiso and had become Chile's naval academy. It is in that capacity that Basil Kendall would have known her. In 1828 she was ordered to be sold, but with no bidders at the auction she was converted into a pontoon, and broken up in 1829. With the academy gone, and the navy dispersed, there was no promising career ahead for Basil. He returned to Sydney in 1828, aged 21.[23]

He appears to have had a sufficiency of the maritime life. But clearing paddocks was not a preferred option either. He took employment at Thomas Barker's steam mill in Sussex Street, recently purchased and under expansion: Basil's role was as a clerk. Later events reveal that he was trusted with something more than lowly duties. He was involved in the purchase of quantities of wheat for the mill, and the issuing of notes of credit.

Barker was ever a good friend to the Kendalls. Later John Kendall was apprenticed there, and Lawrence too was apprenticed in 1834.[24] He lived with the Barkers, learned the flour-milling trade and eventually set up his own steam mill in Liverpool.

Basil though was more independent. There is no indication that he skippered his father's cutter, the *Brisbane*, on its monthly trips up and down the coast, despite that vessel being registered in his name. His duties at the steam mill would have kept him anchored at his desk.

At this very time, in 1828, Patrick McNally too was working for Thomas Barker, as a carter. His home then was in the next street, Kent Street. All of this area down alongside what had been known as Cockle Bay, but later raised to a higher eminence as Darling Harbour, was largely commercial and industrial, with workers' cottages between the warehouses and mills and manufactories. The McNallys were well and truly ensconced there; the Kendalls had pretensions to something better.

In 1829 Thomas Kendall's Sydney address appears when he advertised for two bullock drivers. At that stage he could be contacted at 43 Upper Pitt Street, not far from where Thomas Surfleet had his carpentry workshop, and where Joseph sometimes lived too. For whatever reason, Thomas chose not to share his sons' quarters.

He remained as feisty as ever. He would not be imposed upon. He had stood up to Marsden, and defied the sniping and occasional direct hostility of his fellow missionaries in the Bay of Islands. He would kowtow to no one. Once in his anger he had even struck a Maori.[25] He issued through the press a public warning against trespass on his land (assuming that the likely offenders were literate and read their newspapers assiduously); he was angered to find that bullock drovers were making tracks across his lands, and in all likelihood helping themselves to his cedar. Cedar poaching was rife. Then he confronted a bullocky. He would not be intimidated by such a one either, regardless of their reputed toughness and fighting abilities. This bullock driver was not going to turn out of his way and drove straight at Kendall, who was forced to step aside. But only for as long as it took him to summons the law.[26] That was one trespass that would not be forgiven.

Kendall was no vicar of the kind to sit in the front room and eat cucumber sandwiches. Indeed, some of the newspapers identified him as a cedar cutter rather than as a parson. He was a pioneer. He was involved in opening up the country, clearing the dense forests and installing fences. Even if he hired men to do the hard physical work, he too had to be tough and resilient. He lived as the other pioneers, and did as they did. He was wilful, if no longer wayward. According to Ackland, at this time Thomas Kendall continued with the heavy drinking that had been in evidence in his New Zealand days:

> perhaps as a result of isolation and extremely difficult living conditions, the Kendalls of Kirmington nonetheless earned an unenviable reputation for their drinking habits even in those days. Both the Reverend Thomas Kendall and his wife Jane … had already been given to over-indulgence in liquor.[27]

Over several months in 1831 the press carried advertisements for the sale of the *Brisbane*, giving various contact details – sometimes directing enquiries to Joseph, or to Basil, and even to Thomas Barker. Yet Thomas Kendall would still have needed to ship his cedar and his dairy produce up to Sydney. In one of the advertisements the tonnage of the cutter had been reduced from 18 to 15. It is a curious detail. That might, for example, be an indication of some unhelpful modification. It might be a hint of why he planned to sell the vessel. Alternatively, he might have wanted the funds he could realise on that sale to further enlarge his holdings down close to Pigeon House Mountain. Either way, whatever happened to the little ship was his decision even though Basil was the registered owner.

And he was steadily increasing his holdings, by application for further grants and by direct purchase. He had come a long way from those 15 acres in Lincolnshire. If the church would not provide him with a sure foundation, then he would find it another way. Besides, what he was about was not so very different from Marsden's pursuit of pasturage for his sheep.

Kendall now had enough funding, both by his own activity and raised by subscription, to proceed with the publication of his revised New Zealand grammar. But he was defeated in this ambition by an unforeseen turn of events.

In the mid-winter of 1832, with fierce squalls driving in towards the coast, Thomas Kendall took the *Brisbane* out to sea with a load of cedar from his property, cheeses and perhaps kegs of butter from his dairy, valued in all at £200,[28] and turned to scud before the strong winds up to Sydney. At the mouth of Jervis Bay a violent storm caught up with them. The cutter capsized and was wrecked, with the loss of all life. Early reports included among the dead Thomas's son-in-law, Thomas Florance, but that was erroneous for he had not been aboard.[29]

This was the third time Thomas Kendall had met with disaster at sea. Going down for the third time, in a violent and disturbed sea. They were far from any help – it was a case of every man for himself.

The wreckage was found by a party of local tribesmen near Currumbene Creek in the north of the bay, the *Brisbane* half-buried in the sand. Kendall's shoes were picked up nearby, his wig and a small trunk recognised as his property. Some hoped that the shoes had been kicked off so as not to hinder his swimming, and that he would be discovered along the empty shore. No bodies were ever found. The date of his death was agreed as 6 August.

His wife Jane notified the Sydney press soon after the discovery of the wreckage and the failure to discover any survivors. She likewise wrote immediately to their ever-reliable old friend, Thomas Barker. He was quick to reply, with sound practical advice and with an eye on the legal implications. He advised Jane to go at once to Kiama, to stay with her son Thomas. She had no protection and not much comfort at Kendall Dale. But his chief concern for the moment was with the contents of her husband's wooden chest. The Reverend's papers were missing. The chest had been plundered. Deeds, titles and all had gone, and not least important, there was no surviving will.

Even at that distance, Barker seemed to have been remarkably well informed. He knew that a gang of sharks, something like a local variant of the coastal wreckers of England, ranged about that difficult part of the coast, far enough away from authorities to be fairly confident in carrying out their plundering, but not as far as to be wholly absolutely free of the long arm of the law. They were known. They had 'history'. They were led by a man called Morris, who often acted as a decoy, pretending to be adrift in a disabled boat, and enticing would-be rescuers to leave whatever they were doing and to put to sea, to come to his assistance. His accomplices then helped themselves to whatever was left behind, while he would suddenly hoist sail and make off. They were also experienced burglars and thieves.

Several members of Morris's gang had been in and out of the courts in recent years. Barker was sure that these were the rascals responsible for breaking into Kendall's box, and he had no doubt they had likewise plundered the vessel. He recommended that they be offered five pounds – indeed, he would provide that amount – and a pardon for having helped themselves to whatever was aboard the *Brisbane*, provided that they restore the papers. The will had to be found. Of course there was nothing to prove that Morris and his men were the offenders.

The will was not forthcoming. That meant that Thomas Kendall had died intestate – indeed, there was neither a body nor a will – and Thomas Surfleet, as his eldest son, became (according to the British regulation that then applied) heir-at-law, inheriting one-half of the estate. Barker arranged for a man to take over the dairy; the cargo of cedar was sold on the beach at a penny a foot; and the *Brisbane* was patched and sailed back to Sydney.[30]

Samuel Marsden provided a last vindictive epitaph for the Rev. Thomas Kendall: 'He was very much given to indulge in Spirits'.[31] Rubbing Kendall's reputation into the ground, affirming the distance he had fallen from the Wesleys' firm principles.

Thomas Surfleet appears to have avoided this aspect of his parents' disposition, or at least the excess of it. His character was marked by steadiness. Joseph briefly held a partnership in a brewery, the Union Brewery in Pitt Street, which manufactured colonial porter. The brewery commenced business in April 1831, but by mid-September of that year Joseph had pulled out, leaving it to his partner to carry on. He had a more enticing offer, and shipping news shows him returning from New Zealand towards the end of March 1832.[32] That was more his cup of tea.

As for Basil, his activities in Barker's mill did not confine him to the counting house. He had on occasion to negotiate with those selling wheat, he had to negotiate with the settlement of bills and the exchange of promissory notes; and it was not unknown for him to then proceed to a public house with the commission agent when an arrangement had been settled.

And the McNallys? Patrick continued as a carter, sometimes a labourer, and, as it were, indentured to his wife. His eldest daughter, Mary, was listed in the 1828 census as resident in less-than-salubrious Kent Street, housekeeper to the Martins, and identified as Catholic. In 1830 she and her brother William were each granted 50 acres at Bellambi, near Wollongong. By the standard of the day, and certainly by comparison with grants made to the Kendalls, that was a modest allocation. Three years later, in 1833, Mary married James Martin. They moved to her property at Fairy Meadow, just behind Bellambi, and right alongside her brother William's little farm. There was an initial spurt of children, then James sold her grant, took the proceeds and vanished from historical sight. Mary never remarried, perhaps understandably. Nor did she return to her parents' home.

Her sister Matilda, meanwhile, still in her teenage years, remained with the Hills in Castlereagh Street as servant, housekeeper or governess, whatever version of the facts came most immediately to mind. Quite possibly she did learn a little needlework in this time, supervised by Mrs Hill. Quite possibly the Hills did take some pains with a rudimentary education. And quite possibly she was introduced there to the desirable habit of reading.

But they were not quite so comfortable as they had been. The Rev. Richard had been too generous in his support of various charities, and much too generous in supporting his mother, back in England. Nevertheless, they employed Matilda still – she was not 'adopted' by them. The annual returns continued to identify her as a servant there, meaning that she lived in. They continued to list her as Protestant, in spite of her father's manoeuvre to reclaim her to the faith of his fathers. In that particular respect, at least, she was leading a double life.

Servants did not have a lot of freedom or independence. She would have been expected to attend to her duties, and she would have been expected to behave in conformity with the manners and the status of the Hills. Such time as was gradually allowed to her would doubtless have included visiting her parents across town. It is perhaps on these occasions that she began to develop a taste for dancing, for bantering and perhaps flirting with young people of her own age and background. And who knows, developing a fondness for a tipple. For that has to have come from somewhere, and it would not have happened with the Hills.

4

Thirty Pieces of Silver

The Kendall family history persists with the story that, at the end of July 1835, Basil Kendall met Matilda at a dance held in Sussex Street, they fell instantly in love and were married the next morning. Some variants speculate that several returns to the cheering cup were also involved in that train of events.

Certainly, the two were married, but not in such a gay manner as the romantic legend likes to make out. For the marriage certificate shows that they were married by the publishing of banns. That means the impulsive ardour was stretched out by a factor of at least several weeks.

The marriage certificate brings other challenges too. Matilda chose to enjoy yet another name change. She was no longer a McNally but claimed on this occasion to be a McAllan. And she orchestrated for herself a whole string of given names: Melinda Olivia Leonora. Melinda is the name on her baptismal paper, though her family all called her Matilda, and the census taker as well; and her son Henry would continue to believe that was her proper name. He cannot have been the only child to think so, for his siblings would have corrected him if it were otherwise. But Olivia Leonora? Really?

And why did she not sign her wedding certificate? Sins of omission as well as of commission …

There are further questions. The marriage ceremony was not conducted by the Anglican Rev. Richard Hill; yet she had lived under his roof for a dozen or so years and was in some sense his protégée. She was married in the Presbyterian church, which one might suppose would have disappointed him. She was a few months short of her 20th birthday – under age – and the question then is who might have given consent. For her father was emphatically a Catholic and could not have relished this falling by the way. The two witnesses at the wedding were friends of the Kendalls. Matilda married away from her own family, and from her de facto guardian.

A kind of defiance can be deduced hereabouts. Living with the Hills, she would have been carefully watched over. Weekend dances down in Sussex Street could hardly have been acceptable to them. As a servant she would have been allowed only limited time to herself, and they would have required to know just what kind of activity she proposed on such occasions. Similarly, indeed even more so, if she had been taken into their household, then not only did they have the responsibility for her, they had their own image of propriety to maintain.

Yet on this occasion at least she had chosen to go off to the other side of town, away from the genteel addresses of the top end. It was a kind of deliberate transgression. Her parents lived over that way; that is where she went dancing and, given her subsequent reputation, quite possibly drinking too. She had to have acquired the taste for it from somewhere, and it is improbable that she picked up that disposition from the Hills' sideboard.

It is well to remember also that she was not the only young woman living with the Hills. Two other misses are listed in the 1828 census, quite separately from three identified as servants (plus a manservant too). Whatever role Matilda had in that household, she was not unique. But this also means that Matilda was sometimes identified as a servant, and sometimes as not a servant. Mercurial Matilda.

By common consent she was acknowledged to have been pretty, lively, witty, ingenious. And quite possibly disingenuous, given that she kept on recreating not only herself but also her version of the facts. Her liveliness might have been part of her face-to-face charm, but it was misleading, for those she encountered and for literary historians alike. Bertram Stevens, on the other hand, chose instead to read her as of a 'strong constitution', that is, stubborn; and of a 'volatile temperament',[1] which implies much that might be more testing than charming.

However she is to be understood, she and Basil married somewhat precipitately. The family legend emphasises the dashing impulsiveness of this betrothal, an instant love match. But behind it lies a different story: Matilda was pregnant. Her daughter – also Melinda – was born prematurely, just a few months later, and died. T.D. Mutch claims the infant was named Mary, dying at the age of eight weeks, and was buried, on 28 October 1835, at Sydney by the Rev. William Cowper of St Philip's.[2] That invites a different gloss on the puzzling absence of the Hills, effectively her guardians; indeed, the absence of anyone from Matilda's side. It might explain why Matilda took measures to inhibit any link with her past at the Hills'. Whatever the case, the young couple were not off to a good start.

Basil's prospects were not very promising either. He had been employed in Barker's mills, but at about this time, perhaps just a little before it, he branched out on his own and set up shop as a purchasing agent.[3] Marjorie Kendall says that he also tried his hand as a clerk–storekeeper, but that might refer to his employment at Barker's.[4] Ackland is more elaborate:

> Basil ... attempted to establish himself as a minor Sydney merchant in premises rented near Market Wharf, trading as a general commission agent as far north as the Hunter River and as far south as the Illawarra district, while in Sydney itself he tried to build up a viable commercial venture based on flour, bran and spirit sales.[5]

He was unsuccessful. He was no businessman. His son Henry in later years avoided referring to Basil's business failures, and to 'a major reason for his commercial ineptitude – drink'.[6]

But another reason would soon emerge, Basil's weakness of character. For across the next decade, he would twice stand exposed as a petty criminal.

In April 1837 the *Sydney Gazette* announced that a young man, Wilson Berry or Bury, had been arrested on a charge of forgery and was brought to trial. The court proceedings were summarised without the excited nuancing which characterises the newspapers of the day, indeed the press since then. The initial circumstances of the alleged offence were unfolded in full detail; in the days that followed it emerged not only that Basil Kendall was implicated, but he may well have been the chief instigator in the crime. Before long, and rather more sensationally, it emerged that he had misled his younger brothers, who were also caught up in the matter. The Reverend would have been rolling in his watery grave, and not only for the misdeeds of his progeny but also because of the offence given to the Kendalls' well-wisher, Thomas Barker.

The intended deception presented a tangled web indeed. To begin with: Wilson Bury (that slowly consolidated as the preferred spelling, though Berry is the more likely), a commission agent, had brought a bill to Barker's thumping great steam mill in Sussex Street, from its subsidiary firm, the Brisbane Mills, in Parramatta Road. This mill was owned by Thomas Barker's brother, James, along with a partner, Ambrose Hallen; the big steam mill was also being operated at the time by James Barker, as Thomas had departed on an extended recuperative visit to England.

The court reporter had difficulty in keeping tabs on which of the younger Kendall brothers was which, and that confusion lasted right throughout the course of the trial. Lawrence Kendall had been apprenticed to Thomas Barker, and presumably so had John. Certainly, John was employed by him. Lawrence had been intended to follow in his father's footsteps as a minister – not as a cultural transgressor – presumably in the Church of England, though he attended Presbyterian services with the Barkers while he lived with them, and later changed his allegiance to the Wesleyan chapel, becoming a zealous Sunday School teacher.[7] He was a religious youth. He was unlikely to have knowingly participated in any fraudulence. John was invariably steady and reliable.

Basil had also formerly been employed in the mills but had left off working there some 12 months previously. What exactly he had been doing in that interval of independent enterprise does not emerge in the court hearing; but at this same point in time he was suspended from his Masonic Lodge,[8] an indication that he had been involved in some activity they disapproved of. Or that they disapproved of his character.

Initially the reporter thought it was Lawrence who 'had charge of that establishment', the mill on the Parramatta Road, and was consequently 'authorised to draw tickets for money, for purchases of wheat'.[9] But it was John who issued those tickets, and it was John's signature that was forged in this particular instance, for he gave evidence that he had not written out the note, nor had he authorised his younger brother to sign the note in question for him, or any other note. He had not given his brother Basil any such note either.

What Bury presented to Barker was a 'ticket', a kind of account statement, apparently signed by John Kendall. James Barker, who testified that he regularly received such tickets authorised by Lawrence Kendall, accepted it at face value and wrote out his cheque to the Commercial Bank to cover it. Bury's role was to present the cheque, as he customarily did, carrying it directly from Barker and keeping aside an agreed amount as his commission. The forgery, for such it was, was not discovered until the accounts were squared up at the end of the week.

When Bury was questioned before the Bench, he implicated Basil Kendall. There had been a negotiation between the two of them about how much commission Bury was to be allowed. His tried for what he claimed was his usual rate, five per cent. Basil would not concede so much, proposing instead a flat 30 shillings. That was a saving of some 10 shillings on the amount in question. Yet, if five per cent were customary, then Barker would not have been surprised to see his cheque cashed minus two pounds. Which leaves one wondering if there were 10 shillings floating about, and where that ended up.

Bury further testified that Basil Kendall had come to him after the transaction had been settled and wished to introduce him to his (Basil's) brother later that evening, but that he would not use Bury's name, rather an alias. Bury agreed to this, although he thought the concealment somewhat strange. The court thought it was somewhat suspicious. On the basis of this testimony Basil Kendall was apprehended upon warrant, and at the next hearing placed before the Bar alongside Bury as the examination continued. Bury of course already had his 30 pieces of silver.

John Kendall remembered that two or three weeks previously Basil had wanted him to write out a note in Bury's name so that he might obtain the cash for it. And he testified that he had never bought wheat from either Basil or Bury. James Barker produced several 'tickets', or notes of the purchase of wheat, and John was certain he had not given them to his brother.

When Basil was cross-examined, he denied having given the note in question to Bury, and he tried to prove that he had sold wheat to his brother at the mill. Having the brothers contradict each other was hardly going to make for comfortable relations between them.

When the investigation was resumed several days later, John 'exposed a most infamous and extensive system of plunder'.[10] Basil had been exploiting these arrangements for something like two years; that is, from the time he had married Matilda. He had persuaded John to write open tickets, the value not specified; he had assured him that this was his usual practice when he worked at the mills. John had received no wheat for those open tickets, even though the notes had been cashed and the commission extracted.

When Basil Kendall appeared before the Bench it became clear that he had been milking the system for such incidental perks. His argument was that, when the price of wheat fell, as it surely must, John could balance his books, making his accounts square, and nobody had lost anything. Never mind that he was cheating his former employer of the profit margin. Morally evasive at best.

And his final argument before the court was that 'the idea of his forging an order like that ... was preposterous, as he must have been detected at the end of the week'.[11] Which was not what he had been thinking on those previous occasions about which his brother John had testified.

Clearly the authorities had their doubts about Basil Kendall. He was refused bail, whereas Bury was allowed it. Basil spent the next weeks in gaol, awaiting the trial proper.

In the week following, the *Sydney Gazette* reported that Basil had attempted to flee the colony in the steamship *James Watt*. It corrected itself a week later again, informing the public that Lawrence Kendall, not Basil, was the one who had attempted to take passage to Hobart. Then later again, that it was neither of those brothers, but John Kendall, presenting himself as a passenger under his mother's maiden name, Quickfall. Then it became Lawrence again; a Customs officer had recognised him and refused to sign his clearance.

Yet, although a warrant was obtained for his arrest, he had not been discovered by the time of the next sitting. It was all turning into a farce. Without the presence of a material witness the trial could not proceed. This time Basil appears to have been granted bail, whereas Bury's application was refused by the judge.

To muddy the waters completely, the accused were to be tried together; but one of them elected trial before a military jury, the other before a civil jury. That had never happened before. Nevertheless, it was their right to choose whichever judicature they preferred. The press would have to clear their customary side of the court to make way for a second panel of jurors. But until the material witness – still uncertainly either John or

Lawrence – could be found, the prosecution could not proceed; and, as one postponed sitting followed another across the weeks, the case eventually lapsed. The Crown Prosecutor was not prepared to swear that he could obtain the attendance of (maybe) Lawrence Kendall by the next session. The two accused were discharged on their own recognisance to appear when called upon. The whole process had become a shambles.

Basil does not come out of this at all well. He cannot have been pleased that his brothers had testified against him. He cannot have been pleased at the exposure of his questionable practice over a protracted period of time. He was now identified as untrustworthy and the Barkers would certainly prefer to have nothing more to do with him. His brothers likewise chose to keep their distance thereafter, though they did not altogether deny him. But from that time they had little respect for him.

It is not at all clear just what was involved in the matter of the absconding witness, whether that was an independent instance of panic, a premeditated manoeuvre, or a strategy suggested by an unknown party. Lawrence should not have been too difficult to find. He was building his millhouse down at Liverpool. John was at the Hope Mill and did not go back to Ulladulla until about 1840.[12] At this distance it looks as though there was no particular will for the trial to go ahead.

One direct outcome of it all was that Basil and Matilda relocated well out of the public eye, to their portion of his father's estate at Ulladulla, on a section of the land grant noted by the surveyor as Mandnal and just outside the little village now known as Milton. In a very few years the property would be renamed Kirmington, adjacent to Kendall Dale and only a mile or so across the paddocks from Thomas Surfleet's grant, Darling Forest – Thomas had moved there from Kiama in 1838 with his young family and with his widowed mother. This was the Kendall enclave in the making. The different homesteads were close enough to be within sight of each other, but distant enough to be distinct farms. At this time, 'there were three Kendall brothers living within a mile of each other. A signal raised by Thomas at Wapindally could be seen by John and relayed to Basil'.[13]

And conversely. One such signal might have had to do with Matilda's birth pangs. On 18 April 1839, in an elementary and isolated slab-and-bark hut such as settlers used to build for themselves throughout the bush,

Matilda gave birth to twins, Basil Edward and Thomas Henry. Twins had not been expected, and the family legend was that a timber cutter shaped a bigger cedar cradle:

> There was shortage of clothing and bedding, but worst of all of sleeping accommodation for the babies. This was overcome by sheer bush initiative. Some timber-fellers of the neighbourhood went out into the forest and chose a large tree, cut it down and carefully stripped it of the greater portion of its bark. By closing in the extremities the bark was transformed into a capacious cradle, wherein two babies could be laid in comfort, one at each end. The natural curve dispensed with the necessity of adding rockers.[14]

Sometimes the kindly bushman is named, Jim Birkinshaw, and improved carpentry hinted at – he 'fashioned a cradle'[15] – though in point of fact it could have been the same rudimentary item of furniture. Joanne Ewin takes the story one step further: 'He and his twin brother Basil were placed in an aboriginal bark cradle'.[16] It could still be the same bedding arrangement, but it has been identified differently. And that is how legends begin.

Romantic legends begin in a comparable fashion too. In later years his mother Matilda (modestly anonymous but signalling exactly who she was) wrote rhapsodically that Henry was 'born at the foot of the mountain'.[17] That was a figure of speech, for the dominant peak in that region, Pigeon House Mountain, was miles and miles away, a ride of three hours. In the opposite direction, and at something like the same distance, the escarpment could rise to two thousand feet. The hills behind Kirmington are quite substantial too. Matilda – by the stage in her life when she began publishing her newspaper verse, she would identify herself as Melinda – was taking a liberty, although in this instance it might be allowed, as she was beginning to discover poetic aspirations of her own. In the same set of verses she lets us know that her famous son learned his letters in the sand, notwithstanding that the beach was at quite a distance for small legs. More poetic licence. Unless the sand was the dust in the road, as well it might be, in which case that is a different order of poeticism.

No mention of his twin brother however.

By one of those whimsical coincidences, the name of the local area which the Kendalls now owned was Yatte Yatta, meaning twin falls,[18] a feature of the stream that flows through that country. That was a chance analogy that did not get noticed, though Henry Kendall's continuing delight in small waterfalls is marked all through his poetry.

Just as with Melinda/Matilda, so there has been uncertainty about the names of the boys. It became something of a family practice with this set of Kendalls that the children were identified by their second given name – thus Henry, not Thomas; and likewise when the girls were born subsequently, Mary Josephine became Joey, Christina Jane became plain Jane, and so forth. Except for the complication of Basil junior. The commentators mostly identify him as Basil, whereas in a letter to his uncle, Henry referred to his own twin brother as Edward[19]; and that is a good enough recommendation. He became more widely known as Basil after his father died, or when, as happened, he too came to official notice.

The two of them were baptised by a visiting Presbyterian minister 15 months later (26 July 1840). The old Rev. Thomas Kendall had well and truly succeeded in his intention of settling in a situation where no other clergyman resided. It was still a far stretch for gentlemen of the cloth. The other brother, Basil Edward, was listed ahead of Henry; his father Basil was identified in the baptismal record as 'Settler'. And Matilda gave her name as Millinda McAllan, possibly to maintain consistency with the form of her hasty Presbyterian wedding.

The Kendalls were now living on land in Thomas Surfleet's purview. As the eldest son in a case of an intestacy, the substance of the property would in the end be assigned to him, although he could not claim title to it until 1840; and nothing could be done formally until that time, or indeed not until a year later again, when the livestock was divided up between the family.[20] Until that time Basil's commitment to life on the land was less than strenuous. After that time, although a portion was now his, he continued on it with modified enthusiasm. His youngest brother Edward remembered that he and John assisted Basil 'more than once, leaving their own work – which they could ill-afford to do – [to] put in Basil's crop'.[21] Edward was no more than 17 at the time, and had not his own property. John acquired his in 1843. It was presumably Thomas Surfleet's employment they were setting aside for the time being.

John, be it noted, was one of the two brothers who had been caught up in Basil's court appearances.

Edward's remarks were prompted by Alexander Sutherland's sequence of articles about Henry Kendall. He, Edward, was particularly incensed by the maudlin sentiments about Basil's frail being:

> of the deepening cough wherewith, as slow midnights passed over, the father shook its frail walls, and of the ever more frequently smuggled black bottle which the mother brought from the grog shanty two miles off. The people of the district were then, with few exceptions, emancipated convicts, and the children's two uncles, Edward and John, though they lived not far away, scarcely ever visited the home of the luckless pair.[22]

Edward and his brother had not neglected Basil and Matilda – but they had kept at some distance, given 'with what brutal candour the failings of Basil Kendall and his wife have been laid bare'. He denied that Basil was in ill health at the time. Basil's loss of one of his lungs must have become apparent only subsequently. The cough which was stated 'in all soberness' to have shaken the walls of the hut was likewise non-existent at the time. In all soberness indeed.

And Edward could not bring himself to write Matilda's name. Patently, the family did not approve.

In a short piece on Matilda (though the formally correct name Melinda is used, not her more familiar name), Marjorie Kendall summed up the pair of them. The work Basil and Matilda had to undertake when they settled on his father's grant was 'backbreaking, the farm isolated, and the young couple totally unsuited to the task. Family legend has it that they both took to drink'.[23] There were good enough grounds for that. Their move to life on the land had coincided exactly with a three-year drought.

Marjorie Kendall remained steadfastly loyal to the Kendall legend, however: Matilda/Melinda, she claimed, was gay, talented, pretty, a writer of pleasant verse, and totally impractical. There is certainly continuing evidence of this last; but despite the commonly repeated assertion of Matilda's writerly accomplishments, the evidence for it at this early stage in her life is simply unavailable. It is an unsupported assertion. Such evidence as did become available only emerged later, and after Henry's death, when she began publishing small poems in the local papers. Marjorie Kendall is not the only one to have accepted at face value the proposition that Matilda had poetic talent, however.

Basil in his turn is said to have been charming, intelligent and scholarly.

That does not square with his earlier misbehaviour in Sydney, his weakness of character, his moral unconcern. Given the family investment in the legend of the coming poet, they were hardly likely to promote Basil's fall from grace. The version that is pushed rests ultimately on an assertion by Henry long after the death of his father. 'He was an accomplished scholar; but an indifferent man of business. He was always speculating; he died poor.'[24] Mrs Hamilton-Grey was so adventurous as to set down that he had a college training, though how and where that might have happened defies credibility. It is true that he had acquired some facility with Maori, and possibly learned enough Spanish to get by in his time in the Chilean navy; but that is not quite what constitutes mastery of several languages. And Basil's reputed scholarship seems to rest on his acquaintance with a selection of the Greek legends. That could have come from his reading of popular books of translation – much as Henry Kendall himself later relied on Lemprière's dictionary.

When Sutherland came to write his piece some 50 years after the event, he had visited the sacred site, so to speak, a grassy knoll in a paddock near the Shoalhaven road. There was no sign of the lonely little hut, nothing but a stunted willow, fit emblem as it turns out. Given that Edward had taken over Basil's allocation (Edward bought it and extra acreage from his brother Thomas Surfleet, the property now known as Kirmington – Thomas had resumed some sort of notional control, or stewardship, of the vacated land when Basil left the South Coast to return to Sydney), and given Edward's attitude, as indicated in the riposte to Sutherland, he would scarcely have gone out of his way to preserve the rough and ready cabin.

Edward was not indifferent to a romantic conceit of his own. In 1847 he married Mary Jane Ridd, recently arrived in Australia and said to be a direct descendant of John Ridd and Lorna Doone. Lorna Doone was a figment of the imagination. Richard Blackmore's *Lorna Doone: A romance of Exmoor* was fiction pure and simple; however, the John Ridd in it was modelled on a real John Ridd. But that well-known novel did not appear until 1869, more than 20 years after Edward tied the knot. Just where and when this whimsy first started is not known, but it has proved as persistent and adhesive as so many of the other Kendall whimsies.

When in 1843 Thomas Surfleet determined to return to Kiama, taking his elderly mother with him, the other brother, John, a 'gentle giant', bought an acreage from the estate for £10 (John Milton earned that much for writing *Paradise Lost*), and renamed it Kendall Dale. The eldest brother, careful as ever, was managing his affairs to ride out the economic troubles rolling over Sydney, especially the collapse of the banks. Even the biggest of them, the Bank of Australia, failed in 1843. Basil and his family however chose to return to Sydney at this time. Given their circumstances, given the unforgiving seasons, there was little else they could have done.

That is to say, Henry knew the Ulladulla landscape for only the first five years of his life. The country was at that time still heavily treed, with great dark rainforests towards the escarpment, and shady fern gullies, and leaf litter underfoot. The bird life was concentrated along the creeks and waterways. Stiff eye-watering breezes came off the ocean, though the hut was far enough back from the beach that the sound of surf would not often reach there. Possibly the idea of mountains began to work its way into his imagination from this time, but there is little indication of precise inspiration from these very early years. That was to come later, and from a different source. Yet it is true that he was a son of the mountain forests, and he had played along swift-flowing mossy creeks from his earliest days.

These were not the best of times to look for employment. In Sydney Basil found work as a 'writing clerk' to begin with, and then as a schoolmaster, just as his own father had done. The evidence for this is from the baptismal certificates for the children, dated 29 October 1844, when Matilda had her children recommitted, this time to the Anglican faith. The family historian, Marjorie Kendall, claims that that ceremony was conducted by the Rev. Richard Hill, Matilda's old employer or patron, whichever the case might be, in St James' church.[25] That would indicate that Matilda had found favour with him again. But Hill had died eight years earlier, in May 1836, of apoplexy, in the vestry.

There is another curious echo here. Matilda had been baptised twice, and now so were the twins. That begins to look less like affirmation and more like its opposite. Matilda never quite sure just what she stood for.

It seems that Basil and his family lived in Sydney for the next few years – though a counter-chronology also circulates, that they all went up to the Clarence River, where Basil took on a position as a shepherd. Either way, hard times. There is one very sure indication, however, that they were in Sydney at this time, and not up on the northern rivers. Basil, weak-willed or desperate, or both, had returned to his old ways. Just three months after his youngest daughter (Edith Emily) was born,[26] increasing the strain on his meagre resources, he forged another cheque and with it he bought a bag of flour. At the price he paid, it must have been a substantial quantity. He kept 30 shillings in change, again that fraught quantity of pieces of silver. Some versions of this episode invest it with an almost Dickensian inevitability. He was arrested on Christmas Eve in 1847.[27]

Enigmatically, as much about the Kendalls is enigmatic, the report of Basil's arrest identifies him as 'Thomas'. More identity slipperiness. And astonishingly, he had again offended against his own family. He was either shameless, or reckless, or insensitive. He forged the signature of his brother-in-law, Thomas Wheaton Bowden, married to his elder sister Susannah; perhaps it had been convenient for him to practise copying the signature of someone close to hand. Or perhaps he thought his brother-in-law, who had prospered as an ironmonger in George Street, would not notice a mere five pounds.

Basil was arrested at his then place of residence at South Head, and tried three days later. He pleaded guilty and was sentenced to hard labour for two years,[28] to be served in Parramatta prison.

Which would leave Matilda to cope as best she could on her own. The daughter of a convict, her husband likewise convicted, five children, the twins not yet old enough to earn more than a pittance, if they could get the work. However frivolous and impractical she may have been, she would have to buckle down and earn whatever she could. Given that in later years she supported herself by sewing, she could have resorted to such piecework in these difficult times. And there would have been little to offer the children in the way of an education.

That is, if Basil actually served his time. For the documentation about this has not been found – just as he managed to avoid actual imprisonment in consequence of his first trial. One explanation in this second instance, and a likely one, is that instead of breaking rocks in Parramatta prison he was sent off to the Clarence River as a government man, assigned to Dr Dobie, to serve out his time there. Up that way was new country, and well beyond the 19 counties, the limits of location. To say nothing of beyond the pale.

If that is how it was, then it was undoubtedly a very expedient move for the Kendalls. Basil's reputation around Sydney would not have been improved by those recent events. He was an embarrassment to his family. He had been tried and sentenced before the end of the convict system of transportation; he was as one of them in the eyes of the law, and not much better in the eyes of the respectable community. He would be out of sight, if not out of mind, along the Clarence, which was only just opening up – the first flocks of sheep had been driven from the Hunter and over the ranges with great difficulty only a matter of years before.

The vast forests were all around but there was inviting open country thereabouts too. Cedar cutters were already into the valley. They brought down their rafts of cedar to what would become known as Grafton. A thirsty lot, too, given the dearth of public houses. The first to establish itself as a point of legal supply was a store known as The Settlement, on the south bank of Grafton. Of course, any number of illegal stills were tucked away in the bush.

One of the first to take his flocks up that way was a Dr John Dobie, formerly a naval surgeon, who overlanded his stock from near Maitland. He started his run at a place called Ramornie, close to Kendall's beloved Orara Creek, but then moved his selection downriver and on the opposite side, to Gordon Brook, where perhaps the grass was greener. Here he needed someone to keep an eye on his property, as well as his sheep. This was difficult country, with the local Indigenous community both hostile and resistant to white incursions; with bushranging gangs in the area; and with a good many tough ex-convicts. The axemen and sawyers were not much better, especially once they broached a barrel of rum. When people moved about on the river in their whale boats, they were always fully armed.[29]

Dobie employed Basil Kendall and his family to take up that caretaking role. Theirs was a very rudimentary and remote kind of life, their accommodation not much more than a shelter. For the year or so that they were at Gordon Brook, the boys, aged 10 or 11, had an extended experience of the banality of minding sheep; but of the beauty of the Orara too, carving its way through a deep valley. And if Basil were working off his sentence in such a way, then that was not something Matilda was going to talk about subsequently. It was not consistent with the romantic image of the tubercular scholar teaching his children at his knee, deep in the backwoods. Worse, it was too much like a repeat of her own convict father. And she did not talk about him either.

Then they moved closer again to Grafton, to red-headed James Aitken's Bushy Park on the Orara, and then (at the expiry of Basil's time?) closer to The Settlement, but still outside the nominal township. Here he is said briefly to have taught at a school.[30] It must have been at this time that Henry endured a smattering of formal education – for the most part, his education was irregular. He wrote later of how:

> Occasionally I [presumably his twin brother also] went to school, where my aptitude for picking up the facts of history and the elements of geographical knowledge surprised my teachers. But I always hated grammar ...[31]

and that he could never 'cotton' on to the didactic abominations of the standard textbook of the day. That was something else he apparently shared with his paternal grandfather.

Basil, though, was sickening. The conditions did not suit him, and by this time his tuberculosis was making serious inroads on his health. He was thin, and one of his lungs was almost entirely ravaged – consumption indeed. According to Henry, he had been unwell for five years. That means that his final sickness commenced at about the time he was sentenced.

Alexander Sutherland, who was not an eyewitness and whose source of information was Henry's wife – who was not present either – recounted the last moments of the unfortunate man:

> On a little station out in the bush the invalid father made a struggle to secure a living; but soon the utmost he was fit for was to gather his boys around his feeble knees and give some thought to their growing need of education. The little fellow Henry was the object of his earliest and most especial care. When at last the father was able to do no more than crawl out into the sunshine or crowd close in to the fire, the boy sat by his side, an affectionate companion, holding his hand and listening to the history of bygone ages; the myths of Greece, the exploits of Rome, the glories of England. Some little attempt was made at more systematic education; but the lad was barely eleven when his father became too far spent to be able to leave his bed. Here the boys tended him, assisted only in fitful turns by their mother. On a winter evening he grew manifestly worse. He told his two eldest lads they had better hurry to the township for the doctor. As they were leaving he called them back. 'Henry, hide that bottle', he said,

> pointing to the mournful cause of the family misery, and ere the little lads departed they made all seemly for the eyes of a stranger. It was a long and eerie journey, and the night was far advanced when they returned with the physician. There upon the bed lay the thin and chilly face of the dead father, and by his side a huddled heap, the equally unconscious mother.[32]

He was 42; his 'little fellow' Henry was 13.

All too patently Sutherland was indulging himself in his mawkish if not sordid sketch. If Matilda had passed out at the time, then the only witnesses were the two young boys. They may very well have seen something of what is set down here, but its reliability is questionable. Especially if, subsequently, Matilda endorsed and contributed any of the detail, given her record of outlandish stories.

As it stands, that death scene is a virtual parody of the sentimental tableaux the nineteenth century delighted in, in their novels and operas. Dickens would not have dared to write it.

What can be safely garnered from this, however, is that Henry Kendall's first acquaintance with Orara and the Grafton area did not extend over much more than two years.

James Aitken's Bushy Park was somewhat more than a little station, and extended along the banks of the Orara. When the Kendalls moved closer to South Grafton, they were only just 'out in the bush', as Henry claimed; he too was inclined to romanticise. When years later he came to write his poem about his father's death, 'A death in the bush', he represents his father's grave as 'In the depths of a forest', in secluded and wild woodland. Thomas Bawden, a local historian of Grafton, begged to differ: 'His [Basil's] remains lie in the cemetery at South Grafton'.[33] Supposing that to be so – and there is no reason to dispute it – then Henry Kendall's poem continues in the same chimerical manner, with the remembered grave identified by no 'time-shattered stone'. Basil's burial plot is unmarked, which is a saddening image for quite a different reason.

Whichever was the case, through the example of Henry's memorial poem it can be seen that what he wrote was not in the strict sense of the term biographical. His poems start from his experience, but the images are conflations of what he knew from his lot in life and of what he had read. More, they are attuned to what he thought of as poetical. There is nothing wrong with that, provided it is not presumed that the poems are grounded in factuality. They are equivalents of emotional states of being, remembered after the event, sometimes many years afterwards. That is not to say they are imaginary or unreal; they are poignant, and more often than not they represent Henry yearning for something else, yearning for what is for him now lost, or yearning for some ideal beyond his reach. That is what sets the mood, and defines the characteristic tone of his verse.

It is all too likely that, with Matilda unconscious alongside her husband's body, the children were at least for the immediate present cared for by neighbours, who, according to Sutherland, 'brought the little family their food, and made all needful arrangements for the burial of the father'.[34] She would not have had the wherewithal for an elaborate funeral – nor a headstone, no stone in the forest depths for time to shatter. Perhaps the neighbours were responsible for arranging the sale of his slender belongings. Sutherland is not clear on that.

Matilda forgot to complete the registration of her husband's death. Possibly at the time she was in no fit condition to do so, though it might be more kindly supposed that she did not know what she was required to do. For, really, she had very little knowledge of the way of the world. And she had almost nothing in the way of assets, no income, and a brood of children. She would have to fall back on the charity of her relatives.

5

There Goes Mad Harry

There was not much to leave behind, apart from Basil's mortal remains. From this point on it was up to the 'totally impractical' Matilda to make the decisions. But from this point on, too, she was free to reconstruct the past as she wished. Far from leaving her husband to moulder in his grave, she encouraged the view of him as the very type of a 'delicate, sensitive soul'.[1] A poetical sentiment, one might say – especially if one were a poetess in the making.

Henry had a different reason for elevating his father. If he was to be taken seriously as a poet, then it would hardly do to pretend that he, Henry, was self-taught, or had learned all he needed to know by immersing himself in nature. Wordsworth, by way of comparison ('Nature never did betray/ The heart that loved her'), had an Oxford degree. Young Henry Kendall had to have acquired some rudiments of an education, in which case it suited his cause to assert the cultural depth of both his parents. He inherited from his mother 'what talents I have ... My father was a scholar ...'[2]

Somehow, they all made their way back to kith and kin. The children were parcelled out to various relatives. Initially, according to Reed, the three girls lodged with Joseph Kendall and his new wife at their home in Macquarie Street, Sydney.[3] By the time the twins had entered their teens, Matilda had reacquainted herself with her father, Patrick McNally, on his small property at Fairy Meadow, just outside Wollongong, taking the boys with her. McNally was a tenant farmer there, on the estate of Dr Cox. His wife, Judith, had passed away probably about 1840 – the record is unclear. The girls were subsequently dispersed through the Kendall side of the family, but they were hardly welcomed into the bosom of doting aunts and uncles.

Thomas Surfleet Kendall placed 10-year-old Jane in a boarding school in Sydney; Josephine, two years younger, went to a school at Kiama. At least that was not quite so distant from Retreat Farm. Emily, scarcely more than a tot, was handed over to the care of her uncle Lawrence at Campbelltown, where she committed the cardinal offence of not knowing her place. She joined with her cousins in referring to their grandmother as 'Granny'. She was a poor relation, and should know it.

There must have been more to it than that, though, for when she gave an account of her early days to Mrs Agnes Hamilton-Grey, she conceded that she might have been 'too much trouble'[4] and was sent on down to Thomas Surfleet at Kiama. She was being treated as a 'charity child', accepted as a familial obligation but bundled about whenever she became inconvenient.

At Retreat Farm she was not permitted to join in with her cousins as they played about the place. She was confined to a garden and, left to herself, took to talking to the flowers and the trees. As she recalled, if her aunt overheard her, she would be confronted with "Talking to the devil again, are you? Just like your mother!'[5] Which is patent evidence that Matilda had not been and was not liked. For that was a comment built upon acquaintance from at least five years previously, when Basil and Matilda were living on the Kendall estate down at Ulladulla. Uncle Lawrence's wife had likewise made disparaging remarks about Matilda. A drinker and a convict's daughter.

Emily's long curling black hair was cut off. It was too much to manage. Cropped, it might have looked somewhat convict-like.[6] She stayed at Kiama until she was seven.

Thomas Surfleet's formidable wife was one of the three Rutter sisters, who had their own interesting history. Their mother, a widow named Charlotte Flower, had been appointed governess to the children of John Blaxland, and it was on the long voyage out from England that she met another new employee, William Rutter, from Lymington in Dorset. With nothing better to do they became attached to each other and agreed to marry. Blaxland was furious as he had been to some expense in shipping out Mrs Flower; but he could not afford to alienate Rutter, who was a specialist in making salt from seawater and an invaluable acquisition to Blaxland's workforce. Blaxland needed Rutter's skills to provide the means of salting down his beef. Indeed, Rutter was of crucial importance in his opening-up of this venture in the colony.[7]

Three daughters resulted from the union of Rutter and Mrs Flower, all three of them sharing the initial C, which must have made for confusion over their monogrammed handkerchiefs. Thomas Surfleet married the second sister, Caroline. Another sister, Cecilia, had married Michael Hindmarsh, and it was at Miss Hindmarsh's school in Kiama that uncle Thomas arranged for Josephine to be placed as a boarder. The third of the Rutter sisters was named Charlotte.

Although Fairy Meadow lay closer to Sydney than did Kiama, at this time it was still largely undeveloped land. It is close up against the escarpment behind Wollongong, with then pristine creeks, waterfalls and tumbled rocks. Great trees supporting staghorn and bird's-nest ferns were – still are – assailed by strangler figs, looking like giant pythons writhing up their trunks. The heavy underbrush was draped in flowering vines, so dark as to allow in no light. Only ferns and moss grew along the creeks, though butterflies found patches of sun there too. Towering over all is a massive rocky prominence known as Broker's Nose. The Illawarra countryside was then heavily timbered, with cabbage palms predominating in thick scrub, yet with patches of naturally open meadowland for dairy cattle. Here and there the landscape was punctuated with magnificent specimens of the local flame tree.

Clearing the cabbage palms was especially difficult. They would not burn, one of the readiest means of land clearing; they had to be cut into lengths and rolled to the nearest stream. Pigs ate chips hacked out from inside the trunk, and the foliage was put to various uses, especially the new growth, which was edible. For other kinds of tree, ringbarking was the common practice. Dead trees stood forlornly in the newly opened paddocks, gesturing hopelessly to empty skies.

Not only did Patrick McNally have a small property here, but so too did his elder children, Matilda's brother and sister. William's grant extended almost to the slope of the mountain behind, Mary's was alongside his.

Fairy Meadow is an unlikely name for any stretch of land in the Australian bush; and unsurprisingly this turns out not to be its original form. It had changed – apt enough for the capricious Matilda, one might think – from Ferrah Meadow (in 1824), presumably a corruption of Para Meadow. The meaning of Para is 'water', and that was also the name of the creek there.

In a similar vein, the origin of 'Broker's Nose' is at best tentative. There may have been an early settler with Broker as a surname. Or Brooker.[8] Or it may have referred to the poor miners (brokers) in the area; or again, and even more unsatisfactorily, the great uplifted rock outcrop might have been named by its resemblance to a broker's nose – whatever kind of nose might be thought distinctively characteristic of a broker. None of these explanations is especially convincing. Clearly, with all this imprecise definition, Matilda would have been right at home. In a prose piece she wrote for the *Illawarra Mercury*,[9] a local had told her the *eminence gris* was named Brooker's Nose, but she went on to write of a broker's nose, paying no heed to the distinction. Which might tell us something about her lack of attention, or her casualness about detail.

The McNallys, unlike the Kendalls, were modest in their aspirations. They did not share the Kendall pretensions, they did not give names to their properties. Besides, they were by comparison latecomers to the land. The Kendalls had established themselves down on the South Coast some decades earlier, and were on their way to becoming something like local Establishment. The McNallys were close to the great escarpment behind which the sun sets early, and down which great falls of fog tumble in the cooler weather, and from where strong winds buffet the forest canopy, making a noise somewhat like the distant surf's roar. It was chilly there in the winter months, less than Arcadian.

Mary McNally had been abandoned by her husband James Martin for the best part of 10 years. With some version of the seven-year itch, he sold her acreage and absconded with the proceeds, possibly to New Zealand; which meant that Patrick would have had to support her. Patrick was reputed as having been somewhat severe at the best of times. The arrival of additional poor relations, Matilda and her boys, must have tested his patience. He put his grandsons to work; that is, when they were not at school. These were the years when Henry Kendall and his identical twin brother – both were left-handed, they looked alike, and they shared some, but not all, characteristics – acquired what little formal education they had, at a privately run bush school, not much more than a shingle-roofed bark-and-slab hut.[10]

They differed in one marked respect. Edward seems to have been much more self-sufficient, much more outgoing. By way of contrast, a local historian recounts that, as Henry was shy and lacked confidence: '[he] was allowed to stay at home where he was tutored by his mother'.[11] From incidental details it seems that Patrick McNally had little time for this delinquency, or for this mummy's boy. If he were not at school then he should be put to useful work, minding the stock.

And if that were not carried out with proper attention, then Patrick was all too ready to thrash his diffident grandson with a stick. Mrs Hamilton-Grey enlarges on this detail by saying that it became a point of confrontation between Matilda and her father – she 'upbraided him for it'.[12] He was remembered as a hard and not particularly enlightened man.[13] Many years later Henry's widow, Charlotte, wrote of this time: 'My husband's life as a boy from his Father's death ... to the time he went to sea ... was a very wretched one indeed'.[14]

Kendall himself recalled that his early teenage years were less than pleasurable: 'from my eleventh to my fifteenth year I had been following sheep: illiterate and friendless indeed'.[15] Illiteracy hardly squares with his father's vaunted scholarliness, unless Basil kept that to himself and shared none of it with his son. Henry cannot have it both ways.

If we accept the timeline he provided, he must have made his acquaintance with the intrepidity of sheep during his brief stint on the Clarence, not in the fields behind Wollongong, for that was dairy country. So it is not entirely clear (once again) from his own account exactly what Henry was doing in lieu of attending to his lessons.

Nor should it be understood that he lived all this time on his grandfather's property in some kind of thrall to the acerbic old man – Patrick McNally thought him 'the most stupidest ass of a boy he had ever set eyes on'.[16] At some stage Matilda and Henry and two of his sisters took up a lodging in Tarrawanna Lane, near the former Church of England.[17] Here Matilda briefly tried her hand at schoolteaching. It has to be deduced from this that Matilda had plenty of confidence in her own abilities. She is never alluded to as a scholar, yet Henry acknowledged she was a reader – wherever, in her circumstances, she could lay her hands on such an indulgence as books.[18] In her time with the Hills, they would have ensured that she was fully literate, and they would have encouraged her to read. Doubtless she was familiar with the standard texts, such as *Pilgrim's Progress*, from her time with them. From what we can deduce from her own subsequent poetic practice, her tastes were for magazine verse, and that taste was passed on to her son. He found his way later to Tennyson and Longfellow, again more appreciated for their technical mastery than for depth of perception.

Interestingly, young Edward is not mentioned in Mrs Hamilton-Grey's reference. That is the first hint of a separateness from the rest of his family. He had no such objections to life on the land as did his twin brother. On the contrary, he quite relished it, helping out while Henry traipsed about in the bush, evading – if only temporarily – his grandfather's harsh discipline, and imagining every bush an Achilles or a giant.[19] If he would not go to school, Henry was a delivery boy for a local store – H.M. Green, in his authoritative *History of Australian Literature*, claims that Henry slept under the counter.[20]

Sutherland writes of Henry as a 'solitary, shy, and awkward lad, a stranger in the school'[21]; but at least he went to the Church of England Sunday School, with his brother and with another boy (George Millard), who in later life relayed to Mrs Hamilton-Grey that Henry was a 'very agreeable and interesting companion, exceedingly good-natured and amiable, very fond of legends and whatever was wonderful and a bit of a naturalist, being intensely interested in any living thing but at times odd in his tastes for almost all sorts of living creatures'.[22] That did not augur well for the Sunday School lessons. But it shows him more energetic than Sutherland's preferred vision, with young Henry drifting off to 'a listless, dreamy life of his own, beside a sunny lagoon, the never-failing streamlet, the deep turn up among the solemn stillness of the hills'.[23]

The idyll was quite bluntly shattered in 1855, when Kendall's uncle Joseph gave him a berth on his whaling ship the *Plumstead* – though Kendall himself wrote of the *Waterwitch*. For two years he was out at sea. Some have argued that not one but two separate voyages might have been involved, one immediately subsequent to the other, and hence the two vessels. In either case, his absence was yet another degree of separation between the twin brothers. Henry was essentially a cabin boy for the duration, sailing in both Antarctic and tropic waters, and finding both disagreeable. Edward, meanwhile, was out and about doing what he liked best, working with his grandfather's stock, poking about in the gullies, well away from the built-up areas. Edward's nature, wrote the gushing Mrs Hamilton-Grey elsewhere, 'was for open country. He would have loved a farm, and to be among cattle and horses'.[24]

Henry's new tour of duty would seem to have been more a decision by the uncles than the realisation of a boyhood dream. It is not impossible that the widespread shortage of manpower because of the goldrushes also played into their decision. Henry might have been plugging a gap in the ship's complement. Where Edward seemed to have measured up to his elders' expectations, Henry – as may be seen by his subsequent life – was not adventurous. Nor would we expect that from one who was innately shy. It would do him good to go out to sea, toughen him up a bit, make a man of him. Kendall had no heart for it though, perhaps no stomach either if he were anything like his missionary grandfather.

His role as cabin boy was to fetch and carry; but all hands were required to turn out when the chase was on. It is unlikely that he would have pulled an oar, for he would not have been strong enough, nor skilful enough, and besides that was decidedly dangerous work. Uncle Joseph would not have pushed him that far. But Henry had to take his turn looking out for whales ('thar she blows'), and the family legend is that he hated the long hours up in the rigging; even more, that he so disliked the actual chase that he sometimes chose not to call out.[25] That would have been a different kind of risk, for he could have been severely punished for denying the captain and the crew that share of the profits. And whatever part he played in the flenching, he could not have escaped the disgusting reek of the boiling down, the dirty smoke of it, the foul stink of the immense carcasses. There was not a lot to like about all of that.

Given that he later wrote a poem about remote Kerguelen, deep in the Antarctic Ocean, the whaling voyage must have taken him well south. But other details show that the *Waterwitch*, or *Plumstead* – Kendall inhabited a universe of imprecision – sailed out past Norfolk Island and to the whaling grounds well north of New Zealand. There he encountered something of the Pacific islands too, rather more to his taste. After all, he had connections with Polynesian culture through his father and grandfather. He could claim some kind of familiarity with it. Yet, when he wrote of the islands and their declining populations, he was more in touch with a literary fashion of the time and what he wrote in no small part derives from that. Those poems are, it has to be conceded, derivative. They do not draw on any precise knowledge, any actual experience on his part.

In the second half of 1856 his ship tied up in Mauritius, taking aboard a cargo of sugar for Melbourne. By the New Year it was swinging at anchor in Port Melbourne, awaiting an on-cargo, but in March as none was forthcoming it sailed for Sydney, with only ballast in the hold. That was hardly a heroic homecoming.

Interestingly, his poem 'Beyond Kerguelen' (when he eventually published it, close to the end of his life) is about what that remote region might have been like once upon a time, and about the ghostliness of its landscape. He writes of it in terms of insubstantiality, as a place out of this world. More indefinition.

He came ashore again in 1857. If he had been so diffident, so nervous and delicate as to have stayed away from school before he went to sea, it must have been very trying for him to be constrained aboard ship for all that time, among a crew of uncouth types. He could not wait to part from them or, according to family lore, from the cruelty of the captain. As Joseph was captain of the *Plumstead*, the family is unlikely to have preserved that image of him, so that the fingerpointing is towards the captain of the second ship, Captain William Lee of the *Waterwitch*.

Henry came ashore to join his mother and brother and the second sister Jane, already in Newtown. Matilda had withdrawn from her father's sheltering roof, leaving the hardships of scratching for a living on a small farm and returning to the more sociable though equally testing circumstances of the village of Fairy Meadow. Now she moved all the way back to Sydney town. No clear cause for this relocation has come to light. It may have been that her father was too testy; or that he was ailing, or unable to keep up with the demands of his farm. He may even have died, though no Patrick McNally is recorded as dying at about that time in the Wollongong area; he is unlikely to have been the Patrick Mcanally who died in 1858 in Goulburn. Among the local community, Patrick McNally's unmarked grave is believed to be in the Catholic section of the Corrimal Cemetery, alongside that of his daughter Mary Martin.[26]Whatever happened, Matilda's father disappears from the story at this point.

It may be too that Matilda thought her chances at teaching would be enhanced in Sydney. She and Jane took on a few pupils in the growing suburb, just outside the old town; and Edward came with them. That is a further hint at his grandfather's possible demise. Edward was employed briefly as a shop assistant to Price the draper, in Newtown, while the family reassembled and established new roots. But then he found a job that suited him down to the ground, working for Anthony Hordern's at a time when that firm was just commencing, and had only the one shop, at what was called Brickfield Hill, between where the Sydney Town Hall stands and Central Railway Station. Strong winds carrying dust from there down the length of George Street gave the southerly buster its colonial name, the 'brickfielder'.

Edward's role was as offsider to Hordern's travelling salesman, helping him on his rounds of country properties, distant settlements, out-of-the way sheep stations. They travelled in a covered wagon, sometimes down to the familiar grounds of Shoalhaven. It was slow work, and they had frequently to camp out. That was the attraction for Edward. He was much more a putative bushman than his twin brother.

Once, so Mrs Hamilton-Grey recounts, Hordern's two agents found themselves in floodwaters when they tried to cross a swollen stream. Edward had charge of the money they had taken for the goods they had sold. Holding the money bag in his teeth, he managed to swim across the swiftly flowing current and make his way to the higher bank.[27] That would have been old-style swimming, breaststroke, English style. The Australian crawl was not demonstrated until a decade or so later. But the native-born children were so adept in the water that in the early days they were nicknamed 'ducks'. Young Edward had evidently shared that kind of boyhood. The South Coast surf, after all.

Edward had not been sent off to sea to make a man of him. Henry's was a different case altogether. Indeed Frederick, Henry's son, later wrote that in 1857 his father was 'then a delicate, nervous lad of only 16'.[28] Yet that is an instance of hearsay, of family lore being reasserted, some 20 years after Henry's death. What the family knew, or thought that it knew, and what were actually the facts of the case were not always the same thing. Frederick, for example, accepted Henry's self-chosen given name, Clarence, and his revised date of birth. Why not? Should he not believe his own father? Besides, he himself had been given Clarence as his second name. That somehow consolidated the fiction.

Whether Henry was so delicate and nervous or no, some change, a very sea change, took place in the two-year interval he was at sea. On his return the family began to turn to Henry, not Edward, as the man of the house.

He displaced his twin. The commentators subsequently erased Edward's presence, or his contribution, laying down as absolute that it was Henry who found them all the cottage in Newtown. His earnings could not have been much different from his twin brother's, however.

There was what turned out to be a more important change too. Henry started to write poetry or, it might be safer to say, to compose rhymes.

One of the jobs he took up was with Biddell Brothers, confectioners. Louisa Lawson, mother of another poet and in the manner of Matilda determined that her own son should become celebrated as the Australian poet of his generation, watched closely over the evolution of Henry Kendall, searching out whatever she could find of his story. She tracked down a co-worker at Biddells who remembered when Henry started as an errand boy after his return from the sea. His duties included being sent out into the streets with a tray of tarts and cakes balanced on his head.

> Already he was composing juvenile poetry, and, as he walked along, with half-seeing eyes fixed in a vacant stare, you could see his mouth working as he mumbled over his lines. People would turn and look at him: 'There goes Mad Harry!'[29]

Not quite talking to the devil, but different from what was generally accepted – different from the man or woman in the street, careless of their opinion, absorbed into himself. Like his mother.

Henry Lawson would in his turn become known as 'barmy 'Arry'. It seems that was the singular disadvantage of being a poet in the colonies. (The general principle stands, even though Lawson was by far a better writer of short stories than of verses.)

The Kendalls lived in a little cottage backing on to Camperdown Cemetery. It was hardly the most desirable precinct, but at least it was affordable, assisted by interest from their late father's share of the invested estate. For in July the Ulladulla uncles arranged the sale of Basil's Mandnal property and placed the proceeds in the hands of Thomas Bowden – the very man that Basil had attempted to defraud by forgery. Bowden was as forgiving as he was honourable, and reliable as well. For years he had managed this investment through a trust fund and forwarded interest to Basil's widow and children, as required. It was little enough, but a surety of a kind. Briefly the Kendalls seemed to have settled.

Here Henry began to coalesce into his idea of a poet. Matilda kept her little day school in the cottage, with the girls helping as they could. Josephine was somehow starting to develop her musical gifts – she would become quite accomplished at playing the piano. Not that there could have been much room for that in their tiny home at that stage.

Where Henry had written skittish verses for his workmates, now he tried his hand at more earnest themes. He had taken to reading the leading poets seriously, studying them; and then he followed their lead as best he could. His first poems were, it has to be confessed, vapid in the manner of the day. But he had a grand theme almost handed to him on a plate, so to speak; for deep in the midwinter of 1857, in Sydney's greatest shipping disaster, the *Dunbar* was wrecked at night off the South Head of Sydney Harbour, driving not into the entrance but in fact straight on to the rocks at the foot of the notorious Gap. All hands and passengers were lost, save one crew member who was hurled up on to a ledge along the sandstone cliffs, and clung there until daybreak.

The whole of Sydney was shocked by the calamity. The bodies of the victims, passengers and crew alike, were buried in Camperdown Cemetery, just over the Kendalls' back fence. That, one might presume, would have focused the young poet's imagination. In fact, he was more taken by the existential reflections that could be extracted from the disaster, the sudden reversal of human happiness, the overthrow of expectations, than by the drama of the tragedy itself. His poem, when eventually it was published (in March 1866) was entitled 'The merchant ship'.

Those reflections were, unhappily, no more than platitudes. Kendall had not found his way into the deeper signification of his material. His verse sounds fatuous, with a bouncy metre much like a popular recitation piece, and a moral reflection no more penetrating than Adam Lindsay Gordon's 'Life is mostly froth and bubble …' ('Ye wearie wayfarer').

The storm is inescapably the poem's climax, and with it Kendall enters more strongly into his subject matter – though even there he lapses into fashionable poeticisms, such as the Leigh Hunt affectation 'forky-shap'd lightning', or the more ponderous 'refulgently', possibly from Pope's translation of Homer, to which various commentators believe Henry had been introduced by his parents. That did nothing to help him find his own voice. Nevertheless, the poem does rise to a crescendo. But then, either by a lapse of judgement, or by lack of ability, he throws himself back on to the bosom of the now placid sea of existence, and the effect of the poem ebbs away. He still had much to learn. The title was hardly arresting either.

Nearly 20 years later Kendall identified this poem as his very first – even though some three or four had already been published in the local press, six months before the wreck itself. 'My first essay in writing was sent to the "Southern Cross" at the time you [J. Sheridan Moore] were sub-editor. You, of course, lit your pipe with it. It was on the subject of the *Dunbar*.'[30]

In retrospect he could see quite well enough that his earlier works were at best clever imitations, occasionally with happy turns of phrase. These would not define him as a poet; but they were a beginning. What they do show however is that he was already drawn to a poetry of changeable light, and of rapid sound – of effect, rather than of precise definition.

Those first poems had been placed with, of all magazines, the *Australian Home Companion and Band of Hope Magazine*, a most unlikely and ironically inappropriate choice, given the immediate Kendall family history. Over the preceding two years it had reversed its priorities, promoting domestic harmony over temperance, its earlier impetus. That was something of an odd choice, for at the outset it had been a children's temperance magazine (*The Australian Band of Hope Review and Children's Friend*, 1856–59). Henry was 17 at this time, hardly an aspirant to the children's pages. But it did provide an opening for him. More likely he was attracted by the emphatically Australian landscapes depicted on the cover. This was the kind of magazine to encourage his view of himself as the coming 'Native Australian Poet'.

Reed thought that the magazine, or if not the magazine then the Poet's Corner section, may have been edited by Sheridan Moore. If that were so, then the connection between Moore and Kendall commenced from this time.[31]

His grandmother, Jane, the Rev. Thomas Kendall's widow, wrote about the shipwreck too, in a letter to her son John. At the time of the storm she was visiting her eldest daughter Susannah at Kennilworth Lodge, at the top end of Ocean Street, Woollahra, close enough to where the tragedy occurred for her to have taken a particular interest in the event. Her reflections on it are of a kind with those of her poetical grandson: 'the wreck of the [D]unbar ... was a very melanchory [sic] affair so many souls launched into eternity at a moment warning in the midst of life we are in Death'.[32]

By the simplicity of her expression and her experimental grammar, she had derived little benefit from her husband's practice as a schoolteacher. She had preserved an appropriate piety, though.

Susannah was, be it remembered, married to Thomas Wheaton Bowden (the ceremony had been conducted by the Rev. Richard Hill), who had had his own financial misadventures but was now remaking his fortune as an auctioneer, especially of real estate. He was co-trustee with Thomas Surfleet Kendall of the invested proceeds from the sale of Basil's property. It would be to Thomas Wheaton Bowden that Henry must appeal for the eventual release of those funds, presuming a kind of leadership in the family, responsibility for them, after his return from the sea. Not Edward, who had been there all along.

With that the occasion for tension emerges, though whether it was Henry's presumption or at his mother's expectation that he should be the man of the house is at this distance impossible to ascertain. Edward's reaction seems to have been to withdraw, and to have been difficult or at least to have created mischief when he was at home with the others. Whatever there may once have been of a close bond between the twins was put under some kind of strain by the new arrangement.

A different kind of enigma appears at about this time too. For in November, still in the *Australian Home Companion and Band of Hope Magazine*,[33] appeared a set of verses, 'The far future', asserting the eventual independence of Australia. This was very little different from much of the same sort of thing scattered across colonial papers and magazines throughout the mid-century, a kind of rattling of the political chains to an emphatic rocking-horse metre, utterly negligible except for the signature at the end: E.H. Kendall. By rights, that should identify the joint authorship of Edward and Henry. An apologetic footnote, excusing any suggestion of disloyalty, refers to the imagination 'springing from a native-born Australian's brain'. Which suggests not joint authorship but rather an evasion, for why else would both twins' initial be included? When the poem was included in his *Early Poems, 1859–70*, that footnote appeared over Henry's own exclusive initials, 'H.K.'. Edward had been bumped hip and shoulder. Or he had been used as a mask.

Edward started publishing verses of his own somewhat after this, a handful of them in the *Empire* once his brother had established himself in the pages of that paper. Here another oddity occurs. In August 1861 Edward published a poem entitled 'Kembla'. Three months later, Henry published the same poem in the *Illawarra Mercury* (19 November 1861, p. 4), but substituting 'Keira' for 'Kembla' in the title and throughout. The only other difference is tidier punctuation, occasional capitalisation, and removal of the stanza divisions. And it appeared over his own name, not his brother's.

Something very strange has happened here. Either Edward had purloined Henry's poem, or the other way round. Or Henry had pretended to be his brother. It speaks of a distorted relationship and of avoided obligations, and hints at some kind of astonishing disregard, if not of dishonour. It reminds us of the extraordinary unfamilial behaviour of the previous generation, at Basil's first trial – though the ramifications here did not reach to comparable matters of legality. Ethics, yes. The Kendalls kept on showing across the generations a penchant for wandering afield in such matters.

Agnes Hamilton-Grey recorded a story from this time that hints at further differences between them. Her chief source was either Matilda, who had a vested interest in promoting her poetic son's reputation, or the younger sister Emily. Mrs Hamilton-Grey writes of Henry's respectability, that he loved his Bible and regularly attended church at St Peters, but that in this respect:

> his twin brother, Basil [that is, Edward], was just the opposite, and made fun of Henry's seriousness in religious sentiment. On one occasion he carried his joke against his brother to the extent of writing a very irreverent verse (of his own composition) on the flyleaf of Henry's treasured Bible.
>
> This was regarded as an unpardonable offence by Henry, and caused a somewhat serious quarrel between the two boys ... they resembled each other physically, so remarkably, that when apart the one could be mistaken for the other.
>
> Basil [was] more prone to the wildness of young blood than the earnest-minded poet ...[34]

The one, we might say, more extrovert than the other. More careless.

Henry's *Dunbar* poem, 'The merchant ship', was published in the following year by Samuel Bennett in the *Empire* (8 March 1860). He began to make his mark there, transferring his allegiance from the *Australian Home Companion and Band of Hope Magazine* – which in any case did not last long, ceasing publication in 1861. Edward likewise contributed poems to the *Empire* throughout 1861, some half a dozen of them; but it was Henry who declared himself 'N.A.P.', Native Australian Poet. Which is not entirely inconsistent with his acknowledged shyness. He could declare himself in a collective allegiance.

Once again the record turns up an oddity. The poems from both brothers at this time were as often as not about Illawarra settings, though they are said to have been living in Newtown with their mother and sisters. They could of course have been drawing on exact memories. However, according to Jan Keith, citing an essay accepted by the Royal Australian Historical Society, Henry Kendall was serving in Mr Allan's store in Jamberoo in 1860,[35] about six miles from Kiama. He could hardly have been in both places at the one time, in Sydney and in the Illawarra. And further, as there were no McNallys for him to stay with down that way, he would have had to call on the goodwill of the Kendalls. From whom his parents had distanced themselves.

Unlike Edward, Henry began to have poems published in the *Sydney Morning Herald* as well. That was the way to bring himself to the attention of the public. It brought him more prominently to the notice of J. Sheridan Moore, the literary figure to whom he had first sent his poem on the *Dunbar*. Moore took up Kendall's cause, and eventually encouraged him to publish his first volume of poems, undertaking to raise subscriptions to pay for that publication, and acting as his editor. He placed an advertisement as early as January 1861, though there was no unseemly rush of supporters.

There is, inevitably, an alternative account. Bertram Stevens accepted Mrs Hamilton-Grey's detail that it was Kendall's mother, Matilda, who took him to see Mr Sheridan Moore.[36] The source for that has ultimately to be Matilda herself.[37] How Matilda Kendall would have had access to Sheridan Moore defies probability. He was passionately pro-Irish, as her by then deceased father, Patrick, had been. Yet there is no hint that she had returned to the attachments of her forebears, nor to their religion. She was not in her own right a literary presence, such as Moore pursued. She had no obvious grounds for knowing him.

Or she was an embarrassing, forthright and impetuous mother, towing a reluctant poetical son to someone who might be helpful. As indeed proved the case. She appeared to know enough about the literary scene to identify Moore as a man to approach.

Moore had been trained as a priest at the leading seminary in England, the Jesuit stronghold Stonyhurst, and had so distinguished himself that, when he arrived in Sydney as a young man, the very age that Henry Kendall now sported, he was appointed headmaster of Lyndhurst College in Glebe. This was in 1847, before the Catholic hierarchy had been re-established in Britain, and begs the question of what kind of future he had envisaged for himself.

In Sydney he was attached to the Benedictine order, an English order headed in Australia by Archbishop Polding – the yet-to-be restoration of the hierarchy notwithstanding. With Moore's profound attachment to Ireland and things Irish, it was all but inevitable that he would fall out with Polding. He left his situation, and his church, and the priesthood in 1856, and a year later married one of the principal singers in Sydney, a prominent concert and oratorio singer; yet he continued his association with Catholicism, editing the *Freeman's Journal* between 1856 and 1857.

He supported himself by, amongst other intermittent endeavours, tutoring young men who hoped to enrol at the new university; he managed to make himself familiar with those who were the leading champions of the university, of education in the colony, and active supporters of the literary life in the community. They had formed themselves into a circle of the illuminati, a significant coterie around the central figure of Nicol D. Stenhouse, founder of the Sydney Free Library, president of the School of Arts, and whose own substantial collection of books ultimately became the nucleus of the later Sydney University's Fisher Library.

Moore introduced young Henry Kendall to this charmed circle. Stenhouse was always generous with lending his books. The principal of the university, Professor John Woolley, subsequently made the university collection available to Kendall. Professor Charles Badham was another of the group. And not least in terms of immediate import, he was introduced to a lawyer and litterateur, James Lionel Michael, who had cachet from his acquaintance with Millais and Ruskin. Suddenly Henry Kendall was amongst real scholars and gentlemen. It was all a bit heady. And not least, that on the strength of this acquaintance Michael invited him to the Clarence River, where he was about to set up a new law practice.

Moore took it upon himself to promote Kendall's poems, to encourage the publication of a small collection of them and to push Kendall's cause amongst likely subscribers, even to the point of puffery. The subscriptions were not forthcoming though, an early foretaste of Kendall's subsequent misfortunes. So was Kendall's despondency. In an anxious frame of mind, he wrote to the editor of *Cornhill Magazine* in London, including in his letter copies of several of his poems. Appealing for sympathetic consideration, he over-emphasised his youth, claiming to be four years younger than he actually was, and asking that the immaturity of his verses (he calls them 'effusions', an arch poeticism of the day and unlikely to have inspired the editor with confidence) be forgiven on the grounds that his education had been neglected.[38] Once again, so much for the claim that his father was a scholar.

Further, he tugged at the editor's heartstrings (another inept move), complaining that he had only intermittent time to devote to his poems, given that he had such limited income and yet had to support his mother and three sisters. What, we may ask, of Matilda's school? And what, indeed, of his twin brother, who once again does not appear to signify.

The letter was sent from his Newtown address, not Kiama or Jamberoo. And it was sent on the eve of his departure for Grafton. For he had accepted Michael's offer with alacrity. His Newtown responsibilities were not going to curb this opportunity. Matilda could have the roost to herself.

6

The Twofold Life

James Lionel Michael had come out to Australia in May 1853 to make his fortune on the goldfields. Never one for an active and physically demanding life, he quickly appreciated that he could make his way more comfortably, and more assuredly, practising law, to which he had been brought up by his solicitor father in London. Within just a few months of his arrival, he was admitted to practise in New South Wales. In the following February he was married. Which represents activity of a kind. Within a tongue-clickingly foreshortened period of gestation, at a time when respectability was esteemed, his wife delivered him of a son, of whom he became very fond. The same could not be said of his feelings towards his wife. Theirs was not a happy marriage and they drifted away from each other, their separation made absolute in 1864.[1]

All this becomes pertinent to the Kendall story in a roundabout manner. Michael's transfer of his law practice to Grafton was consequent upon his bankruptcy in 1858. He was notoriously inept at managing money. Notwithstanding, this reversal had not prevented him from publishing a couple of volumes of reasonably accomplished verse. He delighted in hosting literary dinners too, neither of which activity would have enthralled his wife, given their circumstances. Young Henry Kendall, who was being touted as the coming Australian poet on the basis of poems now appearing regularly in the press, attended some of these dinners once Moore had made the introduction.

When Michael decided to re-establish his law practice in Grafton, he generously offered Henry a position as his clerk; which is how Henry Kendall came to cut his own losses, shake the dust of Newtown from his shoes, and return to the Clarence River.

He followed Michael up to Grafton at the commencement of 1862, his duties being to copy legal documents, but also to copy out Michael's poems for him. Kendall was often the recipient of long discourses from his employer too, about all sorts of matters, literary, artistic, cultural, philosophical. Michael liked an audience.

Lionel Michael was living bachelor-fashion,[2] for his wife had remained in Sydney. That meant that his association with his young clerk could extend beyond office hours, though Kendall appears to have lodged in a boarding house.[3] Michael may not have had the wherewithal to be a generous employer, but he was most certainly generous in allowing Kendall unfettered access to his library. He guided the young man's reading, to Wordsworth and Shelley, Elizabeth Barrett Browning and Swinburne, 'not all of whom were a good influence on a young man with a fatal facility for easy words and easy sentiment'; and, so the story goes, he assisted in teaching him French to the extent that Kendall read both Béranger and Hugo, or enough of them at least to prefer the latter. Michael himself wrote verse translations of Béranger.[4] Tom Inglis Moore spoils the story somewhat, by noting that in fact Professor Woolley had already taken it upon himself to teach Kendall both Latin and French.[5]

The basis for Kendall's preference is not exactly stated. The one was a poet and songwriter, the other a writer of massive novels. Furthermore, this expertise is said to have been achieved within an unlikely seven or eight months. Possibly Michael was a very skilful instructor; or perhaps the story is unreliable. In any case, Kendall's postulated mastery of French had virtually no impact upon his writing.

The arrangement between Michael and Kendall was somewhat like his grandfather's youthful experience, when Thomas served as tutor to a solicitor's children and drew benefit from the experience of such a household. Just possibly Tilly McNally's years with the Hills offered a comparable opportunity for improvement and advancement.

Certainly, Henry found himself immersed in a congenial milieu. Lionel Michael knew about the Pre-Raphaelites, he knew about European, as well as English, art and culture. Indeed, the law was of secondary interest to him. Kendall learned much from Michael's own poetic practice, and flourished under his encouragement. That is a point that all the commentaries make of his time in Grafton. Not only was he enabled to read widely, in Michael's company he was brought to make confident and discerning judgements about the accomplishments of the great poets. This would stand him in good stead when he began to write articles on them, and to give public lectures – hesitant, as his confidence did not extend as far as to self-confidence.

It should also be acknowledged that his employment in a law office served him in another capacity for, as it turned out, that prepared him well enough for future employment in the public service.

It also provided him with a watertight alibi. For in April 1862, the Brisbane *Courier* court reports named Henry Kendall as guilty of an offence:

> Henry Kendall, charged with furious riding in Queen-street, alleged that his horse had bolted, and that he had used every exertion to stop the animal. The latter portion of the statement was contradicted by a constable, and defendant was fined £[illegible].[6]

As Henry was at the time in Grafton, not in Brisbane, he could not have been the offending party. Rather, someone who looked very like him had used his name. Basil Edward, without a doubt. That impersonation used to work for him in Sydney. At least this time he paid up. And that also indicates where Basil had gone. He was in the new colony, in something like a frontier town, racing up and down the main street like a larrikin. Playing fast and loose with the truth, and not quite imaginative or creative enough.

Henry was enough of a Kendall to play fast and loose with the facts too. Hearing nothing from the *Cornhill Magazine*, he wrote in July (when most unambiguously he was at Grafton) to the *Athenaeum*, submitting several manuscript poems, as well as another plaintive letter, in which he reduced his age by a further year again. Even his mother, who was an experienced hand at this kind of adjustment, was not so shameless as to amend her age by one quarter. Michael would not have appreciated Kendall's further complaint that he was 'not in a position to afford to buy books' – likely enough – 'and living out of the reach of them' – patently untrue – 'in the backwoods of the colony'.[7] It is one thing to be selective about the evidence, another entirely to utterly misrepresent his circumstances.

The letter, together with three poems, was published in the *Athenaeum*, and friendly encouragement came with it:

> Mr Kendall has much to learn; but he has received from nature much of that strong poetic faculty and power which no amount of learning can bestow … The manuscript he has sent us contains … a certain portion that is very good indeed.[8]

That welcome response could not have reached him until about October. Which means that he must have been busy in his own interest locally as well, and had been taking up Sheridan Moore's suggestion. Even before he left Sydney to go to Lionel Michael's office, the advertisements for his forthcoming volume, *Poems and Songs* (another unprepossessing title) began to appear. The heralded work itself did not emerge until about the time the first copies of the *Athenaeum*'s review reached the reading public in Sydney, and the Stenhouse circle, and other well-wishers. It is a small detail, but another that has been misrepresented by his son, Frederick, for example, that the publication of *Poems and Songs* by a Sydney publisher (J.R. Clarke) was a consequence of that London review.

Despite favourable notices in the local papers, his first volume did not sell at all well. Poetry rarely does. Of the 500 copies printed, 369 sold – which left him out of pocket. Given his limited financial position, this was a hardship he really could not afford, and various letters hint that he began to borrow from acquaintances to cover his costs.

The *Athenaeum* had seen something it liked in the young colonial, but it also identified weaknesses. His religious allegorical poems were run-of-the-mill, such as anyone might write and such as nobody much would bother to write. G.B. Barton in his survey of literature in New South Wales agreed with that: Kendall was not varied enough, his poems were mostly of the same character, the same diction, the same metre, the same thought and feeling, and 'this sameness … is one of the gravest objections that can be urged against them'.[9] Not monotonous exactly, but too much harping on the one theme. Yet Barton too found something to admire. His was a more penetrating notice than the British had come up with.

He acknowledged Kendall's skill in depicting the landscape, even though it was presented as gloomy and despondent. That would not have been a misrepresentation of the towering forests up against the escarpment of the Illawarra. Such country was the true home of the lyre bird, and the mountain streams Kendall was to write of throughout his poetic life could be found everywhere. But Barton had a point: 'No poet in the language … draws such dismal meanings from the external world'.[10]

At the time *Poems and Songs* appeared, Kendall took temporary leave from Grafton to help see it through the press; and, fortuitously, to enjoy the éclat brought about by his notice in the *Athenaeum*. He enjoyed himself to such an extent that Michael complained of his extended absence. 'I trust you are not dead but only asleep. No news of you', he wrote.[11]

Michael was right to have a nagging doubt. Kendall's success was turning his head a little, and his loyalty. For at this time he was attempting to lift his profile a little further again. He had begun a correspondence with Charles Harpur, for example, and was keen to show some independence of thought and judgement:

> I know Mr. Stenhouse: he introduced me to Henry Halloran a few weeks ago. The last-mentioned gentleman magnificently patronises me, and endeavours to impress upon me the 'fact' that it is a crime to write when you can't excel. What a pity it is that he don't follow up his own theory in his own case, and leave me to take care of myself! … Parkes had a poetical temperament evidently, and Michael is not so contemptible as interested critics would have him appear to be. Dr Woolley, a *crammed* man – a man who admires Tennyson by rote, and Browning backwards, is another of my would-be patrons. I have cut them all.[12]

Which does not show Kendall in a good light. He might have been attempting smartness, but instead he displayed a lack of gratitude to those who had gone out of their way to help him; and, although he is not so snippy about Michael, the lawyer is another of those he has 'cut'. It is a regrettable characteristic in Kendall, one that emerged more and more in his correspondence over the years. A kind of two-facedness, which is not exactly what he intended by the phrase 'the Poet's twofold life' ('Adam Lindsay Gordon').

Henry Halloran became grist to Kendall's unkind mill over the next little while, even though he, Kendall, would continue to benefit from him too. Halloran had offered Kendall employment in the public service, in the Surveyor-General's Office, at the very time he accepted Michael's invitation to Grafton.

As so often happens in tracing the Kendall story, contradictory versions are available. Halloran's account of his first acquaintance with the young poet claims the initiative as his own:

> Attracted by some verse published in the 'Herald' I called on the late Mr John Fairfax a friend of mine, and learned where Kendall was to be found – a small draper's shop, I think in Pitt Street. I called and saw him and, learning that his pay was very small, I offered him work (deed engrossing in the Surveyor-Generals Office where I was then Secretary and Cashier). He declined and went with a Mr. Michael, a clever attorney (a poet also of some pretensions) as his clerk to Grafton on the Clarence River.[13]

That does not read as though the connection was through the Stenhouse group; it is also inconsistent with Kendall's letter, written much closer to the time. Halloran would much rather the record showed him searching out the impoverished young man and offering him the help of a poet of some pretensions, a would-be patron magnificent in his own recollection. It is not unknown for minor figures to enlarge their part in literary history. In this instance one is more inclined to accept Kendall's account though, as well as his satirical reflection upon Halloran.

Kendall continued to snipe about Halloran in the same vein in another letter to Charles Harpur, still at about this point in time: 'You need not hope for Halloran's sympathy, he'd see you "blowed first", before a movement was made by him. For Halloran's idol is Halloran, and his admiration does not extend beyond this shrine'.[14]

Kendall, one suspects, was being more smart than insightful; he was flexing his satirical muscles, and would eventually join the fray at *Punch* and elsewhere, writing squibs, mingling in the lightweight literary fisticuffs, scoring unimportant points, and showing questionable judgement. In this instance, he gradually came to appreciate Halloran's good nature, and eventually published a poem in his honour, praising his learning and the quality of his verse. But there was a sting of truth in what he had written to Harpur.[15]

Jogged by Michael, Kendall returned to Grafton on 8 December[16] and was almost immediately pressed to give a lecture at the Grafton School of Arts, just over a week later, the first time he had stood before a fit audience, though few. The lecture itself was published subsequently, and from it we can see evidence of Kendall's distinct uneasiness on the occasion. Local celebrity may even have added to his nervousness. He excused himself right at the outset, saying that when he had agreed to present a paper on Shelley, which he just happened to have upon him at the time, he could not have known that he would lose that essay from his pocket that very evening. What he would present to his audience was a hastily cobbled together version from what he could recollect of it. It is easy to see through this anxious self-excusing; and indeed, the paper as published suggests a wholly acceptable set of observations.

Years later, when Mrs Hamilton-Grey was accumulating material for her recollections of Kendall, she came across one who remembered Kendall's exceeding nervousness on the occasion: 'his gestures were awkward, and he looked shy to the verge of childishness on being introduced to the audience'.[17] He would rather have been anywhere than on the dais. He had not progressed very far from the days of his school truancy down in the Illawarra.

Her own imagined version of this is that Kendall took stage fright: 'and when he was to have made his appearance on the platform he was nowhere to be found. He had bolted. Mr Michael was obliged to fill his place and entertain the audience, which he was most eminently capable of doing'.[18]

Kendall did not stay long with Michael on his return to Grafton, a matter of months only – not that there appears to have been any actual falling-out, and indeed they continued to correspond for the time being. But he left the Clarence on 28 April 1873, possibly spending a little time on the way back with his twin brother in Dungog, or possibly that visit happened on a separate brief excursion once he had settled back with the remnants of his family in Newtown.

Again we see him speaking, or writing, with a forked tongue; for, no sooner had he returned than he was writing to an acquaintance announcing his presence in Sydney and giving the grounds for leaving Grafton, mocking the Clarence as 'remarkable chiefly for its snakes, mosquitoes, floods and dull people'.[19] That is not a point of view that he had shared with his audience at the School of Arts up that way. Nor is it quite the tone to take up in writing to his correspondent, one with whom he had exchanged tender affections previously,[20] before departing so abruptly for Grafton in the first place. Perhaps his letter was a means of ingratiating himself (together with publishing a poem addressed to her), for they picked up again where he had left off, and continued until other subsequent romantic interests distracted him.

Edward was employed in Dungog as a draper's assistant,[21] and would not have contributed to the support of the womenfolk. In advance of Henry's return, Matilda had placed an advertisement in the *Sydney Morning Herald* to announce that her school would resume after the Easter holidays,[22] but that plan had to be set aside. She had to close her school when her daughter and teaching assistant, Jane, went briefly to Ulladulla, perhaps to help with the instruction of her cousins, and Josephine took up an appointment, first at Caroline Chisholm's school in Newtown, and then a year later transferred to Mrs Chisholm's new expensive school at Tempe House, in large grounds between Wolli Creek and Cooks River. Emily was not clever, and was no help.

Mrs Chisholm was in poor health and in need of funds. Her fees were more than three times as much as at other young ladies boarding schools in the township.[23] There was a move to raise a gratuity for her, and Henry wrote a poem, taking as his point of departure Wordsworth's 'She was a Phantom of delight' (a rather epigrammatic commendation, which Kendall managed to step around).

Their collective income was meagre. Henry had little choice – not that he resisted – but to set aside his private disdain and accept the munificence of the poetical public servant, Henry Halloran, who offered employment. Even though it would only further confirm that gentleman's satisfaction at his self-importance, as percipient patron of emerging versifiers. But at least Kendall would have a regular salary now, which was a relief after the vagaries of working for Michael.

The little cottage that Matilda had moved to while the family was largely disbanded was now too crowded. And the situation became worse, not only with their return, but with the arrival of Edward from Dungog. Edward was seriously ill, so serious that they thought him at death's door. In all likelihood this was a manifestation of his weak lungs, inherited from his father. Henry suffered from that too, and Josephine, resulting in phthisis, as it was then diagnosed. In the end that disease would claim all three.

Towards the end of the year Henry found a more comfortable lodging for them all, and where they could find more stability. There was room for Edward, and a study for Henry. At the rear was a large common. They had been moving from one address to another in Newtown and Enmore, but here they had more comfortable quarters, in a substantial cottage with a view from the front verandah across to the broad sweep of Cooks River and easy of access for Josephine to Caroline Chisholm's school, Green Bank, while she held an appointment there. Later, when that prestigious school closed, Josephine took a position as governess – a real governess, not one of Matilda's reconstructed histories – with the family of one of the proprietors of the *Empire*.

Matilda turned her attention to a different outcome, or income as the case might be. She had had to close her Newtown school, and with fewer children in the new neighbourhood she took in several young boys for board and instruction, one of whom was James Lionel Michael's son Jemmy. Jemmy's welfare was a common topic in the ongoing correspondence between Michael and Kendall. The Grafton lawyer was concerned not so much for Matilda's care of his son, and his instruction, as for his safety from visits by his mother.

> If she comes up (as I suspect she intends) with the object of talking against me to him and retailing to him anything like the abuse and falsehood respecting me which she howls all over Grafton she *will* do him a very serious injury by unsettling his mind … So now you know what I am afraid of, besides her strong tendency to carry him off and hide him altogether. I never talk against her but you know yourself that even when we were together she did [i.e. talk against] me, and *now* a chorus of Furies is milk to her.[24]

So much for legal circumspection. This, at the time of their divorce, when Michael had been given custody of their son. And that put the Kendalls in a sensitive position, midway between the aggrieved parties.

With confirmation of his permanent appointment in the public service, Kendall was likewise in an interesting situation at his office. He wrote to his most valued literary acquaintance, Charles Harpur:

> I see Mr. Halloran every day. I am employed at the Survey Offices. H.H. is a queer fellow. Every morning he calls me in, and treats me with an emphatic recital of his latest. I could no more do the like with my verses than fly. I even hate to make the faintest allusion to Poetry while abroad. I am my own critic, my own audience, and live completely within myself. So the epithet 'Silent' has been generally applied to me.[25]

Whatever tasks he was set he apparently fulfilled satisfactorily. His handwriting was always distinctively pointed, almost cramped, but he must have contrived to master a version of the copperplate that was customary in clerical work at the time. Halloran at least made no objection to it. At the end of the year, Henry's temporary clerkship was confirmed as a permanent tenure, and his salary rose accordingly.

It was all too good to be true. Caroline Chisholm's grand school closed early in 1864 and Josephine's appointment there was terminated. Slowly Edward convalesced, though not for some months, and as he mended he became disruptive, as was his wont, possibly from boredom at first. He tried his hand at writing poems in Henry's manner, not very successfully. He began to go out and about, playing tricks upon Henry's acquaintances by pretending to be Henry. His resemblance to his twin was close enough for Edward to succeed in imposing upon them. And while all this was going on, he was a drain upon the Kendalls' combined resources, and a strain upon their accommodation.

About the middle of the year Edward's impositions became totally unacceptable. Henry found himself obliged to place a notice in the *Sydney Morning Herald*[26]:

> *Caution.* – It having come to my knowledge that a relative of mine (taking advantage of a remarkable likeness which he bears to me) has been impersonating me during the past month, and borrowing money from my friends; I am obliged to adopt this course to the public, to prevent further frauds. Henry Kendall, Cook's River.

The Kendalls were at it once again, as though intent upon disproving that blood is thicker than water. Edward left the family home, and never lived with them again, except once when he visited briefly. In fact he headed north once more, to the recently independent colony of Queensland, taking up employment once more as a draper's assistant, and hating the hours behind the glass windows, arranging displays in the broiling heat.

While Henry had been manfully toiling at his desk and listening to Halloran's latest rustling of poetic wings, and while he had been caring for his ailing brother, he had not been altogether well himself. He had begun a correspondence with a friend in Grafton, the wife of the Anglican rector there. The Rev. Augustus Selwyn was a cousin of the Bishop of New

Zealand, whose ministry had commenced at the Bay of Islands, where the Church Mission Society still held sway and with whom he had fallen out over the issue of land ownership – theirs, not his. Those missionaries had remained a power unto themselves, less fractious than formerly but suspicious of church hierarchy, as represented by Selwyn.

Mrs Selwyn in Grafton was a prolific watercolourist. In the genteel manner of the day her drawings were for friends and relations, not for public exhibition: ladies did not display themselves, nor their paintings. She had grown up in Maitland where her father was the Anglican minister, a daughter of the manse, and was reputed to have been taught by Conrad Martens. If that were so, then at that distance from Sydney the lessons could not have been for any long interval.

Which perhaps accounts for at least one distinctive detail. She undertook a portrait of her husband-to-be; when her mother-in-law saw it, she objected to her reverend son's bulbous nose, and Mrs Selwyn was recommended to undertake an amended portrait.

In Grafton, she and her husband set the benchmark for taste and discernment. For Kendall, she represented yet another step up the ladder of cultivated taste, and his letters show him attempting to present himself as both sensitive and aware, to be the kind of person in whom she might be interested. A different Henry Kendall declares himself in these letters. Given her husband's role, and her presumed piety, there is rather more religious reflection in them than elsewhere, both of doubts and of conventionality. It is another example of him trying on a new or modified character, just as he had invented one for the editors of the British magazines. We find him again and again experimenting with different representations of himself and adapting himself to what his correspondent might expect of him. That is not an altogether unknown manoeuvre, but sometimes this second-guessing leads to a false note, as on the occasion of his letters to London.

In his earliest letter to Mrs Selwyn – that is, the earliest that has been preserved – he sets out by informing her that he has recovered from recent depression of spirit and body. His mother too is in better health. No mention though of Edward on the sick bed in the spare room. But then he continues to develop a theme that most of the colonial poets took up:

> Men and women, with the poetic temperament, are generally sorry creatures: if their sense of enjoyment is keen, their sufferings are extreme. They seem to live a two-fold life; constantly over-balanced, and surrounded by exaggerations. In my case, I have enough of that acute sensibility to work myself into a constant flutter with excitement. And therefore, depression of spirits is, with me, the rule, and momentary elevation, the exception. It cannot be otherwise: it should not be otherwise.[27]

The last sentence quoted is another of those false notes, an extended exclamation mark.

What we see here is Kendall's assumption of the egotistical sublime. Mrs Selwyn is going to be made interested in the inner drama of the poet's *angst*; she is going to have to share his interest in it. Moreover, he is presuming that this is what people such as the two of them – presuming, that is, that he and Mrs Selwyn shared an affinity of heightened aesthetical sensibility – are most interested in, the inner worldly, if not the rarefied unworldly.

The less rarefied of us though take up such details as that his mother has been unwell. Given Matilda's history, and her behaviour to come, it is not impossible to read between the lines here. If she has been poorly, that may well have been self-inflicted. For her drinking was, after all, a well-established habit, though delicacy required that this should only to be mentioned indirectly and hinted at obliquely. We remark too that Kendall not only acknowledges his habitual depression here, but canvasses it as a marker of his acute sensibility. Between soulmates there should be no false modesty.

We do not have Mrs Selwyn's replies. Nor is it known whether she ever sent him any of her watercolours.

His subsequent letters to her are more refreshingly to the point about his circumstances. For example, three months after this first letter he wrote again:

> I suppose you have heard that Master Michael has been placed with my mother with a view to his education. It is a good change for him: he would, most likely, have been ruined *physically* as well as morally in Grafton, if that home had been *his* home for much longer. He is a very delicate lad:

> remarkable for the intense love he bears for his mother. Is he not worth saving? My mother, I am glad to say, is in better health now than that she has been in for many years. I can't say the like of myself. I have never been well since leaving the Clarence.

That is hardly loyal to Lionel Michael. It reads as though he expected Mrs Selwyn to have a disregard for the Grafton solicitor. It shows Kendall as it were changing sides. The two-fold life of the poet indeed.

And he is persistently interested in his own ill health, which suggests as much about his state of mind as of his physical condition.

A year later he took a harder line on his erstwhile employer and poetic mentor, again in a letter to Mrs Selwyn. When Kendall writes like this, the expression is very sharp. They are prose equivalents of the satirical squibs he took to sending off to the lighter journals and papers.

> My mother is not able now to walk far, and hence she was obliged to wait and hope for other means of seeing you than that of calling upon you. Indeed she was ignorant of your town address – else she would have sent my sisters.
>
> ... The more I know of men and books, the less faith I have in Mr Michael's abilities. He appears to me to be a smart chatterbox who has a happy knack of persuading everybody that he knows everything. He is undoubtedly clever, but not original in the least particular. I have never heard him say a beautiful thing yet, that was his own. The man of thought is after all far beyond the man of books ... I think Mr Michael, by reason of his extensive reading, is likely to prove a most useful man in Grafton ... Yet, it must be confessed, I have not the ancient faith in his gifts. His verse is feeble and his prose, flippant.[28]

That is close to cruel. It is designed for Mrs Selwyn's eyes only, just as her watercolours were for her correspondents only. Whether she altogether admired this ambitious young man for his smartness, we cannot know. We can certainly interpret that he was showing off to her. On the other hand, his paragraph about his mother is all a fudge. It covers over the potential embarrassment of his mother waiting upon her (in what capacity? She had not made Mrs Selwyn's acquaintance, as she had left Grafton, widowed and destitute, two years before the reverend's appointment there as rector).

Kendall is going through the motions of politeness. Why, if Mrs Selwyn was in town, did not Kendall himself call upon her? That would have made much more sense than sending one of his sisters.

Late in the year the family heard from Edward. He wrote not from Brisbane but from out to the west, from Jimbour on the Condamine, the very edge of civilisation, the furthest outpost – one could hardly call it settlement – at the time Ludwig Leichhardt chose it as the starting point for his first expedition into the vast unknown (1844). Patrick White wrote a somewhat satirical account of the slab hut which constituted the original Jimbour homestead in *Voss* (chapter 8), giving the property the name Jildra.

Edward confessed that he had succumbed once again to drunkenness, thus maintaining the family likeness, and had resolved to remove himself as far away from temptation as he could. Former friends, fellow window dressers in fact, had come up to Brisbane to visit him. They went on a spree, he was fired, and he became the subject of spiteful gossip. Quite possibly, that was not all about drunkenness. His reputation had followed him from Sydney, and Brisbane was not an overly populated place then.

Bertram Stevens adds yet another dimension to this episode, that Edward had also given way to his hasty temper.[29] That is an echo from his paternal grandfather Thomas. Matilda too was quick-tempered.

Edward left town on foot, picking up odd jobs along the way, fleeing into the wilderness. Out on the distant Darling Downs he found work as a stockman and had raised himself to the more responsible role of storeman. Perhaps that might put him beyond temptation. On the other hand, in that new role he would have had the supervision of stores, measuring out the rations for the men on the outstation.[30] Which would have included an ample supply of beer and spirits to tide them over. He had struggled, he had lived with his misery, and now he had put all that aberrant behaviour behind him, or so he claimed. Edward's contrition reads as tactical. Another Kendall putting himself in an improved light.

In that same letter, in part self-exoneration, he insisted that he had 'never committed anything that would bring me within the walls of a prison',[31] which must have made Matilda wince. It might have been an innocent slip, but then again it might not have been so innocent. A remembrance of his forebears. Tactless, without a doubt.

When next they heard from him, two years later, he had moved further out, quite as far again, on to the Maranoa, away from whatever residual temptation lurked in the storeroom, away from his fellow man, to go droving cattle.[32] Like Clancy of the Overflow, letters would have followed him about the bush in a haphazard way, and he would have been the last of the clan – if at all – to learn of the death of his elderly grandmother, Jane, down at distant Kiama (1866).

Where Edward was losing the battle for respectability, and possibly for self-respect too, Henry was well on the path to the kind of conventionality expected by Halloran and others, those in the public service. Halloran cramped his style somewhat, though. He approached Henry Parkes, newly promoted to Colonial Secretary, and sought a billet in his office. Parkes was pleased to take him under his wing, just as Halloran had originally, and Michael before that. The new arrangement came with an extra £50 per annum to his salary, and the extra prestige too.

His letter to Parkes was another of those servile Uriah Heepish letters that do Kendall's reputation no credit. But he had no alternative. His mother and his sisters were becoming increasingly expensive to maintain. They expected better clothes, they wanted better furnishings, a piano for the girls. And his poems were not going to earn him the means for that.

He was not all folded gloves and furled umbrella at this time. His correspondence with various young women showed that his flights of fancy were not only directed to unattainable shimmering spaces up ferny creeks. He had become interested in the fairer sex, as the quaint phrasing of the period had it. He paid social visits, and amongst his new acquaintances was Rose Bennett, daughter of the joint proprietor of the *Empire*, another of the papers in which Kendall now published his poems. Bennett's partner was William Hanson, and Josephine was governess at Hanson's home, in particular instructing his daughter in playing the piano. Rose Bennett, who also lived in Newtown, was a constant visitor there and became a close friend of Josephine, and joined in musical evenings at the Hansons'.

Rose and Henry fell in love, but it did not end well. According to A.G. Stephens they were engaged to be married. Kendall, he went on to say:

> seemed then quite a desirable candidate for a matrimonial alliance. Good-looking, well dressed, lively and romantic, holding a place in the Colonial Secretary's office at £200 a year, and with the laurels of a 'native Australian poet' green on his brow, Kendall at 27 was attractive to girls of the period.[33]

It should have been a good match, especially for him. Rose Bennett had been given a sound education, she came from a very good home, and such a connection would have done his prospects no harm whatsoever. But they fell out, and there are two stories of how that came about, both of them about pettiness.

In one version, ascribed to Louisa Lawson, Rose Bennett was catching a train at Central Station in March 1867:

> and Master Henry came to the station to see her gallantly off – not himself being a passenger. They exchanged affection through the carriage window, till Rose dropped her gay parasol out of the window and said:
>
> 'Pick that up, Harry!'
>
> Harry said, 'Say please'.
>
> Rose said, 'Pick that up, Harry!'
>
> Harry said, 'Say please'.
>
> Rose wouldn't say please; the train moved off and, though Harry ran after the moving train with the parasol, Rose had taken the huff and Harry had accepted the huff, and the rift widened to a final parting.[34]

Apparently, they were both petulant persons – that is another adjective for Kendall. Miss Bennett undoubtedly had sufficient *amour-propre*. It would be unladylike for her to be the first to apologise.

Years later, Henry's son Frederick dismissed the affair with Rose as no more than momentary. His version of events must have come from either his father or mother, or both. His grandmother, however, kept alive the legend of Henry's deep-seated romantic loss, and after Henry's death wrote a somewhat unsteady memorial poem, in which she claimed that his concealed grief explained the tenor of his verse:

> *Then came to his heart a great first love,*
> *Which could never be conquered by time;*
> *Hence his muse was oft draped in sadness,*
> *And she wore it sometimes in his rhymes …*
> *None knew what it was but the writer*
> *It was a sealed book to the rest.*[35]

There could be no refutation of this. A mother can tell. And try as he might, Frederick would not be able to change her version of history. She knew what she knew. When she republished her poem a year later, she adjusted her phrasing to make a particular emphasis. None knew what it was but *this* writer.[36]

The other story of why Rose and Henry separated stems from the ultraromantic Agnes Hamilton-Grey. A young man, Henry Evans, played a trick upon Henry Kendall. He too had been attending the musical soirées at the Hansons' – his connection was that he had begun paying court to the youngest of the Kendall girls, Emily. The closeness between Rose and Henry was apparent to everyone, and for mischief Evans started a campaign of flirtation with Rose to make Henry jealous. Then somehow he inveigled her to give him a lock of her hair – possibly she was in on the joke – which he presented to Henry as proof of Rose's new preference. It is as well it was not Desdemona's lace handkerchief. When Henry angrily demanded an explanation from Rose, she refused to give him that satisfaction. His jealousy, his suspicion, was contemptible. And that led to their estrangement.

Henry was out of order, whichever version is taken up. He was out of his depth and had much to learn about social niceties, especially about relationships. Whatever his mother had been teaching him, it did not include that kind of sensitivity. He kept his heartbreak to himself, though he wrote a number of poems, chief among them 'Rose Lorraine' (one of the three saddest love songs written, according to Rose's daughter[37]), which drew upon his private hurt, and dwelt on the enduring longing for the unattainable. It suited his dominant mood, for that was, of course, a particular, if sensitive, version of his constant theme.

Through all these travails he was from time to time in financial difficulty, and was struggling to repay various loans, some from friends, some from loan sharks. He had borrowed money from the Rev. Selwyn, from Henry Parkes and others – he had borrowed £25 from Parkes in April and had failed the final repayment of £5 in October, borrowing a further £5 from him instead.[38] It embarrassed him to be so long in honouring his debts. It was even more of an embarrassment when he had to borrow money to pay off a debt. He had of course remembered his father's estate, and in a series of letters to Thomas Surfleet he took to agitating for that money to be released. The sisters all wrote to uncle Thomas too, supporting Henry's application. But the co-trustee, uncle Thomas Bowden, was reluctant because he suspected that the funds would be used to meet Henry's debts rather than shared among the siblings. Interestingly, Henry was against any portion going to Edward. He knew his brother to be a spendthrift, and would waste it.

Through all of the to and fro of negotiations, it was apparent that the older generation knew a good deal more about Henry's circumstances than he was aware, and they disapproved. It also becomes apparent that the clan did not have much to do with each other. In one of the earlier letters (to aunt Caroline – Henry used all routes to press uncle Thomas), some of the distance is quite evident. He expresses surprise that she did not know his mother's address, nor that he and Matilda shared the one address. He makes it known that the others follow his judgement – though that was really part of his campaign to establish that the funds should all come to him to manage. And he makes clear that the coolness between the rest of the clan and Basil's family has continued:

> I am glad you did not answer the note of Mrs Sheen, for it is not my intention to do so. My mother will, I am sure, quite fall in with my views in this respect. Her relatives have been friends only in the same degree as her husband's people. And, with certain exceptions, I care for one set as little as I do for the other. I do not intend the last remark to apply in any way to my Uncle Thomas and yourself.
>
> I may say it will be no fault of mine if we do not continue to be on fair terms with one another.[39]

He cared for neither the McNallys nor the Kendalls, though needless to say he had to present himself as polite to his uncle.

In April the two executors agreed, with misgivings, and the money was paid over by the middle of the year, when the remnants of Basil Kendall's family moved to improved quarters in a terrace house on Enmore Road.

Edward warranted Henry's mistrust, but not quite as had been anticipated. He came down from Queensland to collect his share of the estate, and forged Henry's signature for £45. With the Kendalls – or to be more precise, with this branch of the Kendalls – blood was not thicker than water, it was as thin as ink. Henry had to pay up to conceal the public shame of the forgery.[40]

In September 1867, some six months after Henry's falling-out with Rose, he gave a lecture – somewhat satirically, according to A.G. Stephens – at the

School of Arts in Pitt Street on the topic of 'love, courtship and marriage'. It may not have been altogether satirical but Kendall could not have avoided some sense of irony. 'He had an audience of moderate size', wrote Alexander Sutherland, 'before whom he stood, a spare and shyly-awkward man, in a black frock-coat too large and too loose for him, nervously fingering his manuscript, and pouring forth his words in a rhapsodical flow, to be seen, not heard'.[41]

Sutherland, of course, was not present on the occasion, and we would have to take on trust the rhapsody, along with the awkwardness. He may well have exhibited both. He had already given a lecture on love, or the philosophy of love, perhaps the very same lecture, for flood relief at the school room in St Peters, Cook's River (July 1864),[42] and the ladies in his audience on that occasion had applauded his sentiments about the relations between the sexes.

On the other hand, instead of being ironical in consequence of his jilting by Rose Bennett, he may have been positively mollified. For one of those attending was the fair-complexioned Charlotte Rutter (no relation to his aunt Caroline), the very opposite of darker Rose. She was escorted to the lecture by her brother, who made the introduction between them – and in a year they were married.

That might seem precipitate, but it was as nothing compared with what his mother had been secretly conniving almost under his very nose. The two elder sisters had been able to make arrangements for themselves, they were earning something of a living (which begs the question why Henry had to support them, if in fact that claim was true), but Emily, the youngest and the favourite, was not gifted. She had no independent future. So Matilda encouraged the connection between Emily and Henry Evans, all but urging a marriage. Emily was aged only 16.

Henry was not to be informed of any of this, as they all knew he would have disapproved. He had no particular reason to approve of Henry Evans. He wrote about it two years later:

> My youngest sister was privately married to an unmitigated scamp three months before I was made aware of the circumstances. Then I heard of it from the lips of the minister who applied to me for the marriage fees. The precious bridegroom had left them unpaid. The excuse held out by

> my relatives was a singular one. They knew that I was opposed to the courtship, and the marriage was contracted as 'a safeguard against me'. Of course I was against the courtship. The fellow had no ability, no education, and was, out and out, a petty rogue. Added to this, he was head over ears in debt, and his yearly salary did not exceed fifty pounds. Indeed my sisters bought him his wedding outfit, and their draper billed me with the amount. As I was the nominal head of the house, I was obliged to pay it.[43]

Evidently he was still angry about the secrecy, and the concealment, and about Evans, his words tumbling out – 'head over ears' instead of either 'head over heels' or 'up to his ears'. He must have been shocked at his mother's role in the affair too. Even if Matilda were conniving to secure a future for her extremely young daughter, what was the urgency? And if Henry was providing the financial underpinning for them all, why deliberately alienate him? Her part in the affair was a romantic silliness, another example of her lack of judgement.

Remarkably, in amongst all this personal turbulence, he published what was to become his signature poem, 'Bell Birds', in the *Sydney Morning Herald* (25 November 1867). It is one of his most optimistic poems – and it is not beyond the realms of fancy that 'October, the maiden of bright yellow tresses' owes something to his recent acquaintance with fair-haired Charlotte Rutter, rather more in any case than to raven-haired Rose.

The New Year began with Henry's elevation to first clerk in the Colonial Secretary's Office. Henry Parkes must have been satisfied with his work, and with the steady stream of poems he was submitting to a variety of papers and journals. On the strength of the consequent raise in salary, and having paid down outstanding debts, he married Charlotte Rutter on 7 March 1868, at St John's Bishopthorpe, Glebe.[44] Mrs Hamilton-Grey however, preferred to describe it as a low-key event, in Mrs Rutter's house in the evening. She, Mrs Hamilton-Grey, had a down on Henry's bride, taking Matilda's side in this, or perhaps Emily's, apart from whatever concealed jealousy of her own she may have had.

Charlotte, she recorded, was 'about 18, a well-made girl, and very fair. She looked well, and was what would be termed handsome. The bridegroom came in with Mr Fred Rutter'.[45] And that euphemism for Lottie's build, 'well-made', was unkind. Then the hostility was further unveiled: 'Charlotte's lips were thin and inclined to be snappy'.

Emily supplied the rest of the detail. Astonishingly, none of the rest of his family was present, though Emily apparently (mis)informed Mrs Hamilton-Grey that she and her unwelcome husband, Henry Evans, were there. Henry said differently. Two years later, in his long letter to Dr Neild, the doctor and patron of so many of the Melbourne literary set, and to whom Kendall reached out in those difficult times, he wrote that no member of his family was present. Specifically not his mother – though whether that was by Kendall's choice or hers is not clear. Mrs Hamilton-Grey preferred her own narrative:

> Kendall's little sister observed that his manner was strange, as under the influence of wine, which, hitherto, he had avoided, never taking it even on gala occasions. When the ceremony was over he could not be found anywhere that night. He slept in a vault in the graveyard in the Camperdown Cemetery.

His mother's son, and his father's, after all. Curious. He had walked some distance from the Rutters' place in Glebe over to near where the Kendalls had first settled in Newtown, and that too has an intriguing psychological reverberation. He returned to his mother-in-law's the next day, and made what amends he could.

On the wedding certificate he had signed himself Henry Clarence, not Thomas Henry. He was reinventing himself just as his mother had when she married. He was the third generation named after Thomas, and by this alteration he was denying that ancestry. The sins of the fathers are not so easily sidestepped, however.

And, as Mrs Hamilton-Grey portentously recorded, 'They never lived with his own mother'.[46] Henry had made his choice, and it did not include Matilda.

But that is not how Henry remembered it; and his son Frederick, whose information must have come from his parents, refuted Mrs Hamilton-Grey in a short pamphlet a few years after the final volume of her vapourings on Henry Kendall. It was simply untrue that they never lived with his mother. He took her to their cottage just as he had planned all along.[47] Even though she did not come to his wedding.

7

The Encircling Gloom

If there wasn't uproar in the Kendall family household, then undeniably there was unhappiness. Everything was at sixes and sevens. The womenfolk resented Charlotte taking Henry away from them – they had much preferred Rose. There was anxiety too, for as he was the principal wage earner it was a threat to them that Henry was leaving the household. On top of everything else, he had also manipulated his way into the role of holding the purse strings now that the money from his father's estate had been paid over. That in itself appears to have been the predominant cause of anxiety among them.

To put into plain words what has not been put into plain words, they did not know whether they could trust him. He had his own debts to pay off, but this was their money. They were beginning to suspect what their uncles had already suspected would happen.

That goes a long way to explaining their individual actions. Basil Edward, for example. What he did was to forge Henry's signature to a cheque for the amount he estimated as his due share. He was not going to stand by and watch Henry pay out his own part of the inheritance to the money lenders. That was Henry's problem, not his. Or the sisters: because the furnishings in the cottage had been bought with the newly released money, they pressed him to make that a gift to them. Josephine's piano for instance. They were making sure they had a fair benefit from the inheritance too. They ordered up their finery – silk dresses no less – and presented Henry with the bills for the dressmaking. If he would not hand over the money to them directly, then they were resolved to winkle it out of him another way. And they justified those charges to him by claiming that they had to keep up appearances for his sake.

Simply, they outmanoeuvred him one and all. They pulled the rug from under his feet, or turned the tables; they dispossessed him of his role as nominal head. So much for happy families. Later he conceded that 'my trust in my sisters was folly, but a man with the poetic temperament is generally a thing to play upon'.[1] He was left with less of the investment funds than he had been counting on. He had not as much to get married on, and not as much with which to set up a new household.

He was astonished too when he was prevented from taking anything from his old home to his new lodging; indeed, he felt especially injured because he had proposed to take his mother into his care. Perhaps that was to be her portion of the estate. When he called by to collect his mother and some belongings, as he thought, he was laughed at. Instead, they presented him with his new brother-in-law's entitlement to all the furnishings. They had tricked him when they cajoled him into agreeing to making them a gift of the furnishings, for they then signed them over to Henry Evans, the next male in the household (given Edward's absence).

That can hardly have made for amicable relations between the siblings; that might explain why there is so little reference to his sisters subsequently. As for Evans, Henry Kendall was unrelenting in his contempt for him, 'a petty rogue'. Perhaps he suspected Evans of encouraging his sisters to take a stand against him, if not actually putting them up to it in the first place.

That is one version of the sequence of events. Another, spelled out in a letter that provides a comprehensive explanation of Henry's reasons for quitting Sydney, was that the domestic coup occurred at some little time in advance of his marriage. He understood immediately that this put him effectively in the position of a lodger, and in a huff he stormed out. He went to Charlotte and offered to release her from her promise, but she refused to give him up. She would not do that; she had given her word, and she would hold true to it. Her own mother insisted that either they married forthwith, or break off the engagement absolutely; and as Charlotte was not one for turning, they married penurious.[2]

It was, or might have been, a more romantic marriage than Matilda's, but she made the better story of hers.

Whichever is the more exact sequence of events, his troubles did not stop there:

> Day after day I was inundated by drapers' and grocers' accounts which I thought had long since been settled. In two cases I allowed the creditors to sue me, but suffered for it. I went to the Jews, and from that time to the date of my resignation, I was in utter depression of body and mind. The moneylenders were like a cancer upon me.[3]

When he invited several of his creditors to take him to court, that presented a difficulty, given his situation in the civil service. He could not afford to be declared a bankrupt, as that would be grounds for dismissal. The bitterness in this was that he had just achieved some status in at the office, with his elevation to the position of chief clerk. He had to look the part and act the part, in his tall silk hat, frock coat and kid gloves.[4] He was expected to be beyond reproof, he had to be impeccable. He just had to pay down those debts.

Once married, Henry and Lottie lived briefly in Sydney, in Bent Street.[5] Shortly afterwards they moved to a cottage in Glebe owned by Lottie's mother; which is where Henry brought his mother to live with them. This was not a well-considered move, as it was right next door to the Rutter household.

His mother proved a difficult lodger. One can imagine she was not a congenial neighbour either. In the new domestic arrangement she had lost her former role, and she had to compete for the attention of her favourite son. She still had to soften Henry's abiding objections to Henry Evans, and to her own part in that overly precipitate marriage. No wonder she turned to her habitual comforter, for it was at this stage that her drinking became a significant problem.

Sutherland later summarised her circumstances sympathetically: 'The poor old lady [she was now 53], even then more than half a wreck, had for a while promised a complete amendment, but after a brief hope of reform, gave way again to her ancient malady'.[6]

Kendall wrote later of how uncomfortable Matilda made her daughter-in-law, whose own family was rather more sedate, more respectable. It would not have helped matters that the Rutters were also more secure financially. Lottie's recently deceased father had been a doctor with a practice in Castlereagh Street; he had been superintendent of the Vaccine Institution and surgeon to the Metropolitan Police force. And Lottie remained close to her mother – it was clear that she was not about to move into the Kendall clan. Everything about her must have seemed a criticism of the feckless Irishness of Matilda.

Not just fecklessness. Matilda had begun breaking out rather badly. She was an embarrassment at home – years later Henry wrote about the domestic complications Matilda set loose:

> During the weary time I was in the Government service I had to keep her [his mother] quiet by bribing her with brandy every night. After my marriage, I tried the plan of restraint, but she became furious; and the result was my wife couldn't stand her; and I had to leave Sydney … I do not accuse the source of my trouble of sin – she is too insane to be responsible for her actions.[7]

Both Henry and Lottie would have met the full indignation of the glint-eyed drinker whenever they dared stand between her and the brandy bottle. And there is nothing to suggest that Matilda was ever reticent. Her own father had come to know that. 'Paddy' is a word that comes to mind, though Mrs Hamilton-Grey preferred 'passionate'. She also conceded that Matilda's 'volubility was not strictly conventional'.[8]

The antipathy between the mother and daughter-in-law was reciprocal.

When Kendall wrote to Halloran a decade after these events, he said of his mother that she had been a confirmed dipsomaniac for at least 30 years[9]; that is, from before the time of her husband's death. There was nothing new about her condition when she came to live with the young couple. The astonishment is in Henry's naivety and his tactlessness in imposing her upon his new young wife in this way. Besides, why should he have taken on the burden of care for Matilda, when there were three sisters at the family home? Or did he not trust them?

Matilda was an embarrassment to Henry at work too. Sometimes she waylaid him in the evenings on the steps of the Colonial Secretary's Office, rather much the worse for wear, and in need of a supplementary tipple. Sometimes she even forced her way to his office, unsteady on her feet and with the first signs of a persistent tremor, asking for money, even demanding money. That disorderliness would not have been well received.

And as it happened, although Henry performed his duties assiduously, he was not popular among his fellow clerks. He had no small talk, he was simply uninterested in sport and billiards and horse racing, 'he detested dancing, he was indifferent to music, and impatient of novels'.[10] His lack of interest in horses should in itself to have disqualified him as a Native Australian Poet. He kept himself to himself. His mother's irruptions therefore were doubtless a revelation among them, and then when the novelty wore off, a nuisance. Even Mrs Hamilton-Grey conceded that Matilda was 'somewhat shabby in her appearance ... Civil servants, in those days, were somewhat prone to snobbishness. They saw a shabby, excited old woman as the mother of the poet, hence they laughed at, they ridiculed the poet's mother ...[11]

Yet, as A.G. Stephens put it, Matilda had the constitution to stand a drop or two, or a gallon or two. With Henry now well placed she felt herself entitled to go 'on the spree'.[12] Shades of Basil Edward – a kindred spirit indeed.

But as Sutherland goes on to reveal, Henry himself was turning to his cups. He was in no way as self-indulgent as his mother, nor his brother, nor his father, nor his grandfather – or not yet.

> In general a shy, self conscious man, with little to say for himself in general company, a single glass of wine gave his face a pinker glow, quickened the flow of his thoughts, made his tongue ready and his spirits gay. But for an evening spent in such cheery fashion the morning had to pay the penalty, in a whiter skin, a duller brain, a deep depression of mind. From that listless misery a glass would lift him, and he had none near to warn him what that process led to, how the needless glass expands to two, and then to three; how the general drift of life grows wretched save when the magic but treacherous touch of alcohol gives it a transient brightness. It is strange that, with his mother's fate so urgently before him, he should not have been cautious and full of self distrust.[13]

Given his circumstances, it is little wonder that Henry Kendall resorted to a consoling glass or two. Something else for office gossip. With his mother creating unhappiness in his home and difficulties at work, his sisters evicting him (as he thought it) and sending a ceaseless flow of bills for him to pay, and with debts accumulating, he hardly knew which way to turn. Just as matters had begun to take a turn for the better, they turned worse. As he recalled it, this was a period of utter depression of body and mind.

It was urgent for him to write, though what he earned by his pen was, as one might say, small beer. He took to writing squibs and satirical verses in the manner of the day, for *Punch* and the like, firing off thinly veiled barbs and finding himself punctured if not pinned by retaliatory thrusts. *Punch*, for example, was facetious at his expense, burlesquing the 'deep metaphysical subtlety of his poems'.[14] He had already begun writing prose pieces – unhappily for him, some of these were 'dyspeptic lectures', warnings against the dire consequences all too likely to follow entrance into the holy estate of matrimony. Wedlock, more like.

That was before he had encountered Miss Charlotte Rutter. Now he had all the world before him – where to choose.

Gloom was endemic with him; it circled about him. In April of that year, 1868, his former mentor James Lionel Michael was found dead in the Clarence River, though whether Michael died by his own hand or at the hand of an assailant or by accident was never established. He had a mysterious jagged cut on his head, near his right eye, and his frontal bone was broken, as though he fallen on a broken bottle, or maybe a rotting pile, before he drowned; on the other hand, he had recently written what some took to be a hint of suicidal thoughts. He had also been blamed (wrongly) for not accounting for certain trust funds, and that might have prompted him to take his own life.[15] Kendall seems to have persuaded himself that it was suicide.[16]

The inquest could not resolve exactly what had happened, nor has literary history resolved the matter since then. Closure for Michael, but not for anybody else. Certainly not for Kendall, though curiously he seemed more concerned for the ex-wife when Sheridan Moore began to circulate a proposal for a public lecture to raise a benefit for her and her son, now wholly unprovided for. Stenhouse, a staunch Presbyterian, could not allow himself to be seen possibly condoning suicide, and declined to have anything to do with it. Kendall wrote in a fury to Moore: 'If that d-mned old sham Stenhouse had any kindness in him he would have initiated the step you have so laudably taken'.[17] The historian of the Stenhouse circle, Ann-Mari Jordens, suspected that Kendall revealed just a touch of hypocrisy in this, embarrassed by his own lack of practical interest.[18]

Two months later, the other significant figure in his evolving literary life, Charles Harpur, likewise died. From the time Kendall arrived in Grafton

(1862), he had, for the five years that followed, been exchanging letters and critical opinions with Harpur, learning from his example and from his poetic stature, and growing in confidence as he won the older poet's approval. But Harpur, who had become something of a father figure to Henry, at the end wasted away with phthisis like Basil Kendall, Henry's father. Basil had died a weakened man, leaving the twin boys to enter their formative teenage years without a role model. The uncles had kept at a distance. Neither of the grandfathers stood as an example to follow – indeed, the less said of either of them the better. Now Harpur and Michael, the two men who had given Henry some kind of direction when he needed it, some kind of model to emulate, had likewise died.

Like an adolescent, or an incompletely formed person, Henry indulged himself in sorrow and gloom. That was a familiar, strangely comforting mood, it was self-involving. It was good for poetry, or the kind of poetry he found readiest to write. He wrote two very accomplished memorial poems for his late mentors; and in something of the same frame of mind he submitted three entries for the annual poetry prize awarded in Melbourne for the best Australian poem – *Williams's Illustrated Australian Annual* competition – though these were all previously published poems. They impressed the judge, Richard 'Orion' Horne.[19] Horne wrote to Kendall subsequently (when he found out who the pseudonymous 'Araluen' actually was) that, if he had been free to do so, he would have awarded him with three prizes for his three poems.[20]

Horne seemed unperturbed that they were not freshly minted poems; more likely, he was unaware of it. Two of them were revisions and modifications of poems Kendall had published in newspapers a couple of years previously, in appropriately sonorous blank verse, not his more characteristic running alliterative lyrics. The other had appeared in his volume of poems.

Kendall was in no good frame of mind at the time to embark on a major poem, or three. It is understandable that he should have looked to what he had at hand. He submitted poems that he believed had a good chance, reasoning that revisions to them constituted them as new poems (though 'Dungog' would not withstand scrutiny in that respect); he was in urgent need of money, for now he owed Henry Parkes £30, and he had other debts too. George Gordon McCrae subsequently told Mrs Hamilton-Grey that

Kendall deserved the public esteem that went with the award, but just as important was the pocketful of guineas, 'of which he stood so much in need, and which I really believe was the sole reason he went in for the competition at all'.

The winning poem, 'A death in the bush' (it had originally appeared as 'A death scene in the bush', and then was substantially revised and enlarged as 'Orara – a tale'[21]), was thought at the time to have imitated Tennyson rather closely. Certainly, there are echoes both in expression and motif; and in sentiment. The subject matter nods towards his own late acquaintances – indeed, there is as much Harpur as Tennyson in this poem and in 'The glen of Arrawatta' (previously entitled 'The glen of the whiteman's grave', which the Sydney *Punch* had derided as 'the very blankest verse'[22]). There is even what was claimed to be an accidental appropriation of a whole line from Horne himself, which some hint may have encouraged a more welcoming reading from the adjudicator,[23] though George Gordon McCrae did not think either Kendall or Horne recognised the misappropriation.[24]

Kendall's financial debts kept compounding too. He was repaying the loan from Henry Parkes at about the rate of one-half of his pay, and he could scarcely make ends meet. The strain of his mother reached a crisis point, and she was relocated to Palmer Street in Woolloomooloo, an area already well on its way to becoming sleazy. She would have to fend for herself. Defiantly, she presented herself to the Insolvency Court and on 29 July 1868 was listed as insolvent, with debts of over £80, and assets of exactly £5.[25] Now she would have to keep herself – which she did from her next address, a room in Oxford Street, taking in specialty needlework.

This is the stage at which Mrs Hamilton-Grey might more accurately have announced the break between mother and son; for he seems to have had nothing more to do with her thereafter. As one might imagine, given Matilda's fieriness. She would not have been graceful in her departure; quite possibly her appearance in Insolvency was calculated to embarrass the aspiring civil servant. That would certainly have been the effect.

In late September Henry Parkes resigned, whereupon the ministry of the day fell. Henry Kendall lost powerful patronage, and with that went his chances of preferment, just when he needed it. His mother was still, somehow, 'on the spree'.[26] He continued to be harried by creditors, the threat of bankruptcy loomed large over his head, though as a civil servant he could not take refuge in that,[27] and Lottie was suffering from the effects of her advanced pregnancy as the summer progressed. She did not have an easy time of it. On 2 January 1869, their daughter Lizzie (Violet) Araluen was born.[28] Kendall wrote in some desperation to Dr Brereton, a modest fellow poet, as well as a medical practitioner, stressing how very hard up he was, and in need of every honest penny he could earn, and how he thought that a change of air would be of great benefit to the entire little family.

It is not altogether transparent just what his goal was in writing this note to Brereton. Perhaps he was beginning to canvas the idea of leaving Sydney; but the immediate result was Brereton's practical generosity, the offer of a cottage out along what was then the Great North Road, a cottage known as Osgathorpe, and according to persistent legend Leichhardt's last halt before leaving Sydney on his third and fatal expedition. That connection provides a curious echo to Edward's fetching up at Jimbour.

Dr John Le Gay Brereton was not by intention a colourful person. He was just strongly independent, and true to his convictions. He had won something of a reputation as a champion of the benefits of frequent bathing, especially the Turkish version of that, and had opened a very successful public bathing pavilion. He gave lectures on 'rational clothing', appropriately dressed 'in a suit of light tweed, with canvas shoes, without shirt, waistcoat, cravat, or stockings'.[29] He was sufficiently progressive in his attitudes to attract government attention, and in 1864 he was appointed one of the Medical Visitors of Lunatic Asylums. Osgathorpe was a little further on than the Tarban Creek Lunatic Asylum, more commonly known by its new name, given in 1869, as the Gladesville Hospital for the Insane.

If Brereton had continued in this role, he would have been in position to assist when Henry Kendall was committed to Gladesville Hospital on his unhappy return from Melbourne. But Brereton was dismissed from that appointment after some controversy in 1865, possibly because of his promotion of the homeopathic approach to medicine, but also possibly because he had crossed swords with the Colonial Secretary, Charles Cowper, over the publication of a report he and his fellow Visitor had submitted to the government, prompting unwanted public commentary about the conditions there, and the likely cost of their recommendations. A very terse note of 22 September 1865 informed him that he was disqualified from his public role because he had submitted a tender for a contract at the same time as holding his appointment as Visitor.

For the time being, Kendall was delighted to accept Brereton's generous offer for them to stay in Osgathorpe, as well as his encouragement. They lived away from the confines of the township, and the turbulence of the Kendalls. Lottie, who had had a hard time of the birth, could rest and mend; she continued ill for some months, leading Henry to remark acidly that he may have married a chronic invalid. For the time being he fretted and bided his time as best he could.

He wrote off to various acquaintances, taking soundings as to what he should do next. He was uplifted by his success with the Melbourne poetry prize, and his thoughts turned in that direction as a possible bolt-hole. Brereton is one who encouraged him: 'Melbourne is undoubtedly the right place for you'.[30] Yet, by the time he received that endorsement, the die was already cast. He had sent a letter of resignation on 31 March, it was received the next day, and his old champion Henry Halloran wrote back to confirm that his government appointment would cease three weeks later; though Henry seems not to have waited that long. He had already bolted.

Two years later he wrote a piece for the *Town and Country Journal* (18 February 1871), in which he remarked in passing that he 'landed on an ominous first of April, decidedly ominous for a man starting life in a strange city, with a stock-in-trade consisting of two or three letters of introduction, and a sum of money not exceeding four shillings'. If that date is correct, he must have departed Sydney even before his letter of resignation had been lodged. If it was not correct, then it was selected in order to claim some quirk of fate. Henry Kendall throwing up riddles again.

What is undisputed is that his wife was left with her baby at her mother's place until she heard from Henry. He went ahead on his own, disembarking at the old Queen's wharf towards the mouth of the Yarra, and from where he could cross straight into the city. He could walk to wherever he wanted, but that was the rub – where should he go?

He sent for Charlotte as soon as he had found them a place, although later – in one of the many letters he wrote asking for a modest loan – he changed that detail. He had been put under unexpected financial strain because she and the baby arrived earlier than he had expected, before he had found steady employment. Little by little further detail emerged. The long letter to Dr Neild ends with Kendall revealing that he 'left Mrs Kendall with her mama, but could not persuade her to remain behind me for any time. The truth is she was persecuted by cruel asseverations on the part of my family'.[31] The Kendalls' hostility was palpable, and undoubtedly Matilda was fanning the embers. The Rutters could not defend her from that.

The letter to Neild is both long and revealing and reads as though Kendall was relieved to speak frankly of what he had been holding close to his chest. He asked Neild to keep the contents of his letter to himself, and especially not to let his wife know of it. That became something of a regular revelation. He frequently added a request to various of his correspondents to keep such matters from his wife. He may have thought he was protecting her from the dire necessities of their situation, but in fact he was keeping her isolated. A hard time she must have had of it, lonely and oppressed by the winter weather, being unwell herself, her infant failing, with no acquaintance in Melbourne, and Henry going from one newspaper editor to another, or meeting up with the various literary types; or drinking.

Briefly he held a position in the Statistics Office, adding columns of figures (said to be tally sheets of the numbers of the recently deceased) up and down and then cross-checking his results by adding lines of figures across the pages. Kendall just could not get those two procedures to agree, and it drove him to despair. After three days he took his hat off the peg, drew his pay and left.

His letters of introduction led him to the Yorick Club, and to Marcus Clarke, its leading luminary, and to Adam Lindsay Gordon, another member. Probably he was introduced there by Richard Hengist Horne, whom he had visited at the outset.[32] Given the membership of that briefly famous coterie, a number of epigrammatic descriptions were made of Henry Kendall at his first appearance, and of his manner. A.G. Stephens noted that when Kendall came to Melbourne:

> he clung desperately, poor poet! to his garb of dignity. He could not be separated from his umbrella, rolled tightly in the mode of fashion. Vainly gay sparks at the Yorick Club sought to seduce him from the protection of the umbrella – that badge of professional gentility contemned by Henry Parkes …

> ...
>
> G.G. McCrae, reminiscing, said he looked like an undertaker. In Melbourne Kendall's family and Sydney friends – Daley, Myers, Holdsworth – remembered him as quite a lively chap; in spite of underlying sadness.
>
> ...
>
> Holdsworth pictured Kendall, both hungry and thirsty, sitting in one of the two rooms that constituted the Yorick Club trying to do himself and his patrons credit in his best shabby Sydney clothes. Frock coat, tall hat, gloves and umbrella – the relics of his own Civil Service job in Sydney. Poor fellow! He had no other garments.
>
> ...
>
> Not a penny in his pocket, and hugging his umbrella as his sole defence against the bleak rain of Melbourne because his overcoat was shelved with 'Uncle' and he had no money to redeem it.[33]

Stephens constructed his version of Kendall well after the event, but followed the common pattern of writing of him (Kendall) as very much out of his depth, and somewhat ridiculous. The Yorick fraternity looked for the ridiculous everywhere. They made fun of everything, including Henry Kendall. They expected him to see the comic side of it. He, however, was too introverted, too hypersensitive, too shy to join in their rollicking humour. Ultimately, too serious. Every now and then puffing furtively on a pipe, for the form of it.[34] And depression never far away.

While George Gordon McCrae joined in the high jinks, he was subtle enough to see a little further into the newcomer:

> He was a man about middle height, spare and thin but quite the reverse of athletic. He was pale and somewhat wrinkled, and the expression of his countenance as a rule sad. His hair which was crisp and curly (latterly of an iron grey colour) he sometimes trimmed, but never cut; in fact when I first knew him it used to conceal the collar of his coat. His cheeks were naturally bare but he wore a small rather sparse looking beard though his moustache in after years was quite a heavy one ... Nervous to a degree he never felt at home unless he happened to have something either to touch or to hold, and many will remember the manner in which he used to embrace his umbrella as he conversed with them.[35]

The anxieties of the schoolboy and the novice lecturer were still manifesting themselves. McCrae's description is not unsympathetic. In fact, he was a very good friend to Kendall; but his sense of mischief trembles just beneath the line when he constructs Kendall as a new version of the Knight of the Woeful Countenance; and prompts us to recall Kendall's elected poetic role model, Tennyson, with the same flyaway hair, the same moustache, the same sad visage, but a wispier beard.

And then McCrae offers a detail not commonly remarked. Kendall wrote with his left hand, 'the right hand being, owing to an accident (I think) partially paralysed'. That suggests something more than it actually says. Kendall was not just left-handed, but in some sense one-handed. Which would put his lack of athleticism in a new light, and his incompetence on his grandfather's farm. If it is true. It might even explain his awkwardness, his sense of separateness, something of his essential aloneness. If it is true. Given that his identical twin Edward was naturally left-handed, there is every chance that would be the case with Henry too. But then if so, why would he let people think he had had some disability ('lameness', as he says on another occasion)?

One cannot help remembering Grandfather McNally's beating, and Matilda's fury, too late to be protective of her son. McNally lamming him.

The other telling detail in McCrae's description is the mark of poverty all over Kendall. Though again, that might be somewhat coloured. If he had a civil service suit, or frock-coat, or some such, it had become shabby very quickly – in the eye of the beholder, perhaps. In Melbourne the Kendalls were quickly reduced to the bare necessities, and to visits to the pawnbrokers, handing over their possessions one by one. For although Henry was writing quite productively, and publishing successfully in the leading journals and papers, he was not earning much from this activity. Sometimes he did not earn anything for a month at a time together.

Obviously, they could afford only the cheapest lodgings – they moved from the first place he had found, opposite Carlton Park, to Fitzroy, then to Collingwood, then Richmond. Lottie, her constitution run down by their poverty, was unwell much of the time, and so was the baby. Kendall went without sleep and food, he could not pay the rent (another incidental consideration he hid from his wife – 'the deception is wicked'[36]). Sutherland described them as reduced to squalor:

> Meantime poverty, disappointment, and anxiety wrought an unutterable depression, and slowly the good resolves all melted away. He grew more and more unsteady, became less capable of work, and drifted rapidly into squalor. The wretched family hid their heads in a dingy lane of Richmond, while the poet, whose soul but five years earlier had been aglow with high ideals, and a love for all that is beautiful and mysterious in nature, spent his evenings in obscure public-houses, and his nights too often seated in some lane or right-of-way.[37]

Sometimes Kendall earned £5 in a week, mainly by writing prose sketches, considered much more commercially viable than his poems. And sometimes he found himself shut out from a newspaper office, no longer wanted. He was so down in the dumps that he even – briefly, not seriously – contemplated going back to sheep minding. His move to Melbourne was not paying off as he had hoped.

By September he had both enough poems and an agreement with a publisher to try in effect a last toss of the coin. He would publish another volume of poetry. His *Leaves from Australian Forests* came out in a sizeable run, 1000 copies for the Australian market, 500 for 'home consumption'. In the end, despite welcoming reviews, sales were not what had been expected. Kendall was fortunate, in that he lost nothing by the exercise, but that was very cold comfort. His publisher, George Robertson, lost £90. Melbourne had hardly taken him into its arms – he felt still a stranger in 'a grey gloomy flinty-hearted city'.[38] He seemed defeated at every turn.

Then he began to fall out with Marcus Clarke, who had been his earliest sponsor in Melbourne. Clarke had taken to publishing clever little verse parodies, hinting at Kendall's drunkenness (he likewise parodied Adam Lindsay Gordon, celebrating the same haziness); Kendall began to make comparable comments against Clarke, and step by step a kind of estrangement opened up.

Kendall dedicated his new volume of poems to Charlotte, and acknowledged her steadiness and deep affection, one who:

> *faced for love's sole sake the life austere*
> *That waits upon the man of letters here.*

His was a genuine and heartfelt tribute to her self-denial, to her loyalty. Yet – as there is so often a 'yet' with Henry Kendall – in dedicating the book to her, he noted that the tribute of the book, the act of it, if not the rhymes themselves, is what would touch her heart. The inherent catch was to become clearer years later, when he recorded that he did not read his poems to her, as she was not interested.[39] That too was a part of, even privately a substantial part, of his disappointment. But in his turn, he failed to acknowledge their life was falling short of what they might have hoped for, largely because of his failings. He did not sufficiently appreciate what her life must have been like, quite different from the circumstances in which she had been brought up. If she were disappointed, she did not let on about it.

Their child continued ailing and poorly. By February 1870 her condition had become critical. Dr Neild sent a prescription for the infant, and likewise one for Henry, who had let drop that he had not slept for several nights. Not that he had been angling for this; it was just the kind of detail he inserted in his letters, part of his habitual – if in this case all too readily understandable – despondency. He had to ask yet another acquaintance for the loan of five shillings to pay for the prescription. This was a matter of great urgency, as the infant was in almost a dying state. Indeed, in just a matter of days Araluen did in fact die, from a combination of fever brought on by bad teeth, and malnutrition. She was simply too weak to withstand her final illness.

As is commonly remembered, Kendall did not have enough money to pay for her funeral expenses. It shattered him that he had been the cause of her death, or rather that his incapacity had brought it about. He was haunted, his wife wrote later to Alexander Sutherland, by Araluen's wailing just before her death, haunted ever afterwards – 'she suffered so'.[40] Doubtless Lottie was distressed too, though it is his own distress to which he returned again and again. He wrote a poem to give some focus to his feelings, 'Araluen', addressed to Lottie; and retrieved the sentiments of his dedicatory poem by appropriating a couplet from it, that because her love was noble, she had:

faced with me the lot austere
Ever pressing with its hardship on the man of letters here.

That was a touching gesture from him, though when he turned to the same couplet yet again for his memorial poem for Marcus Clarke (*Bulletin*, 3 September 1881), it began to look like he was repeating himself, or resorting to a formula. It rather spoiled the sentiment.

One difference is that in the 'Araluen' poem he had settled back into his more customary long metre, with the unhappy consequence that the sentiments are in imminent danger of sounding trite. There can be no question about the grief that he felt, but the verse does not always sound so deeply moving.

What is remembered of all this is the ghastliness of the Kendalls' circumstances – the landlord insisting that the rent be paid or they would be evicted, the hearse waiting to take away the child's corpse, Lottie despairing that she could not afford to go into mourning as custom then dictated, and Kendall himself, unsuccessful in all his approaches for a small loan, scribbling away at an article to earn the undertaker's fee.

Kendall was especially incensed at Marcus Clarke, who did not answer a request for help at the time Araluen was entering her last days; then after the death Clarke sent two letters which Kendall declared were brutal. He asked Kendall to send in an account for work he had submitted to Clarke's *Humbug* and agreed that Kendall was owed £5 and promised that the cheque was in the post. It never arrived.[41]

In all their distress, the Kendalls managed to make mistakes of their own over matters of credit, offending their friends; and so the misery continued to circle about them, with Henry spending more and more time, as he subsequently expressed it, 'on the tap-room floor', only occasionally earning a little from his writing. Without her child to care for, Lottie was now the one to carry whatever items they could spare down to the local pawnshop, using the name Mrs Clarence, and returning with five shillings for those worn-out rags. Henry was most likely barnacled in one of the local public houses, the Labour in Vain (where the Irish publican used to quote verses from Tom Moore) or the Perseverance.

Given Kendall's current frame of mind, he was in no fit condition to cope with the next disaster. In his brief time in Melbourne he had established some kind of special connection with Adam Lindsay Gordon. They were linked by their melancholy, by the difficulty of their circumstances, by their poverty, by their disappointment in not being able to live by the pen. They were both uncommunicative, both depressive. They had both suffered from the death of an infant girl – Gordon's daughter had died the year before Kendall's arrival, aged just 11 months. Gordon's distressed young wife had left him for more than a year, but returned when Gordon gave up his livery stable in Ballarat and took a cottage in Brighton. There is no indication that Gordon and Kendall visited one another however; the two men met in the city, walked the streets together, and from time to time wrote notes to each other. The wives were not part of that world.

It was a tragedy for him, then, when Adam Lindsay Gordon committed suicide on Brighton beach at daybreak, on the very morning that Gordon's third and ultimately successful volume of poetry, *Bush Ballads and Galloping Rhymes*, was published. His reasons for doing so have been minutely examined and pondered, and somewhere in all this, so speculation goes, Kendall had a part. He had certainly shared with Gordon the gloomy prospect that volumes of poetry would not sell in Australia; and that they cost the publisher, if not the poet, money. Gordon had borrowed heavily to pay for the expenses of publication; he could not afford failure. Yet he had seemed cheerful at the Yorick Club on the preceding afternoon (unusual for Gordon, who was just as inclined to melancholy as Kendall). Some members wondered if Gordon had suffered some sort of turn from head injuries he had received from his horse riding.

Mrs Hamilton-Grey seems to have been mainly responsible for promoting the story that Kendall was closely connected to that unhappy event. She proposed that the two despondent poets were together on Gordon's last afternoon, but that does not square with other recollections that Gordon had been at the Yorick Club. Mrs Hamilton-Grey's account then jumps ahead to the following days, when George Gordon McCrae had, by his own testimony, offered Kendall a lift in his trap down to Brighton for the funeral, knowing how close Kendall had been to Gordon and likewise knowing that every penny counted with Kendall. He could not have afforded a cab fare. To McCrae's surprise, the offer was declined, on the grounds that Kendall 'couldn't come, not a penny in the house'. Tactfully, he supposed that Kendall may have thought the funeral too much to bear.

But, Mrs Hamilton-Grey continued, McCrae never knew the gruesome truth:

> It seems that Kendall and Gordon had passed the day before the suicide, together, both poets much depressed in hope and faith. Lindsay Gordon, the stronger of the two, and the most daring, conceived the idea of a *double suicide*, both he and Kendall to die at the same hour. They parted, both the worse for drinking. Gordon took his own life, as arranged. But Kendall thought of God, of his child and wife, his mother and sisters, and conscience forbade the act. *He could not do it.* One can understand his refusal to be present at the funeral of Adam Lindsay Gordon, and what he felt about it. He told no one in Melbourne, not even his wife.[42]

So how was this known? 'It was to his mother, on his return to Sydney, that he confided the terrible secret.'[43] And it is difficult to know who had the more fanciful imagination. The story has never been corroborated; indeed, according to Mrs Hamilton-Grey, could never be corroborated. But in the sequence of things, the record contradicts her assumption about Gordon's sorry state of mind, his unmanageable debts [illegible] feeling. And if Henry Kendall had indeed been so depressed as to enter into contemplating suicide, that stage had not been reached just yet either.

It is true though that this was another shattering experience for Kendall. These disasters just kept on coming, one after another. He had felt as close to Gordon as to anyone, a kindred spirit. Yet that must be a qualified comment, for as H.G. Turner said of Gordon, 'he was not quite so depressing as poor Kendall, and despite his grievous lack of pence he occasionally let himself go'.[44]

If Kendall could not bring himself to attend the funeral, he made amends by a sincere and touching elegy, both a personal and a public tribute to 'the late Mr A.L. Gordon', one of that bright company this world could ill afford to lose. He was a poet apart, with Lionel Michael (Michael now reinstated in Kendall's estimation) and Charles Harpur, all three now sadly gone. In particular, 'The mournful meaning of the undersong/ Which runs through all he wrote' was misapprehended, and so too the special doom of the poet, a doom he claimed for himself:

> *The wild specific curse which seems to cling*
> *For ever to the Poet's twofold life!*

With Gordon's death, Kendall resigned from the Yorick Club. He could not afford the membership in any case, and in the past had had to beg for a temporary loan in order to pay his dues. Now step by step he was separating from Melbourne, or being separated from it, though perversely it was at just this stage that he won his greatest acclaim there – he was invited to write an ode to Euterpe, the goddess of music and song and dance, muse of lyric poetry, for a cantata to be sung at the opening of the Melbourne Town Hall. Euterpe with her double pipes, her twin pipes, which combine joy and sorrow ('a subtle sense of pain/ Sighs through thy melodious breathings'). The commission was announced on 1 August, with Kendall chosen ahead of everyone else and acknowledged as one of the prominent voices in Australian poetry. The performance itself was on 9 August, an astonishingly quick turnaround, especially when it is considered that the choir would have had almost no time for rehearsal.

The cantata went off reasonably satisfactorily, and congratulations were spread around in all directions, including by the Lord Mayor. But then, as so often had happened in Kendall's poetic life, complications emerged. It was becoming a familiar pattern. Shortly before Gordon died, Kendall had had to apologise to Adam Lindsay Gordon for approximating, if not appropriating, some lines of his. He emerged from that somewhat scathed. He had tried to smooth his way past Gordon's objections, but eventually he'd had to publish an apology. The absurdity of this habit of his, of usurping the work of others, is that he had no need to. Likewise, with lifting a line or two from Horne. He was perfectly capable of writing his own incisive and often memorable lines, devising his own insightful images. He had no need to lean on anyone. It suggests a latent uncertainty, perhaps deriving ultimately from his lack of a formal education.

The complication about 'Euterpe' was between the differing versions of how the cantata was devised (not to mention the existence of his earlier poem by the same name). Following a benefit concert, the proceeds from which were to be divided between Kendall and the composer, Charles Horsley, the libretto was published – but it differed from what Horsley had actually worked with. Kendall claimed Horsley had rejected what had been submitted; Horsley wrote in astonishment that he had never seen it before, and so the tit-for-tat worked its way through a sequence of letters to the editor. In the engagement it emerged that Kendall had begun their connection as early as May – a much likelier date, but one which also suggests Kendall had an important work in hand at the time he was meant to be thinking suicidally.

A month after the opening volleys the smoke had settled. Kendall's share from the concert was a little over £50. He had not triumphed in his very public spat, and had, on the contrary, somewhat smudged his image, if not tarnished it. But at least he had a sum of money in his pocket. He had enough to pay off those loans and to take Lottie back to Sydney. Without a friend in Melbourne, she wanted to go home, for the birth of her next child.

8

Not in his Right Mind

They arrived back in Sydney on 24 October 1870. First, they took temporary accommodation in Wynyard Square, then moved to rooms above a cabinetmaker's shop further down towards the Rocks, just off Essex Street[1] – closer, too, to the kinds of insalubrious hotels that sailors frequented, and the low life of that district.

Within a matter of weeks, so various friends, acquaintances and relations and expert witnesses subsequently attested at a court hearing, Kendall was showing signs of abnormal behaviour, in public and in private. He was variously encountered on the streets or in public houses, and his claims about himself were in some sense or other delusional. Not only was his conversation eccentric, so was his behaviour. So was his sense of himself. He was not in a good way at all, and it has to be deduced that this was no sudden aberration, a sea change. He must have left Melbourne already somewhat the worse for wear.

His new father-in-law (Charlotte's mother had remarried), William Tindale, was soon providing shelter and accommodation for Lottie and Henry, undoubtedly with rather more an eye on Lottie's wellbeing than Henry's. Kendall was all but unknown to Tindale before his marriage to Mrs Rutter.

The Tindales lived at Five Dock; sometimes the given detail is that Henry was living at Ashfield, just across the Parramatta Road. Tindale's account of Henry at the time is that he was endlessly restless, wandering about the house all night. Tindale obviously thought that was unusual, disturbing if not disturbed; but given the Fagans' subsequent observations of Kendall's behaviour at their cottage in Gosford, it is not impossible that he was in fact composing poems.

At some stage he went missing for two days and nights.[2] On the basis of his prior behaviour in Melbourne, a taproom floor would have been likeliest. He was alternately vacant and overwhelmed with grief, Tindale said, sobbing and sobbing, or evasive and contradictory in his responses to questions. His behaviour was not normal. Kendall's brother-in-law Frank Rutter was so concerned that he was on the point of having Henry confined for lunacy.

The awful brother-in-law Henry Evans, Emily's husband, had been visited by Kendall within a week of the return from Melbourne. Perhaps Jane was there too, but not Josephine, who had left Sydney for Port Macquarie almost as soon as Henry had left for Melbourne. She had been a companion to a Mrs Yates, and she married Mrs Yates's son there (just at the time Henry's son Frederick was being born, in December 1870), and then relocated to Maryborough, Queensland.

Henry would have made an unaccompanied visit to his little sister, given Lottie's condition, as well as her history with the Kendalls. Not very tactfully, Evans asked Henry about the effects of opium. Perhaps that was revenge for Henry claiming not to have known who Evans was. What Evans especially testified at the hearing was that Kendall would burst into tears without cause; that he said his wife was in Melbourne, whereas they had only just returned together from there; and that he had no fear of death, and wished he were dead.

Kendall, it appeared to them all, was profoundly depressed; but that was no new condition.

Other reports came in from a variety of witnesses. On the street, just a week after having landed, Kendall encountered a university scholar, a Doctor of Laws, expert in the classics, who knew him and wished to congratulate him on the prizes he had won in Melbourne. That should have been all very pleasant, but then Kendall claimed to have composed a poem in Greek of some 40 lines, in the Aeolic dialect, and that he had won a prize for it. That was an utter absurdity. Even Henry Evans knew Kendall was ignorant of Greek. Besides, not enough words in the Aeolic dialect had survived for such an exercise to have been completed. Further, Kendall claimed his composition was all in hexameters. Aeolic verse in its classical form is hendecasyllabic. Who can say what was in Kendall's head at the time? Certainly, he was forgetful of the expertise of the university don. What might be speculated is that somehow, in his muddled state, Kendall had a remembrance of tragic Adam Lindsay Gordon, who read Greek poetry and recited great swathes of it by heart (not necessarily in a manner that would have been approved in Oxford. Gordon was also an appallingly bad reader of his own poetry.[3]).

When he met up with the editor of the Sydney *Punch*, Kendall claimed he had been editing a now-defunct comic paper in Melbourne (doubtless a fantasy based upon Clarke's *Humbug*) and that he had written his Town Hall cantata 'Euterpe' in two hours, patently an impossibility. Whether he believed his own fantasies is beside the point; his judgement was so far astray that he seemed to think the preposterous stories were credible. Others saw him toss off two nobblers of brandy, giving every indication that he was in a state of incipient delirium tremens. Kendall was making sure his return had been noticed.

Perhaps he was delusional, but his own mother had been given to extravagant fantasies too. At what point does one become the other?

All of this strange behaviour had been observed up to the eve of Kendall's next transgression. On 21 November, he was arrested for having forged a cheque and presented it to be cashed ('uttered'), both disadvantaged parties being known to him. By comparison with his father and his brother, both of whom had committed the same offence, Henry's delinquency showed almost a lack of conviction. The fraud was for the slightest amount, a mere £1. What is incontrovertible though is that he had in the back of his mind his brother's rather grander larceny, for when they arrested him Henry pretended to them that he had the cheque from Basil, who he said had shipped off out of the colony two or three days previously, to Moreton Bay. The Kendalls. Payback time. They hardly held each other's character or reputation in high esteem.

Kendall was sent to trial on 21 December 1870; and it was there that all this evidence of his strange behaviour came to light. The ever-faithful supporter and well-wisher Sheridan Moore had visited Kendall a week previously and found him abstracted and melancholy. He told how out on the verandah Kendall had begun unbuttoning his waistcoat, and then buttoning it up again. He explained to Moore that a very great cloud had come between him and the sun, and he had thought it must be time to go to bed. He had spoken in a shockingly light-hearted way about Gordon's suicide. And Moore testified that Kendall was about to undertake a piece of literary work, but in his (Moore's) view, Kendall was totally unfit to do it.

Even Moore's wife was so brave as to appear in the stand, making a public spectacle of herself, to attest to Kendall's incoherency. All Kendall's old friends and acquaintances were prepared to speak up, all to the same end, giving evidence that Kendall was not in his right mind, was not himself. Not Halloran though, and not Parkes.

At the time of the court trial, Kendall had been held in a cell for a month. He had tied a handkerchief around his neck one night, but was prevented from taking any more drastic action by the keeper who was in the cell with him. When, next morning, the visiting surgeon asked him why he had done that, he had answered that he was tired of his life. That was consistent with an exchange he'd had with Joseph Harpur, Member of Parliament and brother of the late poet Charles, about a week before his arrest: 'if he were convinced there was a spiritual world he would go into it'.[4] Kendall was pale, nervous, incoherent. His mood would swing from a 'fear of extinction' to 'an unnatural elevation of spirits'. The visiting surgeon noted that he had the appearance of one who had indulged excessively in 'spirituous liquors' and opium. Indeed, he displayed a thirst for opium. Supposing opium came in a liquid form.

During the hearing of the case, Kendall was so overcome – either from his inherent condition or from the public exposure (given his predisposition to shyness) – that he was provided with a mattress and pillow in the dock, in case he were to collapse.

At the committal hearing, when the question was put to William Tindale, his new father-in-law and host, it was made quite clear that he would not be welcomed back into the house at Five Dock without a keeper.[5] That was not asked again at the trial proper. The jury was instructed that a defence on the grounds of insanity must apply to the offence itself. They took exactly 15 minutes to come to their verdict: not guilty on the grounds of insanity. Of unsound mind, as we say today. Kendall's counsel, the urbane William Bede Dalley, was an *habitué* of the Stenhouse circle, where he would have known the young poet in the years before Kendall's Melbourne experiment. Recently he had been elevated to Attorney-General. He was a highly successful barrister – highly expensive too, which raises a question about who was to pay his fee – and had mounted a robust defence to show his client's all-too-evident incapacity. Now Kendall would be held in custody until the Executive determined what should be done with him, and for him. And it was all very sad.

He remained in custody for a month, in the rather impressive, recently built Receiving House for Lunatics, at Darlinghurst, all ornate sandstone and verandahs on a triangular block just behind the Courthouse, a study in the awful symmetry of high Victorianism. It was so new as to be somewhat spartan, with tiny little trees planted alongside the gravel drive. The length of Kendall's stay there is curious, as those who were sent by a magistrate to the Receiving House could be held for only 14 days and would then have to be sent to an asylum if not released.[6]

It is not recorded whether Lottie visited him there, or in the holding cells prior to his trial. That would have been unlikely in the circumstances. According to the birth notice in the *Sydney Morning Herald* on 31 December 1870, their son Frederick was born at Five Dock on Christmas Day; though it is usually held to have been on the 24th. Somewhere a difference of opinion has become established, not that it matters all that much. That is not quite so radical an adjustment as Henry had made to his personal chronicle – but it is another of those destabilising uncertainties that colour the Kendall saga.

Lottie had returned to her mother's fold, and remained there. She had had a difficult time of it when Araluen was born, and undoubtedly she was apprehensive about the coming infant. Of course she would want to be at her mother's. But additionally, by his irresponsibility, Henry had alienated her. He had shown he was unable to support her. When he was arrested, he had just twopence farthing upon him. He was that close to being deemed a vagrant.

For all that his life seemed to have fallen apart, some part of his poetic life nevertheless remained. On 4 February 1871 the fledgling *Australian Town and Country Journal*, founded by Samuel Bennett, the fiddle-faced father of Henry's long-ago love Rose – that was Kendall's caricature of him before he met the incomparable Rose – published his longish poem 'Elijah'.[7] This had first appeared in June 1870 in the *Australian Journal* (where Marcus Clarke was in the seat), and its reappearance at this time is ironic. Its subject is poignant, given the circumstances, a poem about a man of conviction, a man gifted with deep insight into the moral right, a man who shook evil to its foundations. But gradually the concept drifts towards the prophet as poet, a poet not unlike Kendall's own estimation of that role – one who is made

godlike with that scholarship supreme
Which comes of suffering; one with eyes to see
The very core of things ... (ll. 66–8)

The poet as seer – salve to Kendall's unhappy soul.

In light of his real circumstance, the poem reads at this point in time as a moving, truly pathetic revelation, and yet also as an admirable demonstration of his urge to hold on to what he had formerly felt and believed. His suffering was not yet to be so enlightening for him though, and would not be for some time to come.

On the other hand, reprinting the poem revived the difficult episode with Adam Lindsay Gordon, when Gordon had complained that Kendall had plagiarised several lines from his 'The road to Avernus'. That source, but not the offending trespass, is acknowledged in Kendall's note to his poem.[8] The truly discomforting factor here is that the lines in question relate to a young mother's grief at the loss of an infant daughter, painfully personal to both Gordon and Kendall. At such a heartbreaking moment, why would Kendall stoop to petty larceny yet again? It was hardly flattering to Charlotte, it was not handsome of Kendall to have cheated, and the reappearance of the allusion at this time could hardly have been more inopportune. Kendall's sensitivity was towards himself, it seems.

What he did and where he went following his release on 25 January can only be discovered in glimpses. He evidently tried to wean himself off the demon drink, only to relapse. He wandered around Sydney, as he had in the back streets of Melbourne. He was not respectable. In a letter some five years later, when Kendall was in one of his bitter moods, he wrote of having been shown the door at the Rutters' or rather Tindales' house: 'When I have crawled, ill and weak, to her mother's home in order to have a glimpse of her and her child, she has stood and invited her brothers to turn me off the premises'.[9]

There are hints that he slept rough. At least this was the warmer phase of the year, but the way he was living cannot have been much good for his lungs. Unsurprisingly, there are likewise hints that he was occasionally taken into custody. P.J. Holdsworth was one who used to pay Kendall's fines and, on one occasion, reporting at the Central Police Court that Kendall had gone missing, he heard Kendall's voice from the cells: 'My name's Rickeybockey'.[10] Letters survive in which he hopes to cadge a pittance from any likely 'mark', and in which he reveals his various ailments, his aches and pains. There may have been an element of self-pity in all this. He was in no condition yet to begin working through all his inner turmoil.

At some stage, he even made his way to the very outskirts of the city. Parkes recounted that:

> When I lived on Liverpool Road near Lansdowne Bridge Kendall came tottering to our house one Saturday in a state so wretched I hardly knew him. He had been lying out the previous night in the bush. He could hardly stand for debility … We took him in; did the best we could for him. Next day we drove him to Liverpool and engaged a person to board and lodge him, and attend him. When he got well enough, I brought him to Sydney and kept him for a week or two at Miss Horner's Hotel and I got up a small subscription among some friends and reclothed him from head to foot. I really believe he would have perished if these things had not been done for him.[11]

Kendall had become wholly dependent on others' charity, and practical assistance; in his distressed state of mind he was all but helpless, and haunted by that memory of Araluen's wailing. They rallied around him, tousle-headed Parkes in particular, taking active measures to set Kendall back on his feet, to give him some measure of self-respect. That was noble in Parkes, given the exchange of indignant letters a year previously about Kendall's unpaid debt to him, when Parkes threatened to pursue him through the courts, and Kendall's somewhat reckless and unsatisfactory response that if he were to be sent to gaol he, Kendall, should probably be happier there than he was at that time in Melbourne.[12] From Parkes's point of view, he needed to retrieve what monies he could, as he himself was on the way to bankruptcy. Now with Parkes taking him in and feeding and clothing him, it must have been difficult for Kendall to avoid seeing himself as some version of the prodigal.

The next step was all but inevitable. On 5 July 1871 Henry Kendall was admitted to Gladesville Hospital for the Insane, suffering from excessive melancholia and nervous depression, having been brought by friends for examination before a magistrate. In effect they had decided between them that he could no longer be cared for privately, and would be better cared for by a specialist in an institution.

The pertinent hospital records were unearthed and published in 1966 – they make for sorry reading.[13]

His admission sheet shows that he suffered from melancholia, and had been so suffering for three months (that would be the most recent bout, as a previous attack was noted), brought on by a troubled mind. His recent trial for forgery was also noted, and the acquittal on the grounds of insanity at the time; he had been set at liberty when that insanity subsided. Then the admissions sheet elaborates in detail what other sources could only surmise:

> His habits are intemperate and he frequently takes opium and sedatives in large quantities … He is said to have been violent and to have threatened suicide during the present attack.
>
> He is of an extremely nervous temperament and looks worn, thin and ill. He is somewhat melancholic but free from all delusion, quite rational in conversation and correct in behaviour. He is suffering from nervous depression, sleeps badly and his appetite is capricious.
>
> July 12. Remains quite rational and well connected although he feels his position acutely and is most anxious to continue his literary work for the sake of his wife's support, neither his anxiety or mental depression are greater than they would be natural to a man of his temperament under trying circumstances.
>
> July 13. He is writing both for *The Empire* and *Punch* and both his prose and poetic effusions bear all the marks of mental equilibrium.
>
> Discharged July 29 1871.

One could have hoped for something better than 'effusions'.

His poetry was not just a sign of recovered equilibrium; it was the means by which he recovered himself, it was the means of composing himself, or some version of himself. The files of *Empire* for the second half of 1871 do not reveal any success in publication, so that what he was submitting may have been unsuitable. But he did publish two sequences of articles in the *Freeman's Journal*, one on Irish writers, commencing 2 September, and the second – from the beginning of December to 2 March 1872 – under the running title 'Notes upon men and books'. These pieces were quite an accomplishment, and they show balance and a restored continuity of thought. They show Kendall as very much the writer he had promised to be. The *Freeman's Journal* was something of a safe house for him, in publishing terms – Sheridan Moore had edited it formerly, as did William Bede Dalley.

All was not well. Kendall's habitual nervousness was there, even if it did not show in his writing. Ackland notes, without enlarging the astonishing comment, that by the end of 1871 Kendall was incapable of feeding himself.[14] And, although he was concerned that his wife should be supported, it does not seem that he had returned to his in-laws' home. He certainly had no capacity to afford a place of his own for Lottie. He was living an unsettled life, and it must have felt to him that he was on probation.

His connection with Lottie was not completely severed. We know this because in January of 1873 his second son, Frank, was born. Yet there was a separation, at about the time of that birth or before, when late in 1872 he complained that 'nobody – not even my wife who has an income will help me'.[15] Whether he had been abandoned or not is one issue, whether his conduct had become just too trying. The salient point is that he *felt* he had been abandoned. And at some stage he abandoned himself.

He managed to write an essay for *Punch Staff Papers*, 'Men of letters in New South Wales', the gist of which was the very great difficulty under which writers laboured to make a living; then he ceased writing for the *Freeman's Journal* and, apart from half a dozen poems in *Punch Staff Papers* and a song for a benefit concert, nothing more was heard from him for the next two years. The year 1872 cast a deep shadow over his soul. He would never forget it, even though he could recollect very little of it in detail – 'my mind was unhinged nearly all the time', he confided to his steady friend Sheridan Moore.[16] Subsequently, in 1874 and 1875, when he began writing again for the *Town and Country Journal*, he identified these as poems 'Written in the shadow of 1872'.

We can guess at what his life may have been like at that time from the case notes when he was readmitted to Gladesville Hospital on 30 April

1873, diagnosed as suffering from mania, the attack having lasted two weeks. It was supposedly brought on yet again by his intemperance; and his previous two recorded episodes were duly noted.

The admissions sheet elaborated further:

> Since his [previous] discharge he appears to have led the life of a Bohemian and to have plunged deeper and deeper into debauchery. His wife left him some months ago and returned to her relatives owing to his ill-treatment of her and his constant drinking. He has written less and less for the papers and has lately been in a starving condition. He imagined that he was accused of murdering a child.
>
> April 30. On admission. His hair has been cut owing to its dirty condition. He is extremely nervous and in a depressed condition of mind and body. He is fairly rational but there is a jerkiness of manner and a changefulness of thought which is not wholesome. He is sleepless by night and morbid and melancholy by day. He is very emaciated and pale. The secretions are in good order, the appetite is good and he has apparently started on the road to recovery.
>
> May 9. He is picking up flesh, looks brighter and better; takes food and sleeps under the influence of chloral fairly well.
>
> May 31: He appears quite rational but is depressed in spirits and irritable in manner. His general health is better.
>
> June 30: Seems now quite well.
>
> July 7: Discharged.[17]

Astonishing as it must be to the professionally uninformed among us, apparently the assessing officer could discern Kendall's improvement on the very day of his admission. That rather dampens its reliability as a dossier. The commentary on what Charlotte had had to cope with is more reliable, and worth remarking – 'ill-treatment' and 'irritable'. That statement of his mistreatment of her is not open to question. Later comments by Kendall imply that it was very likely so. His constant drinking would have made him nuisance enough, much like his mother. Much like his grandparents too.

The assessment also calls up traits that had been prefigured. Kendall's nervousness dated back to his schooldays, and had continued. So too the enduring depression of spirit, never far away from him. Even accidental details return from his past – the cropping of his unkempt hair, reminiscent of the treatment of his youngest sister Emily, whose head of hair resembled his own. Emily had been made to look like an orphan; or like grandfather McNally in his convict days. Kendall, like McNally, was clipped by a warder, not a professional barber.

But of most interest is what the admissions sheet reveals about his frame of mind. His mania is described as stemming from a belief that he was accused of murdering a child – not a deep-seated conviction that he had been guilty of bringing about her death. In other words, this perception is what followed from his paranoia, not an overwhelming sense of remorse, which would have been rather more creditable in him. The paranoia is another piece of evidence that he had an acute sense of self. So too does his besetting shyness.

At Gladesville he mended. He could be as withdrawn as he wished there; he could walk about inside the walled grounds, on the edge of a short deep gulley surrounded by tall trees, at that time something like a dell of blue gum and angophora, or apple myrtle as it was more commonly called back then. Here he was back in a comforting zone, reminiscent of the big timber country of his childhood, though without the bellbirds. The hospital was on the road to the north, away from the temptations of the city. It had its own provocations though. The superintendent, Dr Frederick Manning, had for reasons best known to himself used the patients to construct a substantial vineyard, a sore reminder of what had brought about Kendall's downfall in the first place.

The hospital overlooked a broad sheet of water, much as down in the Illawarra, much as up at Grafton on the Clarence. From the grounds he could connect imaginatively with his past; from there, he could yearn for the distant reaches as he had always done. That yearning, and the reassurance of the vision, were what his poetry had always been about, and would continue to be once he was up and about again, once he was refreshed; once his spirit had been renewed. 'I recognise in Poetry a revelation of Divinity beyond all revelations: a religion past religion ... The Visible becomes everlastingly new – everlastingly suggestive', he had written in happier days to Mrs Selwyn.[18]

Mending does not come so easily. When after three months he was discharged from the hospital, there came an immediate question – what to do next? He was alienated from his wife and children. They had found him too much to endure, and they were not ready to welcome him back. He, on the other hand, resented being abandoned by them, as he thought it; he had at the time no interest in reconciliation. For how else could he have agreed to the next step, arranged once more by friends, presumably much the same group who had taken it upon themselves to present him to the magistrate in the first place, in order to have him admitted to Gladesville. They engineered an appointment for him in Grafton, where he had once been so much at home, an appointment as editor of the newspaper there, according to one source:

> In 1873 he received the appointment of editor of a newspaper at Grafton, a town where he was well-known and valued. The steamer he sailed in called for a few hours at Newcastle by the way. Kendall was one of the passengers who went ashore, but not one of those who returned on board. His position was soon forfeited; he earned a few shillings from time to time writing poetry for the local papers; walking long distances and hiding from the face of man, living as he himself expressed it, 'In the folds of a shame without end'.[19]

Whoever the friends were, and there can be no disputing they meant well, they were astonishingly insensitive. Their assumption was that the return would be good for him. Yet that was where his alcoholic father had died, and that was where his good friend Lionel Michael had either committed suicide, or was pushed into the river, or had died accidentally, just five years previously.[20] Kendall might have become erratic, but his nerve ends were raw just the same.

Besides, there was the question for him of whether he could perform the role that awaited him. What if he could not, in front of old acquaintances and friends? Patently, he needed a drink, and needed it all the more the nearer he came. When the steamer docked at Newcastle, he took a glass or two at a nearby pothouse, and did not heed the call of 'all aboard'. His ship sailed without him; and Kendall lost that chance of restitution. He cannot have had a good feeling about any of it.

Sutherland recorded that he earned a few shillings here and there, doing whatever came to hand, writing something if he could, though no evidence of any success at that has emerged. He was unsuccessful in finding work, and he had nowhere to stay in Newcastle, no place either in Maitland, further up the river. He had sailed from Sydney with few possessions, and those would have been left on board the steamer. He must have been given just a little travelling money, a little drinking money, to get him to Grafton. His fare had been prepaid, and that was now wasted too. Though some have speculated that he cashed in the remainder of his fare,[21] which provided the *modus vivendi* at least for the next few days, and covered his tab at the bar. His failure to make anything from casual journalistic work only confirmed the bitter experience of his Melbourne days.

If he were to go anywhere, he had to walk. He could walk to Grafton, though that track barely existed; besides, it was 300 miles and more away. Sydney, in the other direction, was just 100 miles.

That was just what his twin Basil Edward had done in striking out from Brisbane; like him, Henry was on the wallaby. He would pick up whatever he could, wherever opportunity came to hand. He was heading back to Sydney, but not to Charlotte, and not to his family. No, he didn't want any of them to know where he was.

9

A Sign of Bad Blood

As it happens, long steady walking through the great swathes of trees was one of the best things Kendall could have done, for that is now known to settle nerves, and quieten disturbed thoughts. On the other hand, his feet would have been sore, his boots rather the worse for wear, and, given the long distances with few villages or settlements, he was bound to have been hungry as well as tired. Thirsty too. In that part of the country he would have encountered timber cutters' camps from time to time, and those of shingle splitters; doubtless he was invited to share their campfire when he came across them, that is, if he could overcome his instinctive shyness.

His likeliest approach to Gosford was down the Narara valley. He would not have been in the pink of condition when he started out from Newcastle, he had to sleep rough, he would have been aching and exhausted. His clothes would not have survived his rambling all that well. His head of hair was already recovering from its temporary institutional arrest; no doubt it was well on the way to becoming dishevelled again too.

All that much must be deduced. What can be confidently affirmed is that on his approach to Gosford he looked very like what he was, in fact – a tramp.

So many versions exist of what happened next that it is impossible to establish exactly how Kendall encountered – or rather, was encountered by – the Fagans. One of Peter Fagan's sons, perhaps Charles, is said to have seen him coming down the track and happened to recognise him. Alternatively, Kendall drifted into Campbell's hotel in Gosford itself, where the Fagans had paused for refreshment. Given that the papers did not feature photographs at that time, just how Charles recognised Australia's leading poet is not altogether clear. Donovan Clarke hints that Kendall may have been in the Gosford region in 1872,[1] though the evidence for that seems to hinge entirely on his particular and uncertain story. A circular proposition.

A different version is laid down by W.H. Wilde, that Charles Fagan, a Justice of the Peace, was at Wyong Creek when he recognised Kendall, and took him to Narara.[2] But then the same questions arise.

And yet another narrative again:

> He was tramping from Maitland to Gosford, following the telegraph line when he became benighted in Allisons swamp at Wyong. He spent a very cold night there but he said he was not lonely because of the croaking of frogs and the howling of dingoes. He found a way out next morning and reached Gosford.[3]

The route sounds probable. Maitland was the biggest town upstream from Newcastle, and the entry point into the Great Northern Road. But the telegraph did not run down that way, as Kendall would have found out.

However it happened, he arrived at the head of Brisbane Water and the Fagans gathered him up and took him home. He was enhungered, and they gave him meat; he was thirsty, and they more likely gave him tea.[4] He was a stranger, and they took him in.

In Greville's New South Wales Post Office directory of 1872 Peter Fagan is listed as a settler. A ticket-of-leave man, originally from County Meath and transported with a seven-year sentence,[5] he had successfully petitioned for 100 acres of land (near what is today called Point Clare) as soon as he was eligible, and by steady and sustained effort he accumulated enough money to purchase a further 60 acres, close to the top of Brisbane Water. There in 1838 he built himself a sandstone, rubble and mortar cottage somewhat in the manner of cottages of his native Ireland, and in which there was not a right angle or straight line to be found.[6] The walls were nearly two feet thick, perhaps from over-enthusiasm, and to ensure they stayed in place. Faith of our fathers notwithstanding, in recent times they have acquired the additional reassurance of three stone buttresses. It is still there and now known as 'Kendall's Cottage', again a testament to immoderate enthusiasm.

At the time as he was building his cottage, Peter Fagan applied for a lease of two square miles of land along the Wyong Creek, only to find

Richard Hill had beaten him to it. This was the very same Richard Hill who had taken in Kendall's mother, Matilda, and who was busily investing in property to ensure the support of his own mother back in England. Peter Fagan had intended to run cattle, but quickly realised that it was much more readily profitable to deal in timber. And in time, to buy up and subdivide allotments. The Fagans were later responsible for the subdivision and naming of Brooklyn, on the Hawkesbury.

In 1840 Peter Fagan applied for a publican's licence, and his cottage was transformed into the Red Cow Inn. It catered to timber getters and land clearers, and to those who tied up at the bank of Cooranbean Creek, which gave the property its original name; it was convenient too for those who moored out in the little estuary.

The wider Gosford settlement spread out around the top stretch of magnificent Brisbane Water. Because roads in that part of the country were no more than tracks, people relied on their little boats to move about, and to carry their crops of fruit down to the Sydney markets. They built their own craft, taking advantage of the extensive stands of timber thereabout. Peter Fagan had done so, but his boat, a sloop, was lost at sea, together with his cargo. That was a hard setback, as he had been relying on the returns from that voyage to pay off all the debts from his early investments. Two years later, another boat carrying his farm produce struck rocks near Long Reef. He was helped this time by a public subscription.[7] That was about the time he applied for his publican's licence, a surer way to make a living, and perhaps a popular way of showing his gratitude.

When, whether walking or riding, Henry Kendall had emerged from the bush, he was taken to where the Fagans lived, on the opposite side of Narara Creek from Gosford (Narara is the modern spelling; in Kendall's time it was Narrara). Kendall had come down through enchanting country. He loved the upper reaches of the Narara especially, where the water gurgled around rocks in the river channel and ferns filtered the light. It was bellbird country – he had written a poem about them years before, in 1867, well before he ever came to Gosford. They were here too, and that was an auspicious sign.

Looking upstream, to the rising tiers above, further up the slopes than where the timber cutters had left their crude trails criss-crossing through the forest, it was like the promised land. It looked like the home of something ideal, where poetry not only might be made, but might be found. Something which, in his troubled condition, he might believe in; only, he had resigned himself to never reaching it. For, by his moral scheme of things, he had by his carelessness in Melbourne precluded himself from approaching such a place, the vision and the dream. Which meant that when he came to write about this country, he would write in terms of sadness and disappointed yearning. But he had not arrived there yet.

Where he found refuge was a far cry from the visionary ideal – and yet, not altogether different. The Fagans were all good men, and they were sympathetic. They had had their share of troubles, and they had surmounted them. A few years earlier, they had been involved in a distressing family tragedy. Mrs Fagan, her sister who was visiting from Sydney, and one of the Fagan daughters had all died when Peter Fagan mixed up a tonic dose of port wine and quinine – or so he thought – as each of them had been complaining of feeling poorly. Unhappily, the unlabelled bottle he used contained not quinine but strychnine. The two bottles were different in shape but he had not been to his medicine chest for some time, and had forgotten which was which.

Another sister, the youngest brother, and Peter Fagan himself were also struck down with severe cramps by this pick-me-up. The remaining sons were variously involved in the calamity, rushing to the cottage to hold their dying mother, trying to induce their sister to vomit, assisting their father who had all but lost the use of his limbs.

At the inquest which followed, the proceedings were held up because the eldest son was too overcome to give his statement. It was highly distressing. Peter Fagan had a very good reason to carry a sense of guilt with him; but he did not let that overthrow him. He and his sons maintained a generosity of spirit. They did not renew the licence of the Red Cow, however – valuing their privacy – and it ceased to be an inn in 1868, ceased to be a public house. Which made it a much safer haven for Henry Kendall.

There he stayed for the best part of two years, nourished by their gentle steadiness, calmed by the surrounding vista, uplifted by the proximity and amplitude of the vast forest country about him. The cottage lay nestled at the foot of the sharply rising country behind, below what he called 'steep beetling hills'. This was, in fact, reminiscent of the escarpment behind the Illawarra, and Kendall was once more at what his mother would call the foot of the mountains. It was not unlike coming home again, or where he could start anew.

There the Fagans let him rest, as he needed. They let him do as he liked, left him to ramble about and return, left him to sit below the she-oaks along the river. They accepted him just as he was, they included him. He was inside a family enclave once more, having walked away from his own.

He was determined to keep his distance from that other world. He did not want his own family to know his whereabouts, nor the literary world. He carefully preserved his anonymity when, after recovering some measure of poise, he began sending off unsigned little snippets and insubstantial verses to 'Sydney town talk' in the *Town and Country Journal*. These were light pieces, but not light-hearted. Something inside him had hardened, and that edge shows in what he was writing, as well as in his adamant resolve to stay completely disconnected from his previous world.

He was well content to soak up the sun over that first summer, or to retreat into the cool of the glens whenever it became too hot; and he took to helping the Fagans on their farm when he felt strong enough. Not that that would have impressed grandfather McNally. Henry helped, as they all did, to take the punt across the river. If it were on the far side, he would sometimes jump into the water to swim across and bring it back. That was easier and quicker than the bother of rowing over. Frederick Kendall had a letter from Joe Fagan saying that Henry had been fond of swimming and boating,[8] which seems somewhat at odds with George Gordon McCrae's testimony that Kendall was 'quite the reverse of athletic'. Even if he did walk all the way from Newcastle.

These were days of simple pleasures, in which he enjoyed the company of the three Fagan sons remaining in the family home, and gradually he became interested in their activities. Sometimes he joined George, and more often young Joseph, as they set out on their long mail run – the Fagans had contracted to bring the mail from Wiseman's Ferry to Gosford, a service made necessary when Peat's ferry was discontinued.[9] Joseph recalled that Harry (as he was known around Gosford – another reinvention):

> would come along part of the way, always up the mountain to his favourite spot at the head of the glen, and there would often spend the whole day by the waterfalls or in the darkened fern-grown recesses, coming back to the farm when night fell, while I went on my way.[10]

They in turn joined him on occasional rambles through the surrounding district, if and when their farming duties allowed.

He was so wholly immersed in this out-of-the-way little community that he had no means of knowing that his twin brother, Basil Edward, lay dying at that very time in the Sydney Infirmary. Edward too shared the family predisposition – he had phthisis, tuberculosis as it is now called. For 58 days he lay there, weakening, and eventually died on 21 January 1874. Mrs Hamilton-Grey would have it that he walked down to Sydney all the way from Queensland:

> He died of consumption and weariness. Before he died he wrote to a second cousin of his, in the Ulladulla District, and asked for some pecuniary help, which was immediately sent to him; but it was returned, by a clergyman, with words to the effect that the money was not *merited* by the young patient. This was a strange reply from a supposed emissary of Jesus of Nazareth. Basil [Edward], it is true, was not religiously inclined like Henry, but he was in a dying condition, and should have been born with patiently ...[11]

The Ulladulla Kendalls remained unimpressed by Basil's family. Edward had hardly redeemed himself. He had brought yet another disgrace to his name, and theirs, late in 1872, when once more he was taken to court.

> BASIL E. KENDALL was committed for trial at the Toowoomba Police Court on Tuesday last, on a charge of forging and attempting to utter an order for the payment of £3 14s. 6d., purporting to be signed by Mr Thomas Hanmer. Prisoner, who had been employed at Talgai some eighteen months ago, was given in custody in trying to pass the forged order on Mr Bird, of the Post-office Hotel.[12]

Thomas Hanmer was a partner, with George Clark, in the prize merino stud Talgai on the Southern Downs of Queensland, and it was probably unwise to forge his signature. Talgai homestead is just eight miles from Allora, on the road from Toowoomba down to New England. Basil had found employment (of several kinds, evidently) in a less remote district than the Maranoa; Talgai was a prestigious property. In repeating his earlier offence, Basil showed he was as weak, or as compulsive, or as desperate, as his father. They shared a disposition towards more than tuberculosis.

Now Edward had reached the end of the road, and he had been the cause of his own misfortune. Presumably Matilda visited him, but that is not on record; that is not something that Mrs Hamilton-Grey appears to have heard in her interviews either. It seems that he died lonely. Certainly, his brother Henry kept his distance, preserving his silence. For the family had no way of contacting him.

Joseph Fagan also told Frederick Kendall that Henry 'could ride a horse well and would be up with the best of us when yarding a mob of fractious cattle and was a good judge of a horse and knew the pedigree of every horse racing at Randwick'.[10] That is at odds with Henry's indifference to, if not boredom with, horse racing in his years in the Colonial Office, and in Melbourne.[14] And it is at odds with the recollection of Joseph's eldest brother, Charles:

> Book in hand ... he [Henry Kendall] wandered for hours here and in the gullies. He was an unskillful rider, being, like Carlyle, too often absorbed in reveries, and preferred walking ... He wrote his poems on any scrap of paper or old note-book, jotting down odd lines and words, to write the poem as a whole with scarcely an alteration. He always wrote with his left hand, owing to an accident in his youth, forming each letter separately.[15]

Charles's description was put on record in 1890; his youngest brother's account came not until 40 years later and long after Charles (d. 1915) or any of the other Fagan siblings could contradict him. It is as though Joe were intent on modifying the image of Kendall to make him a skilled bushman, sturdy and at home in the outdoors, much as Edward had been in his younger years; whereas Kendall was in fact rather more the 'alone and palely loitering' type. Tennyson rather than Adam Lindsay Gordon. With a pipe.

Joseph, it appears, is likewise a questionable witness. Matilda, Kendall himself, Mrs Hamilton-Grey, were not the only ones embellishing the record.

Charles remarked on Kendall's left-handedness, that it was not his natural hand but developed of necessity because of some early accident. He might have paid especial attention to that detail, being crippled himself.[16] George Gordon McCrae had likewise drawn attention to it, adding that Kendall's right hand was partially paralysed. What is truly remarkable is how few people commented on this at the time. Certainly, such a liability would not have helped Kendall when wheeling and turning a horse to yard uncooperative cattle. It would not have helped his handwriting either, yet a meticulous flowing hand would have been required of a government clerk. He himself had apologised to Charles Harpur 10 years previously for his awkward left-handed writing, his right arm – not his right hand – being lame.[17] Kendall's characteristic writing was a stylised version of print script, difficult and angular. A handwriting expert might make something of that. But he also had developed beautifully written cursive handwriting, very legible,[18] which is not what one can always say of his manuscripts.

The Fagans had their farm, where they raised orange seedlings; they grew tobacco too, and carried their produce to market on little trading ships they had built. They also cut, sawed and sold timber. Peter Sr had been sure to take advantage of the cedar stands on his land. Indeed, before long the cedar was quite cleared out of the forests in that neighbourhood. Yet there was plenty of other timber available, hardwoods for the wharves around Circular Quay and for trestle bridges along the rapidly expanding railway network, lumber in general, she-oaks for any number of shingles – the Red Cow Inn itself had a shingle roof.

The brothers Peter and William were the primary agents in the Fagan Brothers' timber business, living in the family house in Bourke Street, Surry Hills,[19] and overseeing the storage and shipping at their timber yard, set in the midst of half a dozen competitor yards between Market Street and Druitt Street and stretching from Sussex Street down to their wharf on Darling Harbour. Theirs was a profitable business venture, and expanding. Just at the time Henry Kendall arrived, Michael – the next brother in line – was sent up to Camden Haven to develop a new branch of the family business. He saw there the fortunes to be made in the great forests close to hand, and the additional blessing of a sheltered harbour; he began at once to buy quantities of girders, palings, shingles and laths from the local sawyers to ship back to the family's Sydney depot.[20]

The Fagan lumberyard at Gosford was nowhere near as extensive, nor as complicated, as that on Darling Harbour. It was active enough, though, for the Fagans to offer Henry Kendall work as their storekeeper and accountant. Little by little, they were setting him on the way to gaining his self-respect. They showed they had confidence in him. For his part, he must have overcome his Melbourne mistrust of the obstinate inconsistency of figures.

The two elder Fagan sons, Charles and Edward, had left the family home. Charles had certainly left the Red Cow by the inauspicious year 1872.[21] With Peter and William mostly in Sydney town, Kendall was left to the care of the remaining three brothers, Michael, George and Joe. The surviving sister, Mary, may have had responsibility for running the house, and the kitchen; or as seems more likely, the Gosford home may have become bachelors' quarters, which would have suited Henry very well in his new frame of mind. For at some stage Peter Sr left the old homestead for the new house in Bourke Street – where he died, in 1876. As he was growing quite elderly, Mary had the care of him; and she was still at the town house six years later when Kendall breathed his last there.

It is certainly difficult to imagine all of them fitting into the old place. And in point of fact, what is now known as 'Kendall's Cottage', where he is persistently said to have lodged, was not the only building on the site. The original farmhouse was close by, consisting of a kitchen, dining room and three bedrooms. Like the cottage, it was constructed of stone and rubble, the interior lined with cedar, and it stood until it burned down in about 1901. The stone was repurposed for those buildings that have survived.

There, in the original farmhouse – so Charles Swancott has established – is where the Fagans' long-stay guest was housed.[22] Kendall could not have seen the Broadwater from the current cottage, as Mrs Hamilton-Grey recorded that he did; it was all but impossible. The only view of the water from the existing building would be if he clambered up into the loft and looked out through the gable-end door. His room had to be somewhere other than in the modern 'Kendall's Cottage'.

The little stone building is a very picturesque, more so from the outside. Which Kendall very much preferred, at least in good weather. He was often to be found down by the creek, or on the river bank, absorbed in the view, absorbed in his own thoughts. He had leisure to read, to write, to think – and to remember.

By the middle of the year he had returned to something comparable with his earlier serious poetry, a poem sponsored by his hours beneath the casuarinas along the river bank – 'The voice in the native oak'.[23] (Subsequently it appeared as 'The voice in the wild oak' and with its arresting annotation, 'Written in the shadow of 1872'. It was the first of the poems in which he acknowledged that darkness.) This was the beginning of his restitution and poetic recovery, though it is by no means one of his most accomplished set of verses. Significantly though, he had declared himself in public once again.

Like so much that he wrote, this poem's meaning is overburdened by the metre and the soft rhymes, where the effect is to make the verse run along. Its theme is the loss of his poetic powers, his sense amounting to a conviction that he had desecrated his poetic gifts, and that he could no longer see and respond to the poetic vision of Australia.

> *I, who am that perished soul,*
> *Have wasted so these powers of mine,*
> *That I can never write that whole,*
> *Pure, perfect speech of thine.*
> (ll. 33–6)

He does try to speak frankly of what he has lost. That is what grieves him, though he claims that through his sufferings he has acquired a dignity in grief. But in fact he was still missing the point of his own accountability, for he does not (at least not in this poem) acknowledge his responsibility for the debacle of Melbourne, and for his separation from his family. He cannot bring himself to that point. That was the hard edge in him.

It was a good sign, nevertheless, that he had returned to the public pages on his own terms. So too was his gradual resumption of links, by way of correspondence, with one or two of his former connections. In the middle of the year a minor poet and former acquaintance, P.J. Holdsworth, was visiting family connections in the vicinity. By chance he encountered Kendall and they began to correspond.[24] Holdsworth made some remarks upon that poem's plaintiveness, and Kendall wrote back to him:

> As regards the tone of the *Native Oak*, I cannot help it. *You* know something of my personal history, and you will hardly say that it has been a very happy one. As to my complaints about the waning of power, I have good reason to make them. To the end of the chapter, my expression will take a colour from the great grief which is making an old man of me. The old Passion is past kindling now.[25]

He wrote much the same to his loyal well-wisher, J. Sheridan Moore, who in September had likewise revived their former connection. He hated the sight of a pen, Kendall insisted. He had had quite enough of that 'in the weary years between 1869 and –74'.[26] He would continue to maintain that stance for the next several years.

In September he sent Moore a copy of 'Narrara', a spritelier poem and in the same metre as 'Bell Birds'. In the accompanying note he enthused about the magnificence of the local scenery. He also began to provide Moore with a little detail of what he had been keeping secret, where he was living and how. 'You are wrong in your estimate of the leisure I have here. I am hardly ever idle, and although I am my own master, I work as hard as any Government official alive.'[27] It was not quite true to write that he was his own master; he was by any measure dependent upon the Fagans, but it was more reassuring to Moore if Kendall fudged the arrangement a little. Then in October, as the correspondence continued, and Kendall started to feel a little more confident as well as confiding, he claimed: 'I have taken nothing stronger than tea for the last eleven months'.[28] By which, in passing, we deduce that he had arrived in Gosford the previous October or November.

The trouble is, he was being disingenuous. It is yet another example of Kendall writing to his correspondents what he thought they might want to hear. For at the same time, in notes to the Fagans, he was making jokes about himself and drinking. To Peter Fagan he wrote that 'I am very dickey today – too dickey in fact to write', and to William he wrote that he had earned enough from a piece in a journal for him to go on a bit of a spree.[29] Joe noted that Kendall 'could not take a single glass of spirituous liquor, that another man would make light of, without a collapse'.[30]

Once Moore had Kendall's address, the secrecy of his whereabouts was no longer so secure, though Moore would have been circumspect. Presumably he was the go-between in relaying a message from Nicol

Stenhouse's widow, asking Kendall to write a memorial verse to her daughter. Kendall obliged, completing a poem for her in that same September. Mrs Stenhouse requested some alteration, Kendall complied, and for his troubles she sent him a copy of the Bible. To her, he wrote his thankyou note in profoundly religiose terms; but to Moore he made quite a different commentary on the gift:

> Mrs Stenhouse has just presented me with a Bible. Poor lady – she wants me to swallow the dogma asserting its plenary inspiration. I cannot see it. Setting aside the grand poetry of the 'prophets', the magnificent myth of Elijah, the fine oriental wisdom of the Proverbs, and the sublime code of ethics laid down in the Gospels, it is about the most disappointing book I have ever read.[31]

It is difficult to determine just what Kendall intended by this worldly insouciance. He appears to mock the devotional attitude of their mutual acquaintance and wife of the equally devout former patron of their literary circle; but more to the point, why would he direct these 'clever' remarks to Moore? For Moore had been trained as a Jesuit before becoming a Benedictine monk, and had continued his faith though he had left his order so that he could marry. He was hardly sceptical, in the sense that James Lionel Michael was. Was Kendall trying to shock Moore, or provoke him? Either way, he seems to have been insensitive.

Kendall played other games with Moore too. In the same letter, he wrote:

> God only knows what has become of my mother, for I don't. I have not heard from a relative for the past two years. I have sinned against her more than I have against anybody else. Her behaviour was the issue of insanity; but that of my wife and sisters proceeded from heartlessness.

Yet it was his decision, indeed his demand, that his whereabouts be kept secret, especially from his relatives. He was still enjoining secrecy six months later, when he wrote to Moore: 'I write to you chiefly to beg that you will not divulge my whereabouts to any one of my relatives. I don't want to have anything to do with either the Rutter or the Kendall mob. I am as tired of one family as I am of the other'.[32] They could not have got in touch with him even if they had wanted to – about the death of Basil Edward, for example.

It was hardly a competition, but if he really thought that he had sinned more against his mother than anyone else, what did that say about his ongoing grief over the death of Araluen? Simply, as habitually, Kendall was about casting himself in a new light, feeling perhaps that he might be seen to have walked away from any responsibility for Matilda. Moore would have been aware of the elder Mrs Kendall's weaknesses, her vices and her vanities. He would also have understood about the insanity – for dipsomania was then regarded as a form of madness, hence the name.

What is not clear is how much of his commentary Kendall would acknowledge as applying to himself. He appears to have maintained a dignified distance from all that.

And yet he could turn a question against himself. For in the same letter again, he asked:

> What has become of the poor waif, Mrs Michael? Has the tired heart found rest at last? That boy of hers ought to be able to do something for her. But probably, like your correspondent, he is not a thoroughbred. A strain of bad blood always tells its own tale.

Which is a rare admission of his own genetic history. Then Kendall brought up the occasion of Moore's public lecture on Michael, to raise a subscription for the widow. That in turn reminds us that elsewhere Kendall had remarked she was a nuisance. Both views could of course be held at the same time – they are not mutually exclusive. It does appear though that Kendall had a duplicitous stance, sympathetic on the one hand and irritated on the other.

His life amongst the Fagans was wholly agreeable to him, even if from time to time he looked askance upon the circle of bushmen, the sawyers and splitters and bullockies who collected about them and who worked for their timber company. Primitive types, he thought them.[33] The Fagans he admired for their steady and occasionally forthright integrity. They were by no means simple-minded. On the contrary, they were fairly well educated, and he acknowledged that Charles in particular, a magistrate, was 'a man of more than ordinary ability and attainments'.[34] He spoke warmly of all members of the family – 'they are all noble fellows'.[35] He liked their forthrightness too. George in particular would speak bluntly to Kendall whenever he thought it necessary. 'George did not spare him when the poet needed, sometimes, to be brought face to face with the practical in this material world of ours.'[36] Kendall both respected and rather liked that, observed Mrs Hamilton-Grey, mincing matters in exactly the way George dismissed.

On Christmas Day in 1874 Kendall strolled with the brothers up along the creek above the cottage. In a newspaper report of the unveiling of a memorial plaque in 1931, an elderly Joe Fagan added the detail that they had been roaming the gullies, gathering wild raspberries.[37] On the face of it, that might have been fanciful, for raspberries ripen from the end of summer into autumn. An unimportant issue, other than to raise uncertainty about Joe's testimony.

Trees and ferns hung over the waterway, dappling the light; sunlight glinted from wherever the current made a ripple. A quiet time in the forenoon, drowsy – Kendall's early mentor Charles Harpur had noted how the bush falls into a kind of trance at such a time, when all activity is suspended, and insects and birds alike seem to merge into the general reverie.

Every other thing is still,
Save the ever wakeful rill
Whose cool murmur only throws
A cooler comfort round Repose ...[38]

There, by a rockpool in a hidden glen, the Fagan brothers and Henry Kendall sat quietly, absorbed in the sustaining peace of the place, appreciating its lovely isolation. Henry was so moved by the experience, and by sharing it with those whose company he had grown to appreciate, that he proposed they cut their initials on a large block of sandstone there:

And, in a dream, I stooped to trace
Our names upon a stone.[39]

The action was nothing so delicate as tracery. Joe claimed to have used George's hatchet, or perhaps they each cut their own initials into the rock. Why George should have been carrying a hatchet with him on such an occasion has not been investigated – perhaps the solemn ceremony was not quite so spontaneous as Kendall's poem suggests. On the other hand, it has been proposed that Kendall wished to commemorate that shared special moment, suspecting that they might never all be together like that again.

For there is one very important key in those lines, one detail which had special poignancy for Kendall. As he began composing poems in the abiding presence of the Shadow of 1872, articulating his regret for a transcendence of vision now denied him because he had fallen by the way, here at this moment – so his poem records – his action was actually within a dream, the vision state he so often yearned for. Here, this once, on a harmonious Christmas afternoon, in the company of good and agreeable young men, he momentarily achieved that dream state which he knew was the true source of poetry. That was not just what he believed; here, on this very occasion, he *knew* it. Briefly.

In later years, Joseph Fagan looked back sorrowfully on what the glen had become:

> In the days when Kendall knew the glen it was a beautiful spot, but later the woodcutter found it and laid it waste. Immense trees were cut down, blocking the pretty water-course and it made him sad to see the havoc wrought by careless vandalism.[40]

That much may be accepted without question; but not Joe's remembrance (at the ceremonial unveiling of the memorial plaque) that Kendall had written the commemorative poem that evening, on their return to the cottage below. For the internal evidence of the poem itself declares that four years had passed. Kendall did often enough compose his verses in the evenings, but not this poem on this particular occasion.

Joe's memory was at fault. Nevertheless, he continued to value the poem for its sentimental attachment, and that is what most readers have continued to share. For Kendall though it was an important personal experience, its 'truth' increased, in that he had shared it with those he held in high esteem, especially George Fagan, to whom in particular the poem was inscribed.

Kendall seemed to have held no attachment to his own family. He was content to live as he was, and where he was. He had no wish to return to Sydney town and the dangerous temptations there, he had no wish to submit to the continuous pressure of sustained writing, and he still had not come to terms with his relation to his wife and children, apart from repeated expressions of distaste, and even of bitterness. Astonishingly, in a letter to Moore in October 1874, he accused Lottie's relatives of being 'lewd and heartless',[41] although the Rutter family appears to have been completely respectable.[42] His astounding allegation may be connected to Henry's failed attempt to meet Charlotte at about that time. In a subsequent letter he told how she refused to see him. He accused her sister of heartlessness in driving him away without letting him see his children, and abusing him for being in the neighbourhood.[43]

That resulted in a resort to alcohol, either as some form of revenge, imputing the lapse to Charlotte's stony-heartedness, or as a betrayal of his efforts at reform – though the evidence is that those had been sporadic at best. '[H]e went to the first public house and got drunk. Strong drink with him was the father of insanity.'[44] He was always liable to fall into his old ways, especially if and when that confirmed the adverse circumstances of his life. It proved, while it provoked, his misfortune. His endless self-justification was as much a sign of weakness in him as it was of the strength of his demon's grip: 'When I saw you last, I had for the first time during the last nineteen months taken a glass or two too much. Since then I have not touched anything stronger than water'.[45]

Some months later he tried again to see her, with no better success, and not much difference in outcome. Now he condemned her inhumanity: 'she might have lifted me up out of the pit. As it is, she left me in it; but somehow I have found my way to the top unassisted'.[46] That last claim was patently untrue. And while it was true that she had not corresponded with him, that was exactly because of his own insistent secretiveness.

So when the Fagans proposed that he move further afield, up the coast to Camden Haven, he agreed without hesitation. That would take him well away from his grievances. Or give him more opportunity to air them.

Just before he left for the north, he was presented with a testimonial by the inhabitants of Gosford. They presented him with a watch. 'I only mention these facts to show that I must have been behaving myself properly while I was in the specified district.'[47]

He had lived in Gosford with the Fagans for a year and a half, and they had helped him to turn his life around. But he could not complete his mending until he was reunited with his wife and children, and that was still some little way off yet.

10

A Terrible Agent for Evil

In the middle of the year, William Fagan and Henry Kendall[1] made their way overland up to Camden Haven. In wintry conditions they rode up from the central coast through and then across heavily timbered mountain ranges. William knew the way – he and his brothers Peter and George had established the new branch of their business there and installed Michael to manage it.

At some stage they stopped off at Kempsey. On the face of it, that is an oddity. It means they travelled up to the New England tableland, say to Armidale, or possibly they followed Dobie's route from the Hunter up to Grafton, turning off part-way along and crossing the rugged Great Dividing Range to make the steep descent down to the coastal plains. Whichever way they went, their route was crowded with towering trees, and offers occasional magnificent vistas of the distant ocean, closer views of stunning waterfalls, picturesque valleys, winding streams. When the mists lift. Kendall's kind of country. Birdsong and parrot chatter everywhere, their calls carrying in the cold air.

In Kempsey the news spread, and Kendall was persuaded to give a lecture in the town hall; that is one disadvantage of having been proclaimed the leading poet in the colony. He was driven around the locality and he was pressed to write something for one of the local papers.[2]

He would not have found that an agreeable undertaking. He always shrank from publicity. He had still to recover some semblance of self-possession in front of an audience, never an easy matter for him, and this was his first public appearance since his trial and the experiences of Gladesville. He must have felt particularly uncomfortable. William's role was to be reassuring, as well as to act discreetly as some kind of chaperone.

In Camden Haven, Michael Fagan had already set the family's timber business on a sure footing. Now it was time to consolidate. That was what prompted the decision to send Henry up there, continuing in his role as bookkeeper accountant and serving also as paymaster. It was more profitable for the Fagans to employ him further up the coast than on Brisbane Water. Although it might be that they also thought he needed to be removed further from the temptation of the demon drink.

Given the model of the timber getters in Grafton, however, it is unlikely that Camden Haven was a particularly 'dry' area.

The Fagan Brothers' store and timber-splitting business was first established at a place called Jerry's Wharf,[3] halfway up the Camden Haven river, near Batar creek. Henry's accommodation was in a little wooden hut on the river bank. Now he was really hidden away from the wide world. The inlet was well up the coast, a quiet spot surrounded by tangled forests, but where cedar, red gold, was to be found. According to Alexander Sutherland, as many as 60 or 70 tree fellers and bullock drivers worked for the Fagans, cutting down the massive trees and hauling the great logs to the water's edge, to be sawed into planks and then loaded on to the firm's shallow-draft barges, catching the turning tide. Kendall's responsibility was 'to receive the timber, pay for it, supervise the execution of all contracts, and keep all the necessary books'.[4] That kept him occupied, though he began to weary of it. It occupied his time, not his mind.

He needed distraction. For he was still fuming at his dismissal by the Rutters, and by what he perceived as his wife's disloyalty, her want of sympathy. Her separateness. To say nothing of his own.

In those first months up at Camden Haven, he wrote to his small circle of correspondents, saying harsh things about Charlotte, and doing himself no favours in the process. Yet he had also evidently begun to correspond with her, perhaps telling her of his regular employment with the Fagans, for she had replied with a request for pocket money, even though 'she was not in need of it'. But much more pertinently, she had drawn her line in the sand. She had known the direst uncertainty in Melbourne, where they had been driven out by the landlord on the very day of Araluen's death. She had no wish to revisit such hardship or such sordid conditions again. She would not return to Henry until he could provide her with a home fit for a lady.[5] To live in the circumstances to which she had once been accustomed.

Her point of view is to be understood by changes in her own situation at the time. She had been living with her brother, but as he was about to move elsewhere she had to find her own lodgings. There was nothing for it but to ask Henry to send for her by the end of the year. That gave him three months to provide house, furniture, servant and a ticket to Camden Haven.[6]

He was in no position to achieve that, an impossibility. Which puts a different gloss upon her consequent decision to go to New Zealand, to live with her recently widowed brother-in-law, who had been left with three children. Within the Rutter family this might have been seen as a practical and generous move; the connection there was of long standing, evidently, for according to Mrs Hamilton-Grey Charlotte had said before her marriage that if she did not marry soon she would go to New Zealand.[7]

However, Henry chose to think of it differently. He was furious. And he wrote the vilest things about her. To his mind, she had gone to live in some kind of relationship with her brother-in-law. 'The ruffian she preferred to me is a low-minded sailor', he fulminated, forgetting for the moment that the sailor in question was a lieutenant and held the same rank as his own father. He was 'utterly destitute of the qualities that every wholesome-hearted woman should look for'.[8] What stung him was not so much the imagined betrayal as that another had been preferred to him.

Either he did not know his wife very well, or he had not altogether recovered his reason. He had invented his own scandalous explanation of her behaviour and became outraged by what in fact he had made up. As if that were not bad enough, he then wrote of it as actuality to his old friend Sheridan Moore, a very proper man and an ex-priest.

That was a step too far. It is one thing to alter the record and reinvent oneself, just as his mother had done, but quite another to maliciously libel an innocent party. In his version of events, she left him, and he had heard nothing from her for three years.

When he learned that she had gone to New Zealand, taking the children with her – would he have expected her to leave them behind? – he claimed to have written her a 'terrible' letter, which brought her back to Sydney:

> only to find that her relatives were ashamed of her, and in her desperation she appealed to the Fagans to treat [i.e. negotiate] with Kendall. He arranged with the Fagans to build him a house at Camden Haven and brought her to

> it. He wrote that no reference to the past would be spoken to her by him. The drink had been utterly forsaken. His wife would receive all the kindness that love can bestow, and his children have all the care and training in my power to accord them ...[9]

That is the version he provided to Moore. Goodness knows what Moore made of it, or of Kendall's laying down as a matter of fact that he had 'married into an unchaste, irreligious family'.[10] And if at the time of writing he had managed a respite from the drink, he would continue to relapse. Again and again.

It was not on Kendall's initiative that the Fagans built the house at Camden Haven about a mile and a half further upstream, though certainly it was in their interest, and his, for the family to be reunited. It was not true that he had utterly forsaken the drink. It was not true that the Rutters were ashamed of Charlotte. Indeed, he subsequently wrote a letter of apology to his brother-in-law, Frank Rutter, who had maintained her during her long separation from Henry.[11] Honourably, she had in fact been making an effort to earn something towards her own keep. She took on clerical work, copying deeds – much as Henry had once done for Lionel Michael.

Years later Frederick, their eldest son, unaware of the contents of Henry's recent correspondence, set straight the record as he knew it:

> His conduct during his absence from her was generally correct but his action in leaving her ignorant of his whereabouts is open to discussion if not altogether censure. The fact is he knew her brothers would not let her be in want and left it at that ... he so far forgot his manhood as to throw the blame of his separation on his wife and to abuse her professing at the same time his devotion.[12]

Just as Henry had been busily blackening Charlotte's character to Sheridan Moore, so he (Henry) wrote in the same vein to his other correspondent, Holdsworth. 'The lady has not one drop of feminine softness in her nature', he confided, and conceded he was obliged to love her because 'she is the mother of my children – or of those I suppose to be my children'. Kendall was being really disgraceful. Her language, he went on, was such as would rarely be found 'outside the haunts of the finished courtesan ... Where she acquired it is not for me to say', coming to the ungenerous conclusion that 'She must be either one or other of the two things – a monster or an adulteress'.[13] It is as well that Charlotte did not know of this sourness; she might have been less than willing to reconcile with him. It is as well his son Frederick never found out either. He might have disowned him.

In later years Henry retracted all that he had said about Charlotte and his in-laws. By way of excuse and possibly of self-justification, he pointed to the effect on him of drinking – even though he had claimed in his letter to Charlotte that the drink had been utterly forsaken. He cannot have it both ways. One or the other was a lie. 'Strong drink is the father of insanity', Kendall continued, and it prompted 'mad irresponsible moments', in which he would strike out in revenge for real or imagined slights. [14] Yet he *had* been thinking those hostile and disreputable thoughts, and he *had* shared his suspicions and accusations with others. He had not kept those views to himself. As his son observed, Kendall had indeed forgotten his manhood. His remarks had been as shameful and unworthy as they were undeserved.

The Fagans relocated their business to the little hamlet of Camden Haven (it would be renamed Kendall, in October 1891) and established a new lumberyard with an office and living space. That was where Henry lived while they built a home for him on an adjacent lot, a home to which he could now invite his wife and children, his two sons – with whom to this point he had had very little connection. According to Donovan Clarke, they rejoined him in July 1876.[15]

It was a spacious weatherboard cottage with a shingle roof, and with a very wide verandah on three sides, Frederick remembered, a six-roomed cottage with a hallway and lined with Baltic pine.[16] The slab kitchen was, as was customary then, detached from the cottage for safety's sake. It had an earth floor, a large stone fireplace, and a brick oven for bread. Their accommodation was comfortable, and Henry's happiness was as complete as it was likely to be when his little family arrived towards the end of 1876; though it was shadowed by news from his friend Holdsworth, concerning Henry's youngest sister, Emily.

Holdsworth seems by this stage to have been keeping himself very well informed about the movements and happenings of the Kendalls. His latest information was that Emily's marriage with the blackguard, the unmitigated scamp Henry Evans, was in difficulty. That was bad news for Henry, and made him feel quite ill.

> I cannot see what is to become of her. I hope she will not become desperate and sacrifice herself to that God-forsaken scamp, Evans. My mother, poor thing, has been a terrible agent of evil. Tell Emily to seek employment away from Evans.[17]

From which it can be perceived that he was not in direct correspondence with his sister, nor did he intend to be. And evidently the same was true about his mother. He had no wish to reconnect with them. In assessing her contribution of misfortune to his family ('a terrible agent of evil'), he must have had in mind her immoderate drinking and the death of his father, among other episodes. The immediate connection was, of course, her encouragement of Emily's early and now unhappy marriage.

The new home, set back from the road leading up from the river and in recently cleared country, with the forest all about on the far side of fields and river flats – almost a hut in a clearing – was not far short of an idyllic situation. He gave it the name 'Orara', after the tributary of the Clarence, near where he had lived in his early teens, and which came to symbolise an access to some unspecified source from which poetic inspiration flowed – almost a commonplace trope of the romantic imagination, of a sacred spring or fountain somewhere beyond, which he yearned for but which he knew now that he could never reach. He would certainly have known it from Emerson's essay 'The poet':

> And this hidden truth, that the fountains whence all this river of Time, and its creatures, floweth, are intrinsically ideal and beautiful, draws us to the consideration of the nature and functions of the Poet, or the man of Beauty, to the means and materials he uses, and to the general aspect of the art in the present time.[18]

It was for him a constant reminder of what might have been. The usual source of a river is, however, rarely so resplendent, more like seepage in a bog.

He delighted in the birdsong all about him, during the summer months. Kendall should have been happy enough. His wife too – she had a fenced flower garden at the front of the cottage, a piano, and a nursemaid to help with the new baby, another boy. And two girls after that. Those plants though would have struggled under the trees.

He kept up with the Fagans' business activities, tallying the different kinds of timber brought in from the bush, negotiating with the timber getters by way of a kind of barter system, offsetting provisions from the store against his valuation of the timber, and ensuring (against his own inner impulses) that the venture continued to be as profitable for the Fagans as possible.

He was determined to keep his promise to Charlotte, that she and the children should not know want. To that end, perhaps as demonstrable proof, he arranged for his salary to be paid into her account. She managed the finances; and she managed them well enough that they were for the first time free of debt, and stayed clear of it, stayed clear of the dreaded moneylenders too.

Without that kind of stress, he was free to concentrate on his writing whenever there was a lull through the day, or at night. He needed the additional funds he earned from his writing, much of it rapidly composed prose pieces, or the satirical volleys he seemed to relish, jousting with public figures from behind a pseudonym. He wrote some serious poetry at this time too, some of his best verse. The experiences he'd had to live through contributed to this, for they had not only coloured his imagination, but they had also deepened his understanding. He was surer of what he had to say, surer of himself in that sense at least.

He still had the old habit of walking about as he composed lines in his head, in the dark too, never a good sleeper. In a letter full of memories written to Alexander Sutherland, Charlotte recalled that Kendall began to smoke his pipe more and more: 'he used to say he gathered his ideas whilst he was smoking. He generally in the winter stood in the sun while he indulged in a smoke. I've seen him thinking and shaking his head and reciting something low'.[19] In that chill air sound carries with a distinctive clarity, magpie calls, lowing cattle, small branches snapping in the upper canopy of the forest, and crashing into the understorey.

On warmer days he sat out of doors, muttering occasionally[20]; and he demanded quiet. He was not to be disturbed, his thoughts were not to be interrupted. Perhaps the piano was played only during working hours. Should any of the children irritate him with their squalling, they were sent off with the nurse, perhaps to a farm across the river. There was a continuing prickliness in him.

If Mrs Hamilton-Grey is to be believed, Lottie did not always help matters. Once, when Kendall had to ride in to Port Macquarie, he looked such a sorry sight on his horse that she, Lottie, could not help laughing at the figure he cut.[21] The Knight of the Woeful Countenance once more. The revealing detail is not that she had laughed at his ungainliness in the saddle, but that she had distanced herself from him to see him in that way. If Mrs Hamilton-Grey is to be believed.

His son Frederick – in keeping with the family tradition, Henry called him by his second name, Clarence – acknowledged the prickliness:

> At times my father, like other men of poetical genius, was very temperamental and difficult, to put it mildly, but life as a rule went on smoothly. The past, especially his unhappy early life, weighed constantly upon him ... Even in his final and happiest years, the black moods of retrospection would envelop him, strangely enough after an evening of animated and humanly merry conversation, as if he thought himself guilty of forgetfulness ... At such times he would seek the delusive consolation of alcohol. His best friends and his dearest ones were then open to misunderstanding and even unjust accusation, though all did their best to humour and soothe him. He was not, like some other poets, a hearty, unashamed Bacchanalian, but became for a time, in turns, querulous, sentimental, suspicious, and even insulting. The trouble was not that he drank much but that he was physically unfit to drink at all. In fact he might have been considered temperate, in a quantitative sense, compared with other public men of those days.[22]

Those mood swings, from high to low, are explained here in terms of a kind of moral see-saw, but in modern times can be recognised as a well-known aspect of one kind of depressive behaviour. Kendall was not as well adjusted as he might have thought. They all united their efforts to keep him in good spirit, and especially the valiant Charlotte, on whom the responsibility chiefly fell.

She discovered just how much he liked to keep to himself. 'He was not fond of mixing in society', she wrote to Alexander Sutherland, 'The ordinary drawing-room chit-chat wearied him; dancing he had a horror of, especially for married ladies – although as a girl I could devote an evening to it'. She was drawing on remembrances of her courting days, and the society of her upbringing, more genteel than Kendall's:

> since my marriage I have not spent an evening that way; he disliked it, so I could not have enjoyed myself. I have become accustomed to his way of spending evenings and I have never regretted doing so.[23]

But she had not forgotten.

With such a difficult man, she could not hope always to succeed. Try as she might, she could not always prevent him from stalking off just up the road to the nearby wine shop,[24] conducted by Mrs Logan and her two daughters. They also ran a post office there. Those premises, and doubtless the serving staff too, were a magnet to the sawyers and teamsters and timber getters of the locality, just come in from the steaming bush. For Kendall, the allure was not the unpretentious company but the stock of colonial wine. He would drink until he was intoxicated, stagger noisily back home, awaken the household and collapse into a drunken stupor.[25] At those times too, he would say the stinging, regrettable and unfair things to which Frederick alluded.

Once, Mrs Hamilton-Grey recounted, Henry had taken himself off up the road to the Logans'. He:

> walked into the sitting-room, and there was a decanter of wine on the table. He went direct to the table, took up the decanter, put it to his lips and drank off the contents.
>
> ...
>
> His temper got the better of him on one occasion with Mrs Kendall, and was witnessed by some school children who carried home, in great excitement, the news to their mother (a rather prim lady) 'how they had seen Mr Kendall throw a cup of tea right into Mrs Kendall's face'.[26]

That might seem offensive to some, but the ever-rapt Mrs Hamilton-Grey had a rather different take on the situation. Her view of the matter was that he ambled up the road to escape his wife's tirades.

Kendall's excessive drinking occurred elsewhere too. A.G. Stephens noted in his *Bulletin* diary a story told by Kendall's correspondent and occasional visitor, P.J. Holdsworth, that once on a riding party (which included Charlotte) Kendall went forward on some errand. Two or three miles further up the track, one of the Fagans, either Joseph or Michael, stopped the party and said that he would go forward to shift a log out of their way. 'The log was Kendall, who had imbibed freely of roadside rum.'[27] Bush etiquette dictated that Charlotte was left none the wiser.

It is a tribute to all of the family that they could set aside his intervals of nastiness. Rather, they chose to recall the delights of walking through the forest with him, through the stillness of the towering blackbutt, turpentine, tallowwood and stringy bark, great high trees all of them, and with a thick understorey of scratchy scrub, where small birds flitted, and occasional bush flowers bloomed. This was dryer forest than down along the Illawarra. They loved just as much those occasions when they all went rowing down the river, Charlotte with them too, to a favourite pool – there is always a favourite pool with Kendall, and a bend in the river, with the light filtering down through fern fronds, where moss grows upon a rock. Idyllic indeed, where the purlieus of Gosford had been an Arcadia.[28] Kendall recognised natural beauty, and responded to it. He did not always create such harmony about himself.

Nor did his unhappy mother. On 11 June 1878, the *Sydney Morning Herald* reported on the Monday session in the Central Police Court. It had been a busy weekend – 71 persons were fined for drunkenness, by far the largest number of them (57) were apprehended before 3 am on Sunday. They had made quite a Saturday night of it. 'Melinda Kendall, 70, was found guilty of being an idle and disorderly person, having neither fixed abode nor lawful means of support, and was sentenced to be imprisoned two months.'[29]

That was the most severe penalty imposed. Hers was double the sentence of a woman charged with being a habitual drunkard. Disorderliness seems to have followed her around; but the surprising detail is that she had nowhere to live. Where were her daughters? Josephine was married and living in Queensland, but what of Jane and Emily? Had Matilda – Melinda, formally – been abandoned by them? None of the rest of the Kendall clan had come to her rescue either; and now the Kendalls were back in court again. Given that Henry read the newspapers so thoroughly when they were brought up to Camden Haven, together with the weekly mail delivery, he would have discovered that detail for himself soon enough.

Whatever arrangements were made for Matilda cannot have achieved much in the way of reform, for news of his mother trickled through to him in one way or another. A year later he was still troubled as to what to do (though equally, it might be observed that he had not in that time actually done anything for her):

> Just now I am in very low spirits. I dare say you have heard of my mother. Poor thing – for the last 30 years she has been a confirmed dipsomaniac … I must endeavour to get her into some place where she would be protected from herself. Money would not help her – it would only foster her madness … For obvious reasons, I cannot place my mother under the roof that shelters my wife and children. Knowing what dipsomania is I will not send her money. There is no hope for her outside of restraint.[30]

That is to say, her drinking had been a very serious problem from just after the time of her husband's sentencing for forgery, and certainly ever since his death. Henry could only have sent his mother money with Charlotte's unlikely approval, though sometimes he did have a little about him which he sent on. He was just as likely to want it for himself, though. He knew the insanity that her, and his, particular lack of restraint could lead to. The strangeness is that he wrote about all of this in a manner that suggests perfectly balanced good judgement, and implies complete sober-mindedness.

Through these years in Camden Haven Kendall wrote good work in amongst what he candidly admitted was writing 'for coin'. He had learned a hard lesson in Melbourne – he could not afford to be exclusively high-principled, nor so idealistic as to dismiss the commercial advantage of popular writing, both poetry and prose. For example, he had seen Adam Lindsay Gordon write well-received poems about the Melbourne Cup – he took to composing verses about horse racing too. He wrote semi-jocular verse about local characters, sometimes in questionable taste ('Black Lizzie'). He demeaned himself as much as he demeaned her and her people. He could crank those out with not too much effort.

But with his family all around him now (unless the littlest ones had been temporarily exiled for persistent crying, Athol in particular) and in securer circumstances, he began to publish verses of a calibre that pleased him. His new poems appeared regularly in the *Australian Town and Country Journal*, and he returned too to the fold of the *Freeman's Journal*. Sometimes he placed a piece with other Sydney papers, especially the *Sydney Mail*. Henniker Heaton, the man who had married Henry's former sweetheart Rose Bennett, commissioned him to write a memorial poem for her father, Samuel Bennett, lately the proprietor of the *Town and Country Journal*. It too was a fine poem, 'By the cliffs of the sea', even if the public expression of Kendall's admiration was at odds with what he had written privately about Bennett in earlier times.

Over the space of three or four years, he began to produce the makings of another volume, or so he estimated, but he was also apprehensive given the financial failure of his previous two ventures. In a letter to Moore, in June 1877, he dropped his habitual reserve and let his ambition speak for itself: 'You will excuse me saying that Australia has lost in me the most remarkable writer she ever had'; yet, characteristically, that is couched in terms of what might have been. A boast and not a boast.

He continued to correspond with Moore and Holdsworth, and occasionally Halloran, and renewed his connection with G.G. McCrae. As elsewhere, he showed a double standard. He wrote against the character, or reputation, of some of those with whom he corresponded with apparent amicability. For example, in one letter he chose to assert his independence of his ever-reliable correspondent Sheridan Moore, who had been retrieving old poems of Kendall's and publishing them in his magazine, even though Kendall would have nothing to do with it. 'Moore is sailing under false colours. He is emphatically a mountebank of the first water, still I have known him to do many kind things.'[31] In the same letter he wanted also to show the acuteness of his judgement about William Bede Dalley, who had successfully defended him in court all those years ago:

> With regard to Dalley, I am not exactly an 'iconoclast', I merely object to his cant about culture. He is a brilliant fellow, but certainly not a genius. The peroration of his recent delivery is beautiful; but the rest of the thing is marred by mannerisms.[32]

Kendall could not bring himself to take a clear unqualified stance about anyone or anything.

Dalley, unaware of Kendall's modified regard for him, was still trying to coax him (Kendall) out into the world of letters. He and Thomas Butler, editor of the *Freeman's Journal*, urged Kendall to write an ode for the opening of the Sydney International Exhibition. A competition for this was announced in the *Sydney Morning Herald* on 11 March 1879; Kendall completed a draft inside a week. It was selected but he was asked to submit a revised version, so that it fitted the structure of a cantata. That won him 30 guineas. Then he was further asked by the Commissioner of the Exhibition to write a 'Hymn of praise' ('four verses, clear and simple').

In early July the *Sydney Morning Herald* announced that the Exhibition Committee had selected 'an exquisite poem by Henry Kendall' for a cantata to be sung at the opening. But there was a demand from the management, more anxious about time-saving than artistry. 'The poet has consented to curtail it somewhat in order to bring it within the proportions of the musical setting rendered necessary.'[33] Ludicrous, thought Butler; simply brutal, thought Dalley.

Then he entered a poem to celebrate the International Exhibition: the prize offered for this was 100 guineas. On 17 September, the *Sydney Morning Herald*, sponsor of the prize, proudly announced that Henry Kendall had won – from a field of 250 entries: 'Mr. Kendall, who it need hardly be said has long been known as one of the first of Australian poets, is to be congratulated on his success in a competition which was open to all the world'.[34]

That was a triumph for him to savour. His poem, all in rhyming heroic couplets, was printed in full for all the readers to view, and it rings with confidence. It displays none of the melancholy that had become so characteristic of most of Kendall's verse. The public mode required for this kind of poetry had given him an exact focus, an uncomplicated imaginative space. It kept him clear of his habitual grieving. The poem was published on the day of the International Exhibition's opening, and with it he took up the mantle of unofficial Poet Laureate, as even *Punch* recognised.

And the Fagans had proved helpful once again. They provided him with a separate and secluded dwelling while he worked on his entry.[35]

All this activity – the long hours in the Fagans' office, the preparation for the competition and the nervous excitement that went with it, the restless composing and the broken sleep, the chill he felt in the early morning, being thin as his wife remembered, her illness (she was pregnant yet again, this time with the younger daughter Roma) – took its toll upon him. He had even undertaken a little schoolteaching. It was all very wearing. An acquaintance wrote later of his appearance at this time:

> The furrows of his face hardened like crinkles in molten metal set while in motion. Kendall had the hardest-lined face I ever saw. It was like the 'old Hickory' of Abraham Lincoln, or the chiseled granite of Carlyle. But all the hell he had endured left no bale-fire in his eyes. They showed clear and kindly always, as did Jonathan Swift's, in his worst madness.[36]

Which is hardly the most sensitive comparison to have made.

His recent success encouraged him to be more active in pushing for another publication. He sought advice from publishers and editors; he even wrote to the Attorney-General. The usual arrangement was to find a number of subscribers whose promise to purchase would guarantee the cost of publication. That did not always turn out well. In this instance the Attorney-General urged Kendall to proceed, and he would endeavour to interest his connections so that the work might be brought out without him, Kendall, incurring any expense.

He began assembling the 35 poems which would constitute *Songs from the Mountains*; he copied out the entirety of the text for the publisher, just as he had done for Lionel Michael, and he informed fellow writers and prospective reviewers. He did what he could to 'push' the work. Yet to one of these correspondents he wrote very candidly:

> Mrs Kendall is better; but she is by no means well. We have been eleven years married; and during all that time, I have never read a line of my verse to her. She loves me dearly, but she does not care for poetry. I am glad of it: she is free of the strange wild curse which clings to men and women of my temperament.[37]

That might not be exactly true. Undoubtedly Charlotte was unwell from time to time, not only during her pregnancies. She was often enough unwell for Kendall to remark that he was both interrupted and depressed by that. His own variable and ongoing ill health, not to mention his drinking bouts and his depression, must in turn have exhausted her, but what we hear instead is her patience and loyalty. Too many times Kendall contrived particular effects in his correspondence, by selecting or embellishing the facts.

It may well have been the case that she did not dote enthusiastically enough on what he had written. She had a household to run, and a family to bring up. Besides, he was an intensely private individual, hypersensitive, difficult. She would have had to be very adept in whatever remarks she made about them. He represented her as somewhat simple in her tastes, and certainly not 'literary'. It was better for her to offend him one way than to offend him in the other.

But Mrs Hamilton-Grey could scarcely conceal her glee in recounting that he had said (to whom? How could she have known?) 'I have won the prize for the poem, and given it to the Loafer who never read it', meaning Charlotte, who according to her took no interest in his poems.[38]

While Kendall was occupied with compiling and promoting his new volume of poems, he had one other difficulty to overcome. In his biting facetious verses and notes he had been enjoying himself for several years at the expense of Henry Parkes. He had in fact been quite insulting. Parkes had managed to return to public life after his bankruptcy; Kendall did not care for Parkes's political style, his anti-Irishness (demonstrated after the attempted assassination of Prince Alfred at Clontarf), nor did he care for Parkes's bluster. He scoffed at some of Parkes's parliamentary Bills, and was deeply angered by others ('The gagging Bill'). And he did not think very highly of Parkes's poetry. Now he had to make some kind of amends, for he was approaching Parkes for a government position once more, conscious that his work for the Fagans confined him too closely to one place, to an office, and a long way from where he might encounter real books. He would like a job as a forest ranger.

He mended matters. Old Henry Halloran wrote to Kendall, explaining that the objectionable Bill was not the Premier's, but his political colleague's; and that Kendall should ease up on Sir Henry (he had been knighted in 1877), who was suffering because of the death of his son. That was magnanimous of Halloran, as he'd had an uneasy relationship with Kendall across the years too. He had been embarrassed by Kendall's sudden resignation from the public service and had been left to smooth over the situation – though he may not have known that Kendall had left owing Parkes money. In his bridge-building back then, Halloran had written of 'Mr Kendall's disposition to be thin-skinned and sensitive', and concluded with: 'I saw, in his handwriting, that he *had a hearty damn for the Whole Civil Service of the Colony* – and, I am grieved to add that I have lost faith in Mr. Kendall'.[39]

Ten years later, when Halloran retired after 51 years of service, Kendall wrote a poem in praise, albeit moderate praise, of his dedication not only to his career but to the cause of poetry; and later, an essay in which again he observed Halloran's perseverance rather than any especial accomplishment. It was not quite a case of damning him with faint praise, but Halloran had hoped for a touch more esteem. Yet that did not prevent him from taking it upon himself to advise Kendall just how extremely he had hurt Parkes.

Not that this handsome action helped him when it was revealed that Kendall, not he, had won the prize for a poem on the Sydney Exhibition. Halloran was twisted with jealousy, to the extent of writing spitefully of Kendall's want of a classical education.[40]

Kendall not only desisted from attacking, he wrote a eulogy which touched Sir Henry, and which also included a public apology, differentiating between political belief and private friendship.

Peter Fagan intervened too. He approached William Bede Dalley, and together they approached Parkes, interceding for Kendall.[41] Fagan in particular could speak to Kendall's expertise in the timber business. He knew his way around trees and forests. In fact, he had spent the formative and reformative years of his life in forest country. Mountain forests were in his soul; they were the source of most of his poetic imagery. He had an affinity with that kind of country; he was ideally suited to the role of a forest ranger. Parkes would think about it, though he wrote a memo that while Kendall had treated him with cruel ingratitude in the past, 'life is too short to maintain ill-will'.[42] When *Songs from the Mountains* was at last published (in November 1880), Parkes handsomely ordered 50 copies.

But before that could happen, there was a difficulty. Kendall had consciously selected a variety of poems, lyrical, melancholy, jocular and satirical, so that there might be something for everyone. One of them was a bouncing satire upon a current political figure, Ninian Melville, recently elected to the Legislative Assembly and representing himself as spokesman for 'that immense impostor they call "the working man"'. Kendall could not abide the type, nor the protectionist politics. He fairly sailed into Melville ('a bladder with the title of M.P.'), who is now only remembered because of Kendall's attack.

The book was printed, and William Bede Dalley was sent an advance copy for review. Looking through it, he was horrified at Kendall's 'Song of Ninian Melville', for in his view – and he was a most experienced lawyer – it lay open to the charge of libel. He warned the publisher, who immediately recalled as many copies as he could set his hands upon. Kendall was furious, but eventually he had to comply. That poem was withdrawn, he had to compose a replacement ('Christmas Creek') and the volume was reprinted at his cost. But the story leaked out, the newspapers were full of excited commentary, and Kendall had the advantage of extensive free publicity. His volume was a great success, profitable to the tune of £80.

He was nevertheless watchful. He wrote to his publisher: 'There are some relatives of mine that you may have heard of. Do not entertain applications not endorsed by me'.[43] There were to be no free copies handed out to them. To his mother? To his sister Jane? Emily and her objectionable husband?

And once again he underwent another of those mood swings which marked the course of his later poetic life, if not his personal life too. The success of his Exhibition ode, and the financial gain that went with it, had not persuaded him that what he wrote was of much real value. He wrote dismissively of his own poems to his friend George Gordon McCrae: 'I can write a damned good set of pianoforte verses – nothing more'. Yet he was not entirely disheartened, because at about the same time he wrote to James Brunton Stephens, a contemporary poet he admired, staking his claim not on those pianoforte pieces but on his poetic portraits of Australian scenery, and its effects. He excelled at that.[44]

On 1 January 1881, the Kendalls moved down to Cundletown, some 35 miles away, just as Henry had succeeded in having the post office in the wine shop closed down. He had formally objected to that arrangement. Instead, Michael Fagan was awarded the postal contract, and the office was relocated to the Fagan store.

Cundletown was a much larger village than Camden Haven, almost a little town, on another great river, the Manning; importantly, it had a school for the children, and a library and, for Charlotte, a furniture arcade. There, in Cundletown, Henry awaited the commencement of his duties. He was not accustomed to idleness. He fretted, and was restless. And moody. And sometimes drunk. 'There is a little gully not many yards from the residence, and here he was often observed lying drunk, his hat replaced by one of his babes as often as the wind blew it off'.[45]

But he was pleased to read the reviews of *Songs from the Mountains* as they began to come in. Dalley appreciated the:

> genuine pathos in more than one of the pieces which manifestly owe their origin to circumstances of domestic sorrow ... the veil of home affliction is tenderly and delicately uplifted by the graceful and trembling hands of one who has suffered. The poem entitled 'Araluen' is an example.[46]

The *Bulletin* joined the chorus and cast him again as the uncrowned laureate of Australia (22 January 1881). That should have lifted his spirit, but he was tired, tired from overwork, imaginatively tired too. It was not that his imagination had dried up, but his energy had, and he came to a standstill. He thought he was recuperating, but once he began his active surveys of forests there was not much time for writing anything other than his reports. He wrote very little poetry thereafter.

His first expeditions into the field began at the end of May. The delay was because the governor had had to sign into existence a new position (12 May). Kendall was to be made Inspector of Forests, not just a forest ranger. His salary would be augmented too, an increase from £100 to £500 pa. He had to travel large distances, sometimes by train or coach, sometimes on horseback. His thin legs were chaffed raw from long hours in the saddle, so that a special padding – presumably sheepskin – was made for him. Cervantes yet again.

He had set out at an inconvenient time. His last child, Orara, named for the river that merged into the Clarence, was born just a month later. That was a reminder of happier times for Henry (apart from straggling after sheep); though obliquely it also leads to reflections on his father's illness and demise.

Possibly Charlotte still retained the services of a nursemaid, but they were in a new village now, they were no longer at Camden Haven, where the previous nursemaid lived. In any case Charlotte's pregnancies were always difficult. The baby, another boy, was sickly, and given to convulsions.

Henry's first tour, up to the Richmond River, was completed in October; then he left for Sydney in November, and never returned to Cundletown. His children never saw him again. At the end of 1881, Kendall was about to set out on a long field trip, where he would misbehave as he did when he was away from Charlotte. Indeed, he had grown to live a double life, the outcome not only of his compulsive drinking but of the too many years lived separately from her and separated from a sense of responsibility, and accountability.

She obviously knew her husband. In considerable distress Charlotte wrote to Peter Fagan in January 1882, just before Henry was to set out:

> Will you use your influence with Mr. Kendall in giving up the situation. Let it be on the score of ill health and not able to travel, he'll get the sack no doubt and I *will not* travel any more, and leave my home. I can hear my little one [Orara] calling me in his pain and [me] away from him watching his father from Ruin. I know I must be a trouble to you all but use your influence. What a disgrace to him if he got sacked through drink.[47]

Her anxiety there is written all through her urgent note – anxiety about Henry's drinking, about the danger of his losing his position, about her own security, about the heartache of her baby's illness.

The code of 'illness', Henry's illness, meaning inebriety had become established between Charlotte and the Fagans. Henry himself had often enough resorted to that euphemism by way of excuse in his correspondence. Peter Fagan's reply must have been disconcerting, for almost immediately she arranged for a local girl in the village, a trustworthy servant,[48] to look after her children (that might indicate the Kendalls no longer employed a regular nursemaid), including Orara, who was too ill to travel, while she hastened to Sydney to attend to her husband. They were both away from the household when Orara died.

Her son Frederick recounted many years later his mother's grief, 'vivid, poignant', on her return – Henry had not returned with her, he was out on the Western Plains – and the heartrending funeral at which the baby's coffin was followed to the cemetery by a band of girls in white.[49] She was profoundly touched by the eight schoolgirls carrying the little coffin in turns.[50]

According to Frederick, the unhappy infant died from a gastric attack. His mother however said that the baby suffered greatly from convulsions, which emphasises how dire her husband's condition must have been for her to make her choice. It was like Araluen all over again; though if Henry admitted his guilt to himself on this occasion, it was not registered to anything like the same degree. He seemed by this stage to have exhausted that emotion in himself.

And Charlotte had had to choose between her delinquent husband and her ailing infant. She had decided he needed her more. Not that Mrs Hamilton-Grey would give her credit for that.

Henry was poorly on his return from two gruelling months on horseback, in variable weather. It can be very hot there at that time of the year, and very cold at night. He recuperated in Sydney, and then set off on his next tour of inspection, even though he was not as well as he would wish.

Indeed, his recuperation left something to be desired. One time, when P.J. Holdsworth called in to see Kendall at Peter Fagan's house, he found him in the charge of a servant. Kendall, according to Holdsworth, was practically a prisoner in that household, at that time. He asked Holdsworth for a shilling, Holdsworth slipped him half a crown; Kendall managed to elude the servant, Holdsworth followed him, to three pubs with a drink in each, and brought Kendall back again 'absolutely flaccid'.[51] He and his acquaintances were as irresponsible as each other.

Kendall was nothing if not conscientious about going out on his forestry rounds, however; although as it appears, and as his wife was beginning to fear, he took unscheduled breaks. But his reports were thoughtful, informed, and progressive. It must have been at this time that Charlotte 'commissioned' George Fagan to travel with Henry as a companion and, should it become necessary, as a kind of custodian. She arranged to pay his expenses herself.

The account Frederick Kendall promoted was that they had been travelling out on the plains, and George Fagan had left him at Waroo on the Lachlan river, apparently in fair health. Subsequently, Henry, travelling in wet clothing, caught a severe chill and took himself to Wagga Wagga, reaching there on 5 June. He sent a telegram to Sydney asking for help; George found him and brought him back to Sydney on 14 June.[52]

George found him not in Wagga, but in a less-than-salubrious little inn some distance outside it.[53] Henry was ill again, actually so, although in surroundings similar to those to which he had almost certainly been resorting for his more familiar style of self-medication. That was what he had been doing whenever he slipped George's supervision. Peter's, too. It was no coincidence that his turn for the worse occurred during George Fagan's absence.[54]

He was taken to St Vincent's Hospital in Sydney. Charlotte had been sent for, and she tended him constantly there for the next five weeks, sharing his private ward, according to Frederick.[55] His restlessness showed through again. He disliked the atmosphere of the hospital, and he found the nurses' habits depressing (they were a nursing order of nuns, and wore the intimidating great starched cornettes for which they became known as 'God's geese'). He was transferred to the Fagan house in Bourke Street,[56] and there he died on the first day of August in 1882, an act of will, according to the report that Charlotte wrote to uncle Thomas Surfleet, the elder of the extended Kendall family. Henry had been determined that Charlotte would be entitled to his month's pay. 'To the last his thought was that he had not left me and my little ones unprovided for'[57]; and Frederick's version, which must also have come from Charlotte, was that Henry had said at the last, 'You see Lottie, I have lasted to the end of the month' – the full month's salary was due.[58]

As an accidental instance of tidiness in an otherwise untidy life, he died on the anniversary of his parents' flighty wedding.

His cold had gone to his lungs. He had the family weakness, a disposition to tuberculosis. At the end, according to Charlotte, he had asked for a sip of tea, thereby showing his redemption. He had a sip of champagne too. He passed away with his right hand resting on his cheek, facing the sea. That was a nice poetic gesture, but, as the sea was not in sight from there, his comfort could only have derived from the idea of being turned in that direction. And throughout his career his right hand had been discounted.

The champagne was not an inappropriate concession to a habitual indulgence. It was believed to have medicinal properties:

> Champagne, if pure, is one of the safest wines that can be drunk. In typhoid fevers, in weakness, in debility, where there is a deficiency of the vital powers, there is nothing that can take its place; it enables the system to resist attacks of intermittent and malignant fever.[59]

Their son Frederick added a further intimate detail, that Henry died in his wife's arms.[60] He would have been obliged to his mother for that detail. It provides a much more orthodox sentimental tableau than Sutherland's account of Basil's death. Its function, as all the slight emendations of and deletions from Henry's last days, served to improve the record. Another reconstructed story.

11

The After Life

Henry Kendall's death was announced in the family notices of the *Sydney Morning Herald* on the very next day. He was aged just over 42, almost exactly the same age as his unhappy father. Neither of them had lived into their prime.

Officially, Henry died of phthisis, tuberculosis, just like his father, and just like his twin. His lungs, the doctors had told Charlotte, had 'tumbled to pieces'.[1] A tribute was published on that day's issue of the *Herald* also, possibly ready-written and awaiting the inevitable. For it had been apparent for some time that Kendall was not in a good way.

The unidentified writer developed this theme. It had been apparent to the public at large that:

> Mr. Kendall's career was chequered and gloomy and overshadowed by great troubles, of which he may have been partly the victim and partly the creator, but the few who gained an insight into his inner life knew that he often went out into the wilderness and wrestled terribly with his temper in a mental and physical struggle, of which, happily, few knew the terrors. His work was tinged with the sorrow of his life.[2]

A week later the *Brisbane Courier* made exactly the same point. 'He was no man's enemy but his own, and it is no exaggeration to say that a profound feeling of pity has been excited by his premature decease.'

Right across the colony, and in Victoria too, the common theme of columns reporting Kendall's death was that he had suffered greatly, and that the details did not need to be aired again as they were already widely known. This collective coyness was the beginning of what we might now think of as a sanitising of the record.

The funeral was held on the Thursday. The following day the paper reported that the interment had been witnessed by some of Kendall's closest friends, as well as a number of gentlemen who knew him only through his poems. According to Holdsworth, the funeral procession numbered no more than 20. There would have been two more, but as A.G. Stephens subsequently recorded, a pair of Bohemians, Victor Daley and Richmond Thatcher, determined to remember Kendall in a suitable style, had called in at various public houses on the long walk to Waverley, reviving their drooping spirits in a manner 'poor Harry' would have approved. Not that Daley had ever met Kendall.[3] Thatcher was a publican – which hardly fits the Bohemian stereotype. He was more the patron of Bohemians.

It was not the done thing for women to be at the graveside. But as the first clods of earth were heard falling on the coffin, a lady who chanced to be visiting Waverley Cemetery approached and threw into the grave a profusion of such wildflowers as were growing thereabouts, and which she had picked in passing. Kendall himself had been laid in a bed of moss, ferns and waxflowers. The beatification of Henry Kendall was under way.

Across the city, committees began to form, to ensure some kind of fund for Charlotte and the children ('the widow and orphans'), to provide for an annual poetry prize at Sydney University, and to lay a memorial stone there too. Musicians, both amateur and professional, were invited to participate in a fundraising concert. And once the grave had been filled in, Kendall's opportunistic publisher William Maddock busied himself advertising *Songs from the Mountains* at 6/- a copy or 6/8 by post. Other booksellers were not long behind. Charlotte sat at her desk and wrote to relatives and answered messages of condolence. Alexander Sutherland was precipitate too – he wanted to ensure he collected as much information as he could about Henry's life and circumstances. He proposed that he and Charlotte should put together a selected edition of Henry's works, with a preface by P.J. Holdsworth. There was no point in striking when the iron is cold.

The Rev. G.F. McArthur, of the prestigious King's School, Parramatta, undertook to educate Kendall's eldest son, Frederick, 'a bright and promising lad'.[4] Unlike his father, and his grandfather, and his great grandfather, he would have a good formal education. According to Mrs Hamilton-Grey, the Catholic Church looked after the education of the eldest girl and the youngest boy[5] – that is, Persia and Athol. The resurgence of a Catholic connection after all these years looks odd; but then Kendall had long contributed to the Catholic newspaper, the *Freeman's Journal*, and one of his most loyal and active supporters had been the ex-priest J. Sheridan Moore, who doubtless played a part in instigating this further instance of generosity. There is no indication of a McNally investment in this. Indeed, Matilda – or Melinda as she was more usually identified at this end of her life – is conspicuous by her absence from these last rites. She was not consulted about any of the arrangements, so Mrs Hamilton-Grey recorded,[6] implying that Charlotte was cold-hearted and exclusive, keeping the disreputable Melinda at arm's length.

By December, £700 had been raised, with the press confident that the fund would top £1000. It did. In the end, the public contributed £1200, as much as Henry's salary for six years. Mrs Hamilton-Grey says the amount was a little more than that, but in either case it was not enough to provide both a maintenance and an appropriately elaborate monument. The gestures of practical support, welcome in themselves, had come rather too late in the day. The money was forwarded to the grieving widow, and Kendall's grave was marked by a simple wooden cross.

And Henry Parkes, showing the sensitivity of a poet, or the retaliatory instincts of one, offered Charlotte a position as overseer of cleaners of government offices. As though she had not been humiliated enough. Some amends were made in 1908, when she was awarded a pension for the rest of her life by the Commonwealth Literary Fund (established 1906).

Two years later, when Louisa Lawson came with her two younger children to Sydney, she found lodgings in Phillip Street in the city and then, according to A.G. Stephens, writing in the *Bulletin*, walked out to the Waverley Cemetery to 'worship at Kendall's grave'. She had read as much of Kendall's poetry as she could when she lived on the Mudgee selection and had been enthralled by it. But alas, there was no poetic shrine at Waverley before which she could kneel. She found instead:

> a neglected weed-grown plot, with a small wooden cross on which hung a sagging wreath; and all her soul was aflame with indignation. She

> went to the *Town and Country Journal* ... with a letter of complaint and remonstrance. The editor took fire from her flame, and sent out a designer who made a sketch of the neglected grave. This was engraved and printed, with Louisa's appeal. It made some stir; and Louisa went around raising funds for a monument. Dr Badham, of the University, delivered a lecture for her; Gerald Massey, a visiting English poet, delivered another.[7]

It is difficult to find any published result of her visit in the *Town and Country Journal*, and in point of fact she went instead to the *Sydney Mail*, a stablemate in a burgeoning group of papers. The proprietors – none other than Mrs Samuel Bennett, her sons, and her son-in-law, Henniker Heaton – used the pages of yet another paper again, the *Evening News*, to revive interest in Kendall's grave. Heaton had been responsible for the wooden cross. As the story was told and retold, the sagging wreath became a rusty tin wreath; it was said to be carelessly slung over the cross, suggesting something like a once ornamental hoopla ring. In later versions of the same story, the rusty tin becomes transformed into cans which had once held flowers, strewn untidily about the plot.[8] The grave did not seem quite so unsightly in the depiction of it in the *Sydney Mail*, 8 November 1884 (p. 938).

Mrs Bennett started the memorial fund with a gift of £5, and other prominent citizens followed suit. Several correspondents had already written letters to various editors, complaining of the disgraceful neglect of Kendall's grave, and the difficulty of finding it. Sydney began to pay attention. Professor Badham lectured at Sydney University on the poetic accomplishment of Henry Kendall. That was one of the last he was to give, as he died the following summer. The papers reported on the various committee deliberations, they copied each other's reports and notices, they welcomed letters to the editors. They worked to keep the story 'alive'. But these sporadic efforts did not result in any immediate outcome, and the indignation and embarrassment continued. The Melbourne *Telegraph* wrote of Sydney's neglect. It had compared Kendall to Gordon and found him wanting: 'He lacked the solid qualities which make a man ... He pined and fretted, and neglecting his opportunities for good, sank to an early grave'.[9] And apparently, or at least by Melbourne standards, it was an unworthy one – in both respects.

The chronology in Stephens's *Bulletin* paragraph suggests that in his account he had slightly misrepresented the case, for Louisa Lawson's discovery of the state of Kendall's grave was well after that particular ball had begun rolling. Professor Badham's lecture was not prompted by Louisa Lawson's campaign, but that which began with Mrs Bennett and Henniker Heaton. There it is, another reinvention, a modification of the truth of the matter. An exaggeration at the very least.

But Louisa did busy herself in raising such funds as she could, although her connections were limited. She amassed £22 towards a more appropriate memorial, and a committee to which she handed over those funds managed to augment that to £40.[10]

Fundraising continued apace elsewhere, sponsored not least by and at the University of Sydney, which had also taken up the cause of memorialising Henry Kendall, aiming at something more substantial than a poetry prize. As late as 15 August 1885 a grand concert was given in the Great Hall by a distinguished visiting Hungarian violinist, Edouard Remenyi, together with other artists, and in the presence of the governor and his lady and politicians and just about anyone with a knighthood, raised £105, with that amount increased by a gift of a further £25 by the maestro. That was generous, as he was on the eve of leaving the country and could not benefit from any associated publicity. The status of those in the audience confirmed the cultural importance of both the event and the cause.

At a less elevated level, Mrs Agnes Hamilton (as at that time she was) gave a public lecture on Henry Kendall and his poetry at the Sydney School of Arts (30 August 1884) to much acclaim. P.J. Holdsworth was in the chair at that event.

A visiting English poet, one Gerald Massey, largely self-educated and a populist of spiritualism and of the interconnections between early Christianity and ancient Egyptology, is also commonly reported to have given a lecture in support of the fundraising activity. His interests were unusual. As he was sufficiently prominent a radical for George Eliot to have modelled her Felix Holt on him, he was unlikely to have been given the podium in the Great Hall at Sydney University. He would have been a useful ally for Henry's grandfather, the Rev. Thomas Kendall.

In fact, newspaper reports show no such lecture to have been given. What happened is that, after a well-subscribed public lecture on Robert Burns in the Theatre Royal (30 December 1884), Massey made a few remarks about Kendall's neglected grave, endorsing and encouraging public subscription towards providing a memorial stone:

> I am told that the lamented poet was somewhat of a sinner in his lifetime; but I do hope that this will not be a reason for some people not subscribing, although it is frequently given as an excuse. If Henry Kendall has sinned against himself in his lifetime, he has left you something of his best in his poetry. The least the people of New South Wales can do is to mark his grave, to show at least that he has their forgiveness. I hope that the response to the committee's request will be spontaneous and cheerful. I would willingly give a lecture for the purpose (cheers); but I don't think that I ought to do so. I should not like it to be said that you had to get a person from elsewhere to assist you in putting a headstone to the grave of your late gifted poet.[11]

And then Massey added a curious detail. He had received a letter from 'someone who must be what is called a medium', who had been visited by Kendall's spirit, and described the visitant as with a 'quiet, subdued, purified look about him, as though he had been on a long, long journey'. Given that Agnes Hamilton had visited Charlotte just after her lecture, borrowed Henry Kendall's own copy of *Songs from the Mountains* and declined to give it back on the basis that Henry Kendall had come to her in a dream,[12] it is not difficult to spot who Massey's correspondent was. For Massey, this was corroborative evidence of the spiritual change which he believed took place after death; that was after all one of the fundamentals of his kind of spiritualism. The audience enthusiastically welcomed his remarks.

Subsequently, Mrs Hamilton-Grey insisted that she was not a spiritualist, nor had she ever been one – but her sleep had been disturbed by rattling and rapping, which in turn prompted her to take up her mission of promoting the career and accomplishment of Henry Kendall. This in 1920.[13]

Not everyone was as enthused as Massey and Professor Badham and Louisa Lawson and Mrs Hamilton-Grey may have wished. Provocatively, one report following Massey's performance asked:

> What have the Kendall family been about that *they* have not done something for their illustrious relative? They did nothing for him while living – though

> they are not without means; and to prolong their virtuous anger after death is not by any means following in the footsteps of one Jesus.[14]

For it is true, clan Kendall had been conspicuous by their collective silence in all of this time. Many of the generation preceding Henry had passed away, but the younger uncles were still alive. They, however, were those who had been most offended by Basil, Henry's father, at his first trial, and by Matilda's drinking.

The resurgence of interest in Henry Kendall happened somewhat in advance of Louisa Lawson's visit to Waverley Cemetery – though that just possibly coincided with Massey's lecture – and independent of her exhortations. Louisa was not one to let a good story get away from her, however. Which is just a variation of the Kendall habit of reconstructing the facts. It seems to have been contagious.

Louisa also hunted out any connection she could find with Henry Kendall – those who had known him, those who had worked with him, those who had stories to tell. She searched out what A.G. Stephens would later call 'Kendalliana'. She bought the burial plot alongside Kendall's grave, to ensure that there was sufficient space for an appropriate monument.

Kendall had become newsworthy. His poetry was even alluded to in articles about remote coastlines, or whenever remote wilderness beauty was to be found. His was the very type of melancholy joy, and there was evidently much of that in the natural landscape, as much as the 'weird melancholy' that Marcus Clarke had pointed to.[15] Mostly, the connection between his lonely, untended grave and the pathos of his life was irresistible. It was wholly to the taste of the times, and it confirmed his status in the public mind.

So too did a passing reference to his mother, again in the columns of the *Evening News*:

> The late Henry Kendall derived his poetic nature and aspirations, his dreamings, and even his Bohemianism, from his mother, who taught the young genius his letters by tracing them in the sand, books and writing material being unobtainable. That mother is now 75 years of age, and is friendless, homeless and even without proper food.[16]

There was no suggestion of raising a public subscription for her. But the sentimentality is unmistakable. The origin of that detail, of Henry learning to write, has to come from Melinda's own poem, which, curiously, was not published in the *Illawarra Mercury* until a fortnight after that paragraph in the *Evening News*. As a detail it is vaguely reminiscent of a favourite nineteenth-century image, Millais's 'The boyhood of Raleigh'. On the other hand, there seems something questionable about learning Bohemianism. Its more customary character is rather by reaction to a particular class of behaviour, to conventionality, for example; so that Henry's version of it is rendered equivocal. Obliquely, Melinda is acknowledged as having been markedly unconventional. That would not have been the Rev. Hill's desired outcome for her.

The allusion to an absence of books and writing materials is perhaps the *Evening News*'s marked irony, though it hardly squares with the commentary that both Henry's parents were well read, and that he was brought to Bunyan and to a translation of Homer in his early years. Nor is it clear on what basis the *Evening News* affirmed her friendlessness and her homelessness, her undernourishment. That would have revealed her as still a vagrant all these years after her last court appearance. In actual fact, Melinda made her modest home at Fernhill in the Illawarra,[17] and kept a school for a while with Jane, who never married. They taught in a church Sunday School room when it was unused through the week. And they stayed down that way until they came back to Sydney. Either the pathos of homelessness and undernourishment applied also to Jane, or it was fanciful.

In the Illawarra Melinda composed a series of lightweight poems, published in the local press, almost at fortnightly intervals. These are mostly simple, some no better than adolescent. Conventional, which is at odds with her Bohemian reputation. They do not show anything like the expressiveness, or the range of vocabulary, that can be found in Henry's poems. They are metrically simple too, short-lined, and their subjects are matters of little account. She displays no marked evidence of being his poetic sponsor, though she does claim the title 'The Poet's Mother'.

Yet something of interest emerges. For in several of them she makes specific reference to the 'home of the hopeless', meaning the women's shelter which opened in that very year, 1884; and she writes of the 'Blue Ribbon Army', founded in 1882, with its mission to save fallen and wretched women, and to promote temperance. Melinda had her own Shadow; and it appears that she had somehow found her own way to reform.[18] Indeed, if she herself had been a resident of that home, even briefly, then that would put the reference in the *Evening News* in an entirely new light.

Given that the marked alteration in her behaviour occurs at the time of her son's death, the conjunction sparks all sorts of speculation. In any case, now returned to the Illawarra, Melinda was remaking herself yet once again, retrieving herself more like. She was aiming for respectability. Melinda, not Matilda. But time had overtaken her, for she was almost 70 years old.

Her absence from Henry's deathbed scene, from the funeral, from the fundraising activities, and in due course from the unveiling of the grand monument at Waverley, can all be explained in terms of how far she lived from Sydney, with still no convenient passage there at that time. Mrs Hamilton-Grey notwithstanding, it had nothing to do with Charlotte's fixed resolve to exclude her.

The final ceremony took place on a Saturday afternoon, 20 November 1886, in the presence of Lord and Lady Carrington. Dalley, who had been enjoined to lead the funding drive towards an appropriate and satisfying outcome, gave a long and characteristically mellifluous oration, in which he cemented Kendall's reputation as a gentle singer of natural scenes, and one who knew his own limitations. Charlotte was introduced to the governor, and her two daughters Persia and Roma presented wreaths to Lady Carrington. That was more in line with what Charlotte might have thought were her social aspirations, impinging on gentility. The governor, choosing his words adeptly, remembered to say how gratified he was that the government of the day had 'placed at the disposal of the widow a position of trust'.[19]

Louisa Lawson, who claimed to have instigated the erection of the monument, did not attend the ceremony. The committee had forgotten her.[20] Or perhaps it did not know about her. Or, as a country newspaper reported well after the event (at the time of her death), she was ill and could not attend the ceremony.[21]

The monument, a polished marble column with attendant urns, was erected above Henry Kendall's 'ashes', in Dalley's term. His remains had been transferred a month previously from their original, neglected, site to a more conspicuous location, closer to the sea. For some undeclared reason this was deemed to be important to Kendall's wishes, even though his persistent theme was of forest ways and mountain streams. That was the country where he had intimations of the radiant dream that led him on, intimations and even glimpses of the ideal. At Waverley, there was not much more than low coastal scrub.

The decision appears to have been based on a confusion about Kendall's last utterance. Mary Fagan had been present and, as she relayed to Henry Evans, from whom in turn P.J. Holdsworth heard it, Kendall had asked in a half-delirious moment 'Give me a drink from the sea'.[22] As Holdsworth was assiduous in all the arrangements for the fundraising, the positioning of the monument and the ceremony itself, it is very likely that he had a considerable say in this sentimental decision.

Mrs Hamilton-Gray, however, had her own variant of the story. Kendall's request was prefaced by his favourite term of endearment to Melinda. 'Little mother, give me a drink from the sea'.[23] Yet Melinda was not in attendance – which is the point of Mrs Hamilton-Gray's version. By her account, Kendall's mother had been ousted by his wife, yet he had called on her, his 'little mother', at the very last.

She was not present at the unveiling of the monument either. She might have registered a shock at the verse from Shelley inscribed on its base:

> *Awake him not! Surely he takes his fill*
> *Of deep and liquid rest, forgetful of all ill.*

It was not as though the wording of this epitaph bypassed the attention of the committee. Dalley for one had wondered whether the sentiment there might be misunderstood, and found inappropriate, given Kendall's notorious proclivity. When Melinda wrote her own memorial poem to him, she made specific allusion to 'the tempting red juice of the wine'.[24]

But Charlotte's version is that Kendall had instead asked for a sip of tea, and to be turned on his side to face the tea, not the sea. She should know. In Ackland's view, that was emphasised as a symbolic gesture of his escape from alcohol (ignoring that Kendall also had that sip of champagne).[25]

Also, chiselled into the massive stone base was Henry Kendall's deceit about his age, that he was born in 1841 and not in 1839. Instead of settling Kendall's career into some kind of commemorative finality, it was all becoming more and more a confusion.

There is a further detail to remark about the memorial. The ostentation of it was a far cry from his description of his father's neglected grave in the distant forest. It certainly had nothing to do with what Kendall, who had all his life preferred solitariness, could have wanted. The polished grandeur was all about stroking the self-esteem of the public. In that sense it might be thought a monumental folly.

The relocation of Kendall's grave left an empty plot alongside Louisa Lawson's recent purchase. Perhaps disappointment about that had something to do with her non-attendance too. Brian Matthews, however, notes that 'a photograph in *The Essential Henry Lawson* depicts Louisa and Gertrude [her daughter] "dressed for the unveiling of the memorial"'.[26] While that rather disqualifies that story about being uninvited, it could still be true that she felt left out of the arrangements and the ceremonial aspects of it. Simply, she was not important enough at the time. It is also of interest that it now seemed acceptable for womenfolk to appear at the grave – this was an unveiling, however, not an interment, and that might make all the difference.

Nearly 40 years later, Henry Lawson was buried in the adjacent vacant plot, as distinct from the vacated one, either at his own request as his sister claimed, or at Mary Gilmore's urging, as she claimed. Louisa had been laid to rest at Rookwood.[27] Henniker Heaton had paid the expenses of placing a stone over Kendall's first gravesite. He also had a bust of Henry Kendall placed in the university.[28]

Mrs Hamilton-Grey commenced her visits to Charlotte soon after her inaugural lecture on Kendall's poetry. She wanted to find out everything she could about the late poet. She lived in Redfern, not very far from the Kendalls in Cleveland Street – and that was not too far either from Peter Fagan's house, and where Henry had died. Peter Fagan had been authorised to dole out funds to Charlotte from the public subscription as she needed them; he had been on the management committee from the start, the Fagans still watching over Henry's interests.

The intrusive Mrs Hamilton-Grey was something of a pest. Frederick Kendall later recalled her visits and her relentless questioning, particularly of the siblings, himself included, while Charlotte was making tea and organising refreshments in the kitchen. 'I recall her clearly as a dark, sybilline woman, voluble and neurotic, with large "soulful" eyes, drinking tea *ad libitum*, intoning in a rhapsodical chant endless verses and questioning us on our recollections.'[29]

Mrs Hamilton-Grey had a personal dislike for his mother, he recalled; his own dislike of their persistent visitor is quite evident too. She was invasive, she was histrionic, she commanded centre stage.

Which is not at all surprising. She had first approached Archibald Sillars Hamilton, a phrenologist of some note and questionable past, for a 'reading' of her character.[30] She wished to learn if she were suitably endowed to become an actress. He was most impressed with her poise, her voice, her perceptiveness and her memory. She was clearly intended to become a phrenologist herself; she might like to be his assistant. Within a few months she became his third wife. His first wife had divorced him for his bigamous marriage to the second.

Agnes learned showmanship from him. They gave public lectures and private sessions through most of the colonies, and she learned self-promotion. She was gifted with an extraordinary memory, though that is according to her own evidence. She was very intense, somewhat hypnotic. Petulant too: if the auditorium was not full, she was known to stalk off the stage. Mostly the reports were of the generous reception they received. Quite possibly the Hamiltons provided review copy to the press, for there is an identifiable uniformity to these notices. The lectures were so interesting, the lecturess had a gentle, tuneful voice, she had melodious enunciation, she illustrated her points by ample and appropriate quotation, she had a wonderful memory, her approach to her material was through 'higher emotionalism'. There is not a lot about substance.

She had the exotic looks of a vamp. She was just over 30, recently widowed, dark, something like Thomas Hardy's Eustacia Vye (*Return of the Native*) – she included photographs of herself as well of Kendall in her biographies of him. In looks she was the total opposite of Charlotte, who was blue-eyed and fair-haired. Kendall's mother had once been a raven-haired beauty too.

Jill Dimond has investigated the next phase of the young widow's activities. Agnes Hamilton-Grey had a daughter who died at the age of five months in 1888, well after the death of her husband (he had died in 1884). It seems that about this time she affixed the hyphenated Grey to her name, though no re-marriage has been recorded. She subsequently had a son too, George, born in either 1889 or 1890, whose godfather was George Houston Reid, soon to become premier of New South Wales, and a decade later prime minister. Dimond speculates that Reid was actually the child's father.[31] He was a well-known ladies' man through the 1880s, and married late in 1891. It would have been inconvenient to have any continuing connection with Agnes Hamilton.

Mrs Hamilton (as she was at that stage) made copious notes of her visits to Charlotte's. Perhaps her much-vaunted memory was less secure than she had claimed. She also visited Emily and charmed her. Emily supplied her with all sorts of material at satisfying variance from Charlotte's account (for example, of Charlotte's wedding). It is less clear that Agnes ever visited Melinda. In her various biographical forays, she repeatedly says of Melinda that 'it is said that', 'she has invariably been described', 'all who remembered'[32] and the like. She does not record the experience of any direct encounter. Which implies therefore that her entire account of Matilda/Melinda rests on hearsay, and most heavily on whatever P.J. Holdsworth had affirmed, though his version too would necessarily have been very much at a distance.

Melinda at some stage returned to Sydney with or to Jane, living with her daughter in Ultimo but then, possibly when she turned blind, in a nursing home for aged women in nearby Glebe Point, where in 1893 she died of a stroke.

To the very end Melinda continued to reinvent herself – for on her death certificate her date of birth is wrong. It is given as 1808, not 1815 as on her marriage certificate. She cannot have been born in 1808 because if she were, she would have had to come to Sydney aboard the *Broxbornebury*. But, as she is not on that passenger list, she must have been born after 1814 – and that is affirmed by the early records, which declare her to have been born in Australia. Simply, the date on her death certificate is misleading. It can hardly have been a mere slip, because that invented date is consistent with the *Evening News* report that she was 75. She had been misleading once again.

This final equivocation is like a signature from the other side of the grave. Or like the error on Kendall's ostentatious monument. Like mother, like son.

Her death certificate provides one final twitch – it gives her father's name as James McNally.[33] Presumably, a degree of separation from any ex-convict connection. If Jane and Emily supplied the information, then that is what they must have been told, by none other than the chameleon Matilda. Nobody else would have known any different.

Mrs Hamilton-Grey did nothing with any of her accumulated material until 1920, when she published her first book on Henry Kendall, a comparatively slight work and heavy with quotation. In 1924, the year that Charlotte died, she (Mrs Hamilton-Grey) brought out a second work, elaborating Kendall's 'romantic history', the young poet's life up until the time of his marriage. Her timing may have been coincidental. In 1929, she published the third and last of her biographies, in which, according to Frederick Kendall, she maligned his mother.

Mrs Hamilton-Grey died in 1937; Frederick's refutation was published in 1938. The timing of that was not at all coincidental.

All those women, like so many restless houris, each demanding to possess his memory. All those equally wavering details, supporting a romanticised idea of the poet. The one thing that is securely on the record is the poetry itself, a poetry of light and shade, and uncertain ways. A poetry of the rainforests. A poetry of our place.

Notes

Prologue

1 Francis J. Donohue, 'In memoriam – Henry Kendall', *Freeman's Journal*, 12 August 1882, p. 17.

2 Henry Kendall to Mrs Selwyn, 25 March 1865, Mitchell Library (ML) Ak39.

3 Ian Hamilton, review of Judith Binney, *The Legacy of Guilt: A life of Thomas Kendall*, in *Journal of the Polynesian Society*, vol. 5, 1969, p. 401. He was even more emphatic in a review of the second edition, in 2005: 'Kendall was simply an ill-educated, lower-middle-class amateur, out of his depth in a situation that was completely beyond him', *Journal of the Polynesian Society*, 2005, pp. 428–34.

4 P.J. Holdsworth, ed. and introduction, *Poems of Henry Kendall*, G. Robertson & Co., Melbourne, 1886, p. xiii.

5 Frederick Kendall, *Henry Kendall, his later years*, Simmons, Sydney, 1938 recalls Shelley, Byron, Mrs Browning, Tennyson and Swinburne among others, and Roget's *Thesaurus*.

6 Henry Kendall to Charles Harpur, 25 September 1862, ML C199.

7 A.D. Hope, 'Introduction', in Leonie Kramer & A.D. Hope (eds), *Three Colonial Poets – Henry Kendall*, Sun Books, Melbourne, 1973, p. xviii. Kenneth Slessor, in his brief remarks on Kendall (*Bread and Wine*, Angus & Robertson, Sydney, 1970, pp. 87–8) is much more disappointed in Kendall's meaningless and unfocused imagery, his see-sawing metres, and his frequently 'atrocious rhymes', giving as one example childhood and wildwood in 'Bell-birds'.

8 T. Inglis Moore, 'Introduction', *Henry Kendall*, Angus & Robertson, Sydney, 1963, p. ix.

9 Vivian Smith, 'Poetry', Leonie Kramer (ed.), *Oxford History of Australian Literature*, Oxford University Press, Melbourne, 1981, p. 282.

10 T.T. Reed, *Henry Kendall: A critical appreciation*, Adelaide, Rigby, 1960, pp. 17–18. Henry's son Frederick attests to that: 'my father was decidedly not an orthodox believer' (Frederick Kendall, *Henry Kendall, his later years*, p. 14).

11 Henry Kendall to Henry Parkes, May 1880; cited in Michael Ackland, *Henry Kendall: The man and the myths*, Miegunyah Press, Carlton, Vic., 1995, p. 286.

Chapter 1 ~ Double Dealings

1 Mrs A.M. Hamilton-Grey, *Poet Kendall: His romantic history (from the cradle to the hymeneal altar)*, John Sands, Sydney, 1926, p. 135.

2 Colonel Brock, Quebec, 17 March 1807, on the exemplary discipline of the 100th, in Ferdinand Brock Tupper, *The Life and Correspondence of Sir Isaac Brock, K.B.*, Simkin, Marshall, London 1847.

3 See Simon Barnard, *Convict Tattoos: Marked men and women of Australia*, Text Publishing, Melbourne, 2016, p. 54. By a recent law (1807) deserters could be tattooed with the letter D two inches below the nipple on the left breast. Those who were found guilty of desertion with premeditation might be branded with the letters BC, meaning 'bad character'. It is open to speculation whether a serial offender could have ended up with BCD. Branding of deserters was not totally abandoned until 1879.

4 According to Charles Bateson, *The Convict Ships, 1787–1868*, Library of Australian History, Sydney, 1988 [1983], p. 173, the height between decks was 5ft 8 inches.

5 A substantial account of the disaster is given in 'The *Surry* tombstones', *Australian Town and Country Journal*, 27 July 1895, p. 31.

6 Bateson, *The Convict Ships*.

7 Carol J. Baxter (ed.), *General Muster of New South Wales, 1814*, Australian Biographical and Genealogical Record in association with the Society of Australian Genealogists, Sydney, 1987.

8 Marjorie Kendall, *Kissin Cousins,* The author, Milton, Qld, 1989, p. 85, n. g.

9 *New South Wales, Australia, Registers of Land Grants and Leases 1792–1867*; 50 acres were granted to Julia McNally at Melville, NSW, on 17 August 1819. That is a clerical mistake, not a change of identity. In the 1828 Muster she is listed as Sussanah – who can determine how a mistake like that came about?

10 Named for the Plain of Mamre, where Abraham dwelt, and made his life acceptable to God; see Genesis 13.18. Marsden was not modest in his ambition.

11 Carol J. Baxter (ed.), *General Muster List of New South Wales, 1823, 1824, 1825*, Australian Biographical and Genealogical Record in association with the Society of Australian Genealogists, Sydney, 1999.

12 Carol J. Baxter (ed.), *General Muster and Land and Stock Muster of New South Wales, 1822*, Australian Biographical and Genealogical Record in association with the Society of Australian Genealogists, Sydney, 1988.

13 Malcolm Sainty & Keith Johnson (eds), *Census of New South Wales, November 1828*, Library of Australian History, Sydney, 1985, p. 255.

14 A.G. Stephens, 'The truth about Henry Kendall', *Windsor and Richmond Gazette*, 27 January 1928, p. 5: 'Matilda … in later years, represented herself as having held the post of governess with the Hill family until her marriage with Basil Kendall'.

15 Marjorie Kendall, 'Melinda Kendall: mother of Henry Kendall, poet', in Patricia Thompson & Susan Yorke (eds), *Lives Obscurely Great: Historical essays on women of New South Wales,* Society of Women Writers (Australia), New South Wales Branch, Sydney, 1980, p. 61. She is following A.M. Hamilton-Grey, *Kendall, Our 'God-made Chief', 'A Singer of the Dawn': a Continuation of Poet Kendall, Making a Complete History from Cradle to Grave*, John Sands, Sydney, 1929, p. 13: 'everyone knows [her name] was McNally, her adopted name being Hill'.

16 Marjorie Kendall, *Kissin Cousins*, p. 85.

17 Hamilton-Grey, *Poet Kendall*, p. 147.

18 Stephens, 'The truth about Henry Kendall', p. 5.

19 Bertram Stevens, 'Biographical note', *The Poems of Henry Kendall*, Angus & Robertson, Sydney 1920, p. xv.

20 See his memoir in *The Poems of Henry Clarence Kendall*, George Robertson, Melbourne, 1903, p. v.

21 Alexander Sutherland, 'Henry Clarence Kendall: his parentage', *Australasian*, 8 August 1896, p. 23.

22 R.R. Madden, *The Life and Times of Robert Emmet,* Haverty, New York, 1868, p. 246. There are variants of the final lines of this speech.

23 'Remembering the past: Leonard McNally arch-informer', *An Phoblacht*, 13 February 1997.

Chapter 2 ~ The Sins of the Fathers

1 'The Lincolnshire Poacher' (traditional, 1776): 'Oh, 'tis my delight on a shining night/ In the season of the year' is widely regarded as an unofficial 'anthem' of Lincolnshire.

2 Judith Binney, *The Legacy of Guilt: A life of Thomas Kendall*, Oxford University Press, Auckland, 1968, p. 2, n. 2. Binney's is the definitive work on Kendall and examines the background of his theology comprehensively. The factual evidence in the following account is for the most part extracted from her work, though with a wholly different emphasis.

3 Thomas Kendall to Basil Woodd, 23 January 1813, cited in R.M. Burdon, *New Zealand Notables*, series 3, Caxton, Christchurch, 1950, p. 10.

4 Binney, *The Legacy of Guilt*, pp. 2–3.

5 Quoted in Tom Harpur, *The Spirituality of Wine*, Northstone Publishing, Kelowna, BC, 2004, p. 37.

6 The fifth of the series (of eight), 1735. The tumbledown church, at that time out in what was still the countryside, was pulled down in 1740, and replaced in 1742 by a church that became rather more fashionable, and celebrated, if that is the word, as the place where Byron was christened. At a somewhat later date, Dickens used it as the basis of the christening scene in *Dombey and Son* (1848), for his own son had undergone the ceremony there prior to that date of course. Dickens particularly noted all the cheerful accoutrements of funerals on display at that occasion. These had apparently been removed from sight by the time Robert Browning and Elizabeth Barrett married there (1846).

7 Binney, *The Legacy of Guilt*, p. 17.

8 ibid., p. 24: 'Kendall had had no real training in the Classics and consequently had no knowledge of the structure of any language but English'.

9 Marjorie Kendall, *Kissin Cousins*, p. 28.

10 Technically, they were not missionaries as none of them had been ordained. Their role was to prepare the way.

11 Binney, *The Legacy of Guilt*, p. 21.

12 They joined their parents later. A standard public notice in the *Sydney Gazette*, 22 March 1817, indicates that Susanna and Elizabeth were planning to depart by the *Active* for New Zealand, and called for all claims or demands for payment to be presented.

13 Binney, *The Legacy of Guilt*, pp. 26–7, n. 66.

14 Thomas Kendall, *A Korao no New Zealand; or, the New Zealander's First Book: being an attempt to compose some lessons for the instruction of the natives*, George Howe, Sydney, 1815; Auckland Institute and Museum, Auckland, 1957.

15 King to Rev. Josiah Pratt, secretary of the Church Missionary Society, quoted in Binney, *The Legacy of Guilt*, pp. 39–40.

16 Binney, *The Legacy of Guilt*, p. 54, n. 21: 'she confessed the whole of her shameful conduct and the child remains a spurious brood in Mr Kendall's family until this day [1822]' (Hall to Pratt).

17 1 Samuel 3:7.

18 Binney, *The Legacy of Guilt*, p. 46.

19 Thomas Kendall, *A Grammar and Vocabulary of the Language of New Zealand,* Church Missionary Society, London, 1820.

20 Binney, *The Legacy of Guilt*, p. 59.
21 Baron Charles de Thierry.
22 Binney, *The Legacy of Guilt*, p. 91.
23 ibid., p. 82, n. 58.
24 ibid., p. 76.
25 Frances Larson, *Severed: A history of heads lost and heads found*, Granta, London, 2014, pp. 26–7.
26 Not to be confused with the more culturally significant 'Tangaroa', meaning 'from the sea'. Tungaroa has a more unfortunate signification, something like 'big-bottomed'.
27 Binney, *The Legacy of Guilt*, p. 109.
28 ibid., p. 107.
29 ibid., p. 111.
30 'The Late Mr. John Kendall', *The Ulladulla and Milton Times*, 16 February 1895, p. 1.
31 'It was not until he had left the Bay of Islands that any reconciliation was effected between himself and his wife' (Binney, *The Legacy of Guilt*, p. 159).
32 Marjorie Kendall, *Kissin Cousins*, p. 30.
33 *Sydney Gazette*, 24 August 1827, p. 3. She married Thomas Wheaton Bowden, whose father (also named Thomas) was Master of the Male Orphanage in 1819 but was removed from office in 1825 for drunkenness (Marjorie Kendall, *Kissin Cousins*, p. 34).
34 8 September 1827, 'Shipping news', *Australian*, 12 September 1827, p. 1. The *Elizabeth* brought with her 6000 bushels of wheat and that would 'create astonishment and just dissatisfaction among our agriculturalists', the editor observed (p. 2). Apparently, the captain or the owners had been misinformed that the colony was in want. Another early example of fake news.
35 *Sydney Gazette*, 21 May 1829, p. 3.
36 See the Index to Marjorie Kendall, *Kissin Cousins*, pp. 239–50. A local historian of the Milton district, the late Joanne Ewin, in her chapter 'The Milton-Ulladullah Pioneers', In *Living Echoes: A community project produced by the Shoalhaven Historical Society, Inc., for the Australian Bicentenary* (Nowra, 1996) makes a different claim: 'Kendall and Tungaroa had a son, Kendall, who has many descendants in New Zealand' (p. 127). The evidence for this forthright assertion is not given. The use of the name Kendall does not in itself prove a bloodline connection – it could have been adopted in honour of the Rev. Thomas, who was well regarded among some of the Maori.

Chapter 3 ~ Very Much Given to Indulge in Spirits

1 Marjorie Kendall, *Kissin Cousins*, p. 49.
2 Obituary, *Kiama Independent*, 9 November 1883, p. 2.
3 W.G. McClymont, *The Exploration of New Zealand*, Department of Internal Affairs, Wellington, 1940, p. 22.
4 John Cowell was one of Marsden's lay missionaries, with a practical skill in twine spinning. He and his second wife lived at Kororareka from 1823 with their son John Vittoria Cowell. When John Sr married a third time, he married a Maori woman and, when he was widowed yet again, he took a common-law Maori wife; see Tom O'Connor, 'John Cowell's House at Te Pahu', New Zealand Historic Places Trust, 2017.
5 New South Wales Land Board Report no. 203, 29 October 1827; reprinted in Milton-Ulladulla and District Historical Society, *Nulladolla 1988*, Ulladulla, 1988, p. 6.
6 Marjorie Kendall, *Kissin Cousins*, p. 49. Hamilton-Grey, *Poet Kendall*, p. 32, identifies no. 68 Pitt St as the Rev. Thomas Kendall's Sydney address in 1825; from there he made his regular trips down to Ulladulla.
7 See Alex McAndrew, *The Narrawallee Story Re-told*, The author, Epping, 1995, p. 39.

8 Marjorie Kendall, *Kissin Cousins*, p. 31.

9 'The late Mr. John Kendall', *Ulladulla and Milton Times*, 16 February 1895, p. 1.

10 ibid.

11 ibid.

12 Marjorie Kendall, *Kissin Cousins*, p. 45. Thomas Florance's unfortunate manner had consequences for him later, when he and Elizabeth moved to New Zealand for the sake of his health. He applied for a position in the Survey Department there too, but an unfavourable report from Sir George Gipps tipped the scales against him. He was not an easy man to deal with, and later in his life he became more and more difficult. In May 1860 he was charged by Elizabeth with leaving her destitute, and without means of support.

13 Milton-Ulladulla and District Historical Society, *Nulladolla 1988*, p. 13.

14 *Sydney Gazette*, 9 December 1830, p. 3.

15 'Solicitus' [Thomas Kendall], 'On the origin, language and religion of the language of New Zealand', *Sydney Gazette*, 8 January 1831.

16 His city address is given in these as 43 Upper Pitt Street, not far from where his son Thomas Surfleet Kendall had lived and worked and where Joseph sometime resided too.

17 Milton-Ulladulla and District Historical Society, *Nulladolla 1988*, p. 6.

18 Ackland, *Henry Kendall*, p. 28, says that Kendall received permission from the archdeacon to carry out limited offices of the Church of England in that district, such as burials, baptisms and marriages, which suggests he still had no access to the pulpit.

19 27 May 1827, cited in Marjorie Kendall, *Kissin Cousins*, p. 85b.

20 Henry Kendall, 29 June 1877, cited in Ackland, *Henry Kendall*, p. 4. In the same passage Kendall asserts that both his grandfathers were ministers of the Church of England. His Irish Catholic grandfather Paddy McNally would have been rotating briskly in his grave.

21 Binney, *The Legacy of Guilt*, p. 163.

22 Lautaro means 'swift hawk' but was also the name of a young Aurucanian warrior who had led his people in an indigenous resistance to the Spanish.

23 Marjorie Kendall, *Kissin Cousins*, p. 85. Marjorie Kendall says March 1830, aboard the *Lady Blackwood*, and that he was aged 21. However, he turned 21 two years earlier; and the *Lady Blackwood* had sailed from London, not Valparaiso.

24 Marjorie Kendall, *Kissin Cousins*, p. 136. John, a year older, may have begun soon after the disaster of 1832.

25 '[Kendall] … struck a Maori. The elders complained of his temper to Marsden, who was himself appalled at the lack of respect shown to so well-mannered a people' (Ronald Hyams, *Empire and Sexuality: The British experience*, Manchester University Press, Manchester, 1990, pp. 103–4).

26 'Police incidents', *Australian*, 15 May 1829, p. 3.

27 Ackland, *Henry Kendall*, p. 37.

28 'Distressing occurrence', *Sydney Gazette*, 16 August 1832, p. 2.

29 'Domestic intelligence', *Sydney Morning Herald*, 16 August 1832, p. 2. Ackland (*Henry Kendall*, p. 29), holds that the cutter was skippered by Florance's brother. That is possible, but across those years the shipping intelligence in the Sydney press invariably identified Thomas Kendall as the captain.

30 Marjorie Kendall, *Kissin Cousins*, p. 32.

31 Cited in Hamilton, review of Judith Binney's *Legacy of Guilt*, p. 430.

32 'Shipping intelligence', *Sydney Gazette*, 29 March 1832, p. 3. He was returning as a passenger on the brig *Guide*. Mysteriously, with the eight passengers listed came 'a female native of New Zealand'.

Chapter 4 ~ Thirty Pieces of Silver

1 Stevens, 'Biographical note', p. xv. H.M. Green identified her more temperately as 'happy-go-lucky' (*A History of Australian Literature*, Angus & Robertson, Sydney, 1961, vol. 1, p. 144).

2 Marjorie Kendall, *Kissin Cousins*, p. 86; T.D. Mutch in Charles Swancott, *The Brisbane Water Story: Part four, the rest of the story*, The author, Woy Woy, NSW, p. 130. Even Mrs Hamilton-Grey gets this right, but not too accurately (*Kendall, our 'God-made Chief'*, p. 18). It is noticeable that Rev. Hill was not involved in his protégée's wedding, even though she had lived in his household for half of her life, and neither was he involved in the funeral of her child. Mutch was a fellow of the Society of Australian Genealogists, which suggests his information is reliable; but not his calculations. The child died at 12 weeks, not eight.

3 In the *New South Wales Directory 1835* he is listed as working at the Brisbane Mills in Parramatta Road.

4 Marjorie Kendall, *Kissin Cousins*, p. 85.

5 Ackland, *Henry Kendall*, p. 34.

6 ibid., p. 5.

7 Marjorie Kendall, *Kissin Cousins*, p. 136.

8 Ackland, *Henry Kendall*, p. 35.

9 'Important to mariners', *Sydney Gazette*, 22 April 1837, p. 2.

10 'Police incidents', *Sydney Gazette*, 27 April 1837, p. 3.

11 *Sydney Gazette*, 29 April 1837, p. 2.

12 'The late Mr John Kendall: a pioneer settler', *Ulladulla and Milton Times*, 16 February 1895, p. 1. He settled on Kendall Dale and formalised the arrangement by buying 256 acres from his brother Thomas Surfleet for £10 in 1843.

13 Milton-Ulladulla and District Historical Society, *Nulladolla 1988*, p. 88. Another name with variant spellings – eventually known as Whappindally and given to the property established when he doubled the acreage of the original 'Darling Forest'.

14 John K. Ewers, 'Pioneers of the pen: Henry Kendall', *West Australian*, 21 December 1929, p. 5.

15 Marjorie Kendall, 'Melinda Kendall', p. 61.

16 Joanne Ewin, *Meet the Pioneers: Early families of the Milton-Ulladulla District*, The author, Milton, NSW, p. 115.

17 Melinda Kendall, 'Henry Kendall (by his mother)', *Kiama Independent*, 16 October 1883, p. 4.

18 See Alex McAndrew, *Mollymook revisited*, The author, Epping, 2015.

19 Henry Kendall to Thomas Surfleet Kendall, 22 July 1867, quoted in Ackland, *Henry Kendall*, p. 133.

20 The distribution, by Jane Kendall, took place in November 1841. Basil's share was 25 head of cattle, and an additional 15 as equivalent to one filly (Marjorie Kendall, *Kissin Cousins*, p. 51; Ackland, *Henry Kendall*, p. 34).

21 'The Biographer', *Australasian*, 3 April 1897, p. 27.

22 Alexander Sutherland, 'Henry Clarence Kendall', *Australasian*, 8 August 1896, p. 23.

23 Marjorie Kendall, 'Melinda Kendall', p. 61.

24 Letter to J. Sheridan Moore, 29 June 1877, Mitchell Library; cited in Ackland, *Henry Kendall*, p. 40.

25 Marjorie Kendall, *Kissin Cousins*, p. 86.

26 14 July 1847, according to Marjorie Kendall (*Kissin Cousins*, p. 86). She further details that Emily was baptised into the Wesleyan Church, 29 October 1847. That seems confident. T.D. Mutch confirms the birth date as July 1847 (Swancott, *The Brisbane Water Story*, p. 130). Ackland begs to differ, proposing 1850 instead; and Michael Wilding, *Wild Bleak Bohemia*, Australian Scholarly Publishing, North Melbourne,

2014 follows him in this. That is just six weeks before Basil Kendall passed off the forged cheque. If this later date is accepted, then Emily was conceived after Basil had served out his sentence. Ackland does not say at what stage of 1850 she was born. In support of this later date, when Emily was married in 1867 a large part of Henry's objection was that she was only 16. There is no reconciling those disparate birth dates.

27 ibid.

28 'Law intelligence', *Sydney Morning Herald*, 3 January 1848, p. 4.

29 Thomas Bawden, *The Bawden Lectures: Early days in the Clarence district*, Clarence River Historical Society, Grafton 1979, p. 35.

30 See J.S. Ryan, 'Henry Kendall's vital association with the Grafton area, particularly in 1862–63', in Russell McDougall (ed.), *Henry Kendall: The muse of Australia*, Centre for Australian Language and Literature Studies, Armidale, 1992, pp. 54–79.

31 Henry Kendall to J. Sheridan Moore, 29 June 1877, ML C199.

32 Alexander Sutherland, 'Henry Clarence Kendall', *Australasian*, 8 August 1896, p. 23.

33 Bawden, *The Bawden Lectures*, p. 105.

34 Sutherland, 'Henry Clarence Kendall', *Australasian*, 8 August 1896, p. 23.

Chapter 5 ~ There Goes Mad Harry

1 'Founders of our literature: Henry Kendall', *Herald* (Melbourne), 26 May 1934, p. 6.

2 Henry Kendall to J. Sheridan Moore, 29 June 1877, ML C199.

3 T.T. Reed, 'The life and poetical works of Henry Kendall', DLitt, University of Adelaide, 1953, p. 63.

4 Hamilton-Grey, *Kendall, 'Our God-made Chief'*, p. 18.

5 ibid., p. 19.

6 ibid., p. 18.

7 Blaxland's success in this venture depended on the accomplishment of Rutter, boiling off water in salt pans alongside the Parramatta River. Blaxland's impressive house, Newington, subsequently was leased to the Methodist church and evolved into Newington College.

8 In a series on the local history of the Illawarra, 'The Old Pioneer' confidently affirms that a local resident, old Mr Brooker, gave the name to Brooker's Nose, which is wrongly called 'Broker's Nose' by many ('Reminiscences of Illawarra', series no. 59, *Illawarra Mercury*, 28 November 1924, p. 1). A Brooker Street is now in the vicinity. Brooker's Farm was long established in that neck of the woods, and Matilda's unawareness of it testifies to the limit of her acquaintance with her neighbourhood.

9 Melinda Kendall, 'Brooker's Nose', *Illawarra Mercury*, 24 May 1884, p. 4.

10 'Away back as early as 1843 we have a record of a school (private) at Fairy Meadow. It was situated about where Fern Hill is now named. The first established state school was opened at Fairy Meadow in the year 1800' ('Reminiscences of Illawarra', series 19, *Illawarra Mercury*, 22 February 1924, p. 1).

11 Jan Keith, 'Henry Kendall in Illawarra', *Illawarra Historical Society Bulletin*, 1 April 1984, p. 16.

12 Hamilton-Grey, *Poet Kendall*, p. 158.

13 Ackland, *Henry Kendall*, p. 49.

14 Charlotte Kendall to Alexander Sutherland, 22 August 1882, ML 3775/9–11.

15 Henry Kendall to Henry Parkes, 5 October 1863, ML AK39.

16 Hamilton-Grey, *Poet Kendall*, p. 157.

17 'Reminiscences of Illawarra,' series 59, *Illawarra Mercury*, 28 November 1924, p. 1.

18 'He always acknowledged his mother's love of literature' (Wilding, *Wild Bleak Bohemia*, p. 29).

19 Marjorie Kendall, *Kissin Cousins*, p. 86; Kendall to J. Sheridan Moore, 29 June 1877, ML C199.
20 Green, *A History of Australia Literature*, vol. 1, p. 144. In this he appears to have followed distinguished company, though it may not have felt like it at the time, for Cook and Bligh are said to have done likewise.
21 Sutherland, 'Henry Clarence Kendall', *Australasian*, 8 August 1896, p. 23.
22 George Millard, in Hamilton-Grey, *Poet Kendall*, p. 156.
23 Sutherland, 'Henry Clarence Kendall', *Australasian*, 8 August 1896, p. 23.
24 Hamilton-Grey, *Kendall, our 'God-made Chief'*, p. 51.
25 See Ackland, *Henry Kendall*, p. 51ff.
26 J.S.G.W., 'Henry Kendall – the poet: links with Corrimal', *South Coast Times and Wollongong Argus*, 15 April 1927, p. 10.
27 Hamilton-Grey, *Kendall, our 'God-made Chief'*, p. 26.
28 Frederick Kendall, 'A memoir' of Henry Kendall', in *Poems of Henry Clarence Kendall*, revised and enlarged edition, Longmans, Green & Co., London, 1903, p. vi.
29 A.G. Stephens, 'Kendalliana IV', Red Page, *Bulletin*, 16 July 1930, p. 5.
30 Henry Kendall to J. Sheridan Moore, 29 June 1877, ML C199.
31 T.T. Reed (ed.), *The Poetical Works of Henry Kendall*, Libraries Board of South Australia, Adelaide, Adelaide, p. xxiii.
32 Jane Kendall to John Kendall, 14 September 1857, facsim., in Marjorie Kendall, *Kissin Cousins*, p. 32.
33 E.H. Kendall, 'The far future', *Australian Home Companion and Band of Hope Magazine*, 5 November 1859, p. 475.
34 Hamilton-Grey, *Kendall, our 'God-made Chief'*, p. 17.
35 James Jervis, 'Illawarra, a century of history, 1788–1888', Royal Australian Historical Society, 1943, cited in Keith, 'Henry Kendall in Illawarra', p. 19. Arthur Cousins makes the same claim (*The Garden of New South Wales: A history of Illawarra and Shoalhaven*, Illawarra Historical Society, Wollongong, 1994 [1948]), identifying it as John Allan's store (p. 244).
36 Stevens, 'Biographical note', p. xvii.
37 Hamilton-Grey, *Kendall, our 'God-made Chief'*, p. 160.
38 Henry Kendall to the *Cornhill* magazine, 21 January 1862, ML C199.

Chapter 6 ~ The Twofold Life

1 Ann-Mari Jordens, *The Stenhouse Circle: Literary life in mid-nineteenth century Sydney*, Melbourne University Press, Carlton, Vic., 1979, p. 92. She hints at what may have disturbed his young wife, that he was somewhat of a voluptuary: 'He is said', reported an obviously intrigued lady biographer, 'to have been more than ordinarily fond of the opposite sex, and a "a flirt or gallant" – not always as wise and discreet as he should have been …' The intrigued lady is none other than the ubiquitous Mrs Agnes Hamilton-Grey; see *Poet Kendall*, p. 240.
2 H.G. Turner & Alexander Sutherland, *The Development of Australian Literature*, George Robertson, Melbourne, 1890, p. 247. The letter does not necessarily imply her presence in Grafton, it only says only that she had been busily besmirching Michael's reputation there.
3 Hamilton-Grey, *Poet Kendall*, p. 240.
4 John Douglas Pringle, 'A death on the Clarence', in *On Second Thoughts*, Angus & Robertson, Sydney, 1971, p. 141.
5 T. Inglis Moore, 'Introduction', *Selected Poems of Henry Kendall*, Angus & Robertson, Sydney, 1957, p. ix.
6 'Central Police Court', [Brisbane] *Courier*, 10 April 1862, p. 2.

7 Henry Kendall to *Athenaeum*, 27 September 1862; Kendall's letter, dated 19 July, is reprinted there, together with several of his poems. The *Athenaeum* selected his 'Fainting by the way' as demonstrating just how effective he could be; it met, perhaps, a distant expectation of what the Australian landscape should be like, all red sand and hot weather. To the modern eye, and to the modern mind, it is merely melodramatic, in the manner of mid-Victorian newspaper verse.

8 ibid.

9 G.B. Barton, *Literature in New South Wales*, Thomas Richards, Government Printer, Sydney, 1866, p. 106.

10 ibid., p. 105.

11 Lionel Michael to Henry Kendall, 21 October 1862, ML 3796/2.

12 Henry Kendall to Charles Harpur, 25 September 1862, ML C199.

13 Henry Halloran to Alexander Sutherland, 10 November 1891, ML 3775/9–11; cited in Ackland, *Henry Kendall*, pp. 61–2.

14 Cited in Jordens, *The Stenhouse Circle*, p. 87.

15 ibid., p. 88.

16 'Shipping intelligence', *Clarence and Richmond Examiner and New England Advertiser*, 9 December 1862, p. 2.

17 Mrs A.M. Hamilton-Grey, *Facts and Fancies about Our 'Son of the Woods': Henry Clarence Kendall and his poetry*, John Sands, Sydney, 1920, p. 19. Victor Daley recounted how Kendall 'arranged to give a lecture on Australian literature – an easy matter in those days one would imagine. When the time arrived, he came upon the platform, glared at the audience, gasped and fled. The chairman on the occasion [Michael] rose to the rescue with an address on beetles, and other nauseous but interesting vermin, entitled "Under the Microscope"' (Reed, 'The life and poetical works of Henry Kendall', p. 110). Daley's amusing description of the event rested on the recollection of a local identity a good few years later. The local paper, the *Clarence and Richmond Examiner*, advertised no such address, nor did it report Michael's off-the-cuff talk.

18 Hamilton-Grey, *Poet Kendall, His Romantic History*, p. 239.

19 Henry Kendall to Annie Hopkins, 2 May 1863, ML C199.

20 Ms Annie Hopkins; see Ackland, *Henry Kendall*, pp. 89–90.

21 Reed, 'The life and poetical works of Henry Kendall', p. 114. Dungog was never a substantial place. Given the times, his employment there looks unusual. He may well have been the only one in the village.

22 Advertisement, *Sydney Morning Herald*, 7 April 1863, p. 1.

23 See Sarah Goldman, *Caroline Chisholm: An irresistible force*, Harper Collins, Sydney, 2017, p. 271. Goldman like many others confuses the two sisters – even Reed stumbles over them. Josephine, the elder of the two, had the musical talent; Jane was gifted in mathematics.

24 James Lionel Michael to Henry Kendall, nd [1864?], ML 3775/9–11; cited in Ackland, *Henry Kendall*, p. 103.

25 Henry Kendall to Charles Harpur, 19 August 1863, ML C199.

26 *Sydney Morning Herald*, 5 August 1864, p. 1; 8 August 1864, p. 1.

27 Henry Kendall to Mrs A.E. Selwyn, 2 January 1864, ML Ak39.

28 Henry Kendall to Mrs A.E. Selwyn, 25 March 1865, ML Ak39.

29 Bertram Stevens, 'Introduction', *The Poems of Henry Kendall*, Angus & Robertson, Sydney, 1920, p. xxxviii.

30 'I fled from Brisbane. Then I walked up here, a distance of 200 miles, trying at the several small townships on the way to get some sort of work. Many back doors of misery I had passed through before I got into my present job … It is terrible to starve in the wilderness like Burke and Wills, but it is still more terrible to starve in

a civilized community; but they would not give me work and I could not beg. I fought through it all and got here where, far from all temptation to which I am liable, I raised myself from a stockman to the position I occupy' (12 November 1865; ms in possession of Reed; cited in *The Poetical Works of Henry Kendall*, p. xxxviii).

31 Edward Kendall to Matilda and Henry Kendall, 12 November 1865, ML 3775/9–11.

32 He had 'been constantly travelling with stock during the last four months' (Henry Kendall to Thomas Surfleet Kendall, 22 July 1867; cited in Ackland, *Henry Kendall*, p. 133).

33 A.G. Stephens, 'Kendalliana III', Red Page, *Bulletin*, 9 July 1930, p. 5.

34 ibid.

35 Melinda Kendall, 'Poem: the late Henry Kendall' (16 October 1833), ll. 17–20, 27–8.

36 Melinda Kendall, 'Henry Kendall (by his mother)', p. 4. The revised version of this poem appeared in *Illawarra Mercury*, 19 April 1884, p. 4, over her own name (Melinda Kendall) and re-titled 'The late Henry Kendall'.

37 Reed, 'The life and poetical works of Henry Kendall', p. 133.

38 W.H. Wilde, *Henry Kendall*, Twayne Publishers, Boston, 1976, p. 20.

39 Henry Kendall to Caroline Kendall, 20 February 1867, repr. in Marjorie Kendall, *Kissin Cousins*, p. 88.

40 Wilde, *Henry Kendall*, p. 20.

41 Turner & Sutherland, *The Development of Australian Literature*, p. 263.

42 A succinct notice of his address on this topic, and in particular on the several conditions of that which he called 'a bright truth set against dark truths', appears in the *Sydney Morning Herald*, 23 July 1864, p. 4.

43 Henry Kendall to J.E. Neild, 22 June 1869, cited in Michael Ackland, *Henry Kendall: Poetry, prose & selected correspondence*, University of Queensland Press, St Lucia, 1993, pp. 219–20.

44 This would be the original church, designed by Blacket, which burned down in 1972. The foundation of the handsome existing church, designed by Blacket and Horbury Hunt, was laid on 15 April 1868, more than a year after Kendall's wedding.

45 Hamilton-Grey, *Kendall, our 'God-made Chief'*, p. 49. She may have intended Frank, who subsequently protected Charlotte. If so, she was careless. The Rutters were of no interest to Mrs Hamilton-Smith.

46 ibid.

47 Frederick Kendall, *Henry Kendall, his later years*, p. 17.

Chapter 7 ~ The Encircling Gloom

1 Henry Kendall to Dr J.E. Neild, 22 June 1869, ML C199.

2 ibid.

3 ibid.

4 A.G. Stephens, 'Kendalliana I', Red Page, *Bulletin*, 11 June 1930, p. 2.

5 Wilding, *Wild Bleak Bohemia*, p. 188.

6 Alexander Sutherland in Turner & Sutherland, *The Development of Australian Literature*, p. 267.

7 Henry Kendall to Henry Halloran, 5 July 1879, ML 3775/ 9–11.

8 Hamilton-Grey, *Poet Kendall*, p. 293.

9 ibid.

10 Alexander Sutherland in Turner & Sutherland, *The Development of Australian Literature*, p. 258.

11 Hamilton-Grey, *Poet Kendall*, p. 293.

12 A.G. Stephens, 'Kendalliana II', Red Page, *Bulletin* 18 June 1930, p. 2.

13 Alexander Sutherland, *Australasian*, 22 August 1896, p. 26.

14 See Reed, *The Poetical Works of Henry Kendall*, p. xxvii.

15 See Ryan, 'Henry Kendall's vital association with the Grafton area', in McDougall (ed.), *Henry Kendall*, p. 71.

16 'Kendall had no doubts: "His body was found floating in the river; and the fact that he had destroyed himself was proved by a letter which he had left in his office, and by the character of some verses that were found on his person. The stanzas were syllables of despair, but their beauty was such that it made the heart ache. I am stating a sincere impression when I state that I do not know where I have seen a more touching farewell to men and time, than poor Michael's forgotten lyric"', cited in Wilding, *Wild Bleak Bohemia*, p. 126.

17 Kendall to Sheridan Moore, 22 June 1868, ML C199.

18 Jordens, *The Stenhouse Circle*, p. 89.

19 Known as the Farthing Poet, his epic poem 'Orion' was published for sale at that price. His life was certainly colourful, and his version of it enough to have served as an encouragement to such as Melinda/Matilda Kendall.

20 Richard Horne to Henry Kendall, 19 January 1869, ML 3775/ 9–11.

21 'This long narrative was published originally in the *Empire*, 24 August 1860, and then an enlarged and quite changed version appeared on 15 April 1865, in the *Sydney Mail*, under the title "Orara – a tale". Finally, as "A death in the bush", with some 100 lines excised from the *Sydney Mail* poem, it won a prize offered at the end of 1868' (Wilde, *Henry Kendall*, cited in Wilding, *Wild Bleak Bohemia*, p. 187).

22 *Punch*, 1865; see Reed (ed.), *The Poetical Works of Henry Kendall*, p. xxvii.

23 'Horne was clearly not offended by this blatant piece of borrowing. He may well have been pleasurably flattered to have been a modern poet of influence' (Wilding, *Wild Bleak Bohemia*, p. 187.

24 'Then how Horne came to pass over that third line in the "Death in the bush" before delivering his judgement *without recognition*, is quite beyond my comprehension. I was not cruel enough to enlighten either of them as to my discovery, and now I don't believe either of them ever attained to the knowledge of it' (George Gordon McCrae, 10 March 1927, ML 294).

25 'Insolvency Court', *Sydney Morning Herald*, 29 June 1868, p. 2.

26 Henry Kendall to J. Sheridan Moore, 28 December 1868. He identifies this behaviour as 'a characteristic sequel to her family history'; cited in Wilding, *Wild Bleak Bohemia*, p. 188.

27 T. Inglis Moore, 'Introduction', *Selected Poems of Henry Kendall*, Angus & Robertson, Sydney, 1957, p. x.

28 The name 'Violet' apparently replaced 'Lizzie' when they arrived in Melbourne, yet another example of what one might think of as the family's endemic nominal uncertainty; see Reed, 'The life and poetical works of Henry Kendall', p. 148.

29 *Empire*, 10 January 1861, cited in H.P. Heseltine, *John Le Gay Brereton*, Lansdowne Press, Melbourne, 1965, p. 8.

30 John Le Gay Brereton to Henry Kendall, 17 April 1869, ML 3775/ 9–11.

31 Henry Kendall to J.E. Neild, 22 June 1869, ML C199.

32 See Reed, 'The life and poetical works of Henry Kendall', p. 161.

33 Stephens, 'Kendalliana I', p. 2.

34 Sutherland in Sutherland & Turner, *The Development of Australian Literature*, p. 275.

35 George Gordon McCrae, cited in Reed, 'The life and poetical works of Henry Kendall', pp. 155–6.

36 Henry Kendall to J.E. Neild, 19 August 1869, ML C199.

37 Alexander Sutherland, 'Henry Clarence Kendall: III – In Melbourne', *Australasian*, 17 September 1896, p. 2.

38 Henry Kendall to G.W. Rusden, 29 July 1869, Rusden Papers, Trinity College Archives, University of Melbourne, cited in Wilding, *Wild Bleak Bohemia*, p. 242. Kendall was writing to solicit a loan, in order that he might pay for his membership in the Yorick Club. This was on the very day that he had been nominated to it.
39 Henry Kendall to Nathaniel Swan, 9 July 1880, National Library of Australia (NLA), MS 3227; see chapter 10.
40 Charlotte Kendall to Alexander Sutherland, 6 September 1882, cited in Wilding, *Wild Bleak Bohemia*, p. 274.
41 See Wilding, *Wild Bleak Bohemia*, pp. 275–6.
42 Hamilton-Grey, *Kendall, our 'God-made Chief'*, pp. 80–2.
43 ibid.
44 Cited in Ackland, *Henry Kendall*, p. 182.

Chapter 8 ~ Not in his Right Mind

1 Donovan Clarke, 'New light on Henry Kendall', *Australian Literary Studies*, vol. 2, June 1966, p. 211.
2 'Painful case of mental aberration', *Evening News*, 25 November 1870, p. 2.
3 See Wilding, *Wild Bleak Bohemia*, p. 292, citing Francis Adams: 'to hear him quote from the poets, and his recitations from the poets, used to make me laugh outright'.
4 'Quarter Sessions – Wednesday', *Empire*, 22 December 1870, pp. 2–3.
5 *Evening News*, 25 November 1870, p. 2.
6 'The Lunatic Reception House at Darlinghurst', *Sydney Morning Herald*, 10 October 1871, p. 5. There were rooms for eight males and eight females, bundled five into one room and three into another, though with the comfortable solitude of a padded cell for each sex. Suitable accommodation was of course provided for the superintendent and staff; see Frederick Norton Manning, *Inspector of the Insane Report for 1876*, New South Wales.
7 Henry Kendall, 'Elijah', *Australian Town & Country Journal*, 4 February 1871, p. 4.
8 'These lines were suggested by a passage in an unpublished drama by my friend, the author of "Ashtaroth": "And she who missed/ A little mouth that used to catch and cling –/ A small sweet trouble – at her yearning breast ..." The poem to which I am indebted is entitled "The Road to Avernus." It is only fair that I should make this acknowledgement. – H.K.'
9 Henry Kendall to P.J. Holdsworth, 5 March 1876, ML C199.
10 Cited in Wilding, *Wild Bleak Bohemia*, p. 371. Dr Rickeybockey is a character in Edward Bulwer-Lytton's *My Life* (1851).
11 Parkes to Henry Halloran, cited in Ackland, *Henry Kendall*, p. 188.
12 Henry Kendall to Henry Parkes, 5 August 1870, *Sir Henry Parkes Papers*, ML A871 to A1052; cited in Ackland, *Henry Kendall*, p. 167.
13 Clarke, 'New light on Henry Kendall', pp. 211–13.
14 Ackland, *Henry Kendall*, p. 182.
15 Henry Kendall to L.L. Harnett, cited in Ackland, *Henry Kendall*, p. 181.
16 Henry Kendall to J. Sheridan Moore, 17 May 1876, ML C199.
17 Clarke, 'New light on Henry Kendall', pp. 211–13.
18 Henry Kendall to Mrs Selwyn, 25 March 1865, ML Ak39.
19 Alexander Sutherland, 'Henry Kendall IV – His final years', *Australasian*, 22 September 1896, p. 2.
20 Reed, however (and almost alone), says Tamworth in *The Poetical Works of Henry Kendall*, p. xxxi. Others avoid the difficulty and write the Northern Rivers.
21 Wilde, *Henry Kendall*, p. 25.

Chapter 9 ~ A Sign of Bad Blood

1 Clarke, 'New light on Henry Kendall', p. 213.
2 Wilde, *Henry Kendall,* p. 25.
3 Charles Swancott, *Gosford and Henry Kendall Country (Koolewong to Lisarow)*, Brisbane Water Historical Society, Woy Woy, NSW, 1966, p. 266.
4 See Matthew 25:35
5 Transported on the *Lord Sidmouth*, arrived 1821.
6 Garnet Adcock, quoted in Joan Fenton, *The Fagans, the Cottage, and Kendall*, Brisbane Water Historical Society, West Gosford, 1996, p. 47.
7 Fenton, *The Fagans*, p. 14.
8 Joseph Fagan, appendix to Frederick Kendall, *Henry Kendall, His Later Years*, p. 32. The letter is undated, but would have been written well after the event, between 1921 and 1925.
9 Swancott, *The Brisbane Water Story*, p. 20.
10 E.D., 'Memories of Henry Kendall: the rock pool Near Gosford', *Sydney Mail*, 10 June 1931, cited in Wilding, *Wild Bleak Bohemia*, p. 399.
11 Hamilton-Grey, *Kendall, our 'God-made Chief'*, p. 85.
12 *Brisbane Courier*, 23 September 1872, p. 2.
13 Frederick Kendall, *Henry Kendall, His Later Years*, p. 32.
14 Alexander Sutherland in Turner & Sutherland, *The Development of Australian Literature*: 'Kendall knew nothing whatsoever of any form of athletic sports, had no pleasure in horses, and loathed what he considered the idiotic frenzy of the race-course' (cited in Wilding, *Wild Bleak Bohemia*, p. 230).
15 Cited in Wilding, *Wild Bleak Bohemia*, p. 416. The source is misidentified – it is not, as he says, in A.G. Wise, 'Our special correspondent in Kendall County', *Illustrated Sydney News*, 25 October 1890.
16 Swancott, *Gosford and Henry Kendall Country*, p. 259.
17 Cited in Swancott, *The Brisbane Water Story*, p. 24. It is of course possible that Kendall was amplifying his disability. It was not uncommon for him to augment details in his correspondence.
18 Reed, *The Poetical Works of Henry Kendall*, p. xxi.
19 Fenton, *The Fagans*, pp. 32–3.
20 Obituary [Michael Fagan], *Port Macquarie News*, 21 December 1912, p. 4. Here again Peter Fagan commented that Kendall was left-handed, 'and one can well believe it after inspecting a specimen of his writing'.
21 See Greville's Post Office Directory for 1872.
22 Swancott, *Gosford and Henry Kendall Country*, pp. 278–9. Swancott's deductions were confirmed by a local resident. He (Swancott) was most apologetic about scuttling the popular story promoted by the Brisbane Water Historical Society, of which he himself had been president for some years. It is noteworthy that the plaque affixed to the end wall of the cottage does not claim that Kendall had lived there. The society had been cautious. It reads: 'Here in 1874–5 Henry Clarence Kendall found friendship, peace & inspiration to write "Mooni", "Narrara", "Names Upon a Stone" & other Deathless Verse. Erected by the Brisbane Water Historical Society 1952'.
23 Henry Kendall, 'The voice in the native oak', *Australian Town and Country Journal*, 4 July 1874, p. 25; reprinted in *Empire*, 8 July 1874, p. 4.
24 Wilding, *Wild Bleak Bohemia*, p. 417.
25 Henry Kendall to P.J. Holdsworth, 14 July 1874, cited in Swancott, *The Brisbane Water Story*, p. 28; cf. Ackland, *Henry Kendall,* p. 227.
26 Henry Kendall to J. Sheridan Moore, 19 November 1874, ML C199.
27 Swancott, *The Brisbane Water Story*, p. 28.

28 Henry Kendall to J Sheridan Moore, 23 October 1874, ML 3775/9–11.
29 Ackland, *Henry Kendall*, p. 198.
30 Hamilton-Grey, *Poet Kendall, His Romantic History*, p. 66.
31 Henry Kendall to J. Sheridan Moore, 19 November 1874, ML C199.
32 ibid., 19 May 1875, ML C199.
33 'H.K.', 'Arcadia at our gates', *Town and Country Journal*, 6 March 1875, p. 19.
34 Henry Kendall to P.J. Holdsworth, June 1874, cited in Swancott, *The Brisbane Water Story*, p. 28. He remarks on the Fagans as well informed and educated in his *Gosford and Henry Kendall Country*, p. 260.
35 Cited in Wilding, *Wild Bleak Bohemia*, p. 427.
36 Hamilton-Grey, *Kendall, our 'God-made Chief'*, p. 103.
37 E.D., 'Henry Kendall: The rock pool near Gosford', p. 17.
38 Charles Harpur, 'A midsummer noon in the Australian forest', 1851, ll. 29–32.
39 Henry Kendall, 'Names upon a stone', 1878, ll. 23–4.
40 Cited in Wilding, *Wild Bleak Bohemia*, p. 400.
41 Henry Kendall to J. Sheridan Moore, 23 October 1874, ML 3775/9–11.
42 Ackland, *Henry Kendall*, p. 313, n.14.
43 Swancott, *The Brisbane Water Story*, p. 30.
44 ibid.
45 Henry Kendall to J. Sheridan Moore, 1875, cited in Wilding, *Wild Bleak Bohemia*, p. 426.
46 Henry Kendall to J. Sheridan Moore, 19 May 1875, ML 3775/9–11.
47 Cited in Wilding, *Wild Bleak Bohemia*, p. 427.

Chapter 10 ~ A Terrible Agent for Evil

1 Swancott, *Gosford and Henry Kendall Country*, p. 269.
2 Swancott, *The Brisbane Water Story*, p. 20.
3 'Collindon Sawmill', *Port Macquarie News and Hastings River Advocate*, 2 November 1912, p. 3. Hamilton-Grey says Kendall stayed there for 12 months (*Kendall, our God-made Chief*, pp. 110, 112).
4 Sutherland, 'Henry Kendall IV – His final years', p. 2.
5 Swancott, *The Brisbane Water Story*, p. 31.
6 ibid.
7 Hamilton-Grey, *Kendall, our 'God-made Chief'*, p. 48.
8 Cited Ackland, *Henry Kendall*, p. 230.
9 Swancott, *The Brisbane Water Story*, p. 31.
10 Henry Kendall to Sheridan Moore, 17 May 1876, ML C199.
11 Ackland, *Henry Kendall*, p. 231.
12 Cited in Reed, *Life and Poetical Works of Henry Kendall*, pp. 183–4.
13 Henry Kendall to P.J. Holdsworth, 5 March 1876, ML C199.
14 'I sincerely retract all that I may have said' (Frederick Kendall, *Henry Kendall, His Later Years*, p. 9).
15 Clarke, 'New light on Henry Kendall', p. 213.
16 ibid., p. 11. The house burned down in about 1900 (Wilding, *Wild Bleak Bohemia*, p. 440).
17 Cited in Swancott, *The Brisbane Water Story*, p. 30.
18 Ralph Waldo Emerson, 'The Poet', *Essays: Second Series* (1844), https://ebooks.adelaide.edu.au/e/emerson/ralph_waldo/e53e/part13.html
19 Charlotte Kendall to Alexander Sutherland, 6 September 1882 (Wilding, *Wild Bleak Bohemia* p. 442). Hamilton-Grey says in *Facts and Fancies* (pp. 45–6) that he would

'lean against a verandah post, in a patch of sunshine soaking up the warmth (a halfpenny clay pipe and tobacco his comfort)'. A few pages later she remarked that Charlotte thought he smoked 'a great deal too much', with the consequence of diminishing his already meagre appetite (p. 50). Frederick Kendall also remembered the clay pipe (*Henry Kendall, His Later Years*, p. 13).

20 Hamilton-Grey, *Poet Kendall*, p. 99.

21 'He was a most distressing sight as an equestrian. Mrs Kendall found much amusement in watching his start on his excursion, and laughed heartily at the poet's sorry figure, where others would have cried' (Hamilton-Grey, *Kendall, our 'God-made Chief'*, p. 114). Frederick Kendall took specific exception to this. What or who could have been Mrs Hamilton-Grey's source?

22 Frederick Kendall, *Henry Kendall, His Later Years*, pp. 9–10.

23 Charlotte Kendall to Alexander Sutherland, 6 September 1882; quoted in Wilding, *Wild Bleak Bohemia*, p. 442.

24 ibid., p. 17: 'When my father in one of his darker moods would adjourn to this resort it was only after the remonstrances and pleading of his wife had failed to restrain him'.

25 Ackland, *Henry Kendall*, p. 237.

26 Hamilton-Grey, *Kendall, our 'God-made Chief'*, p. 113.

27 A.G. Stephens, *Bulletin* diary, 20 May 1896, quoted Wilding, *Wild Bleak Bohemia*, p. 468.

28 See Henry Kendall, 'Arcadia at our gates', *Australian Town and Country Journal*, 27 February, 6 March 1876.

29 'Central Police Court', *Sydney Morning Herald*, 11 June 1878, p. 3.

30 Henry Kendall to Henry Halloran, 5 July 1879, ML 3775/9–11.

31 Henry Kendall to W.H. Traill, 15 February 1879, cited in Wilding, *Wild Bleak Bohemia*, p. 478.

32 ibid.

33 'The International Exhibition', *Sydney Morning Herald*, 5 July 1879, p. 3.

34 'The prize poem', *Sydney Morning Herald*, 17 September 1879, p. 5.

35 Ackland, *Henry Kendall*, p. 253.

36 Frank Myers, 'The other Kendall', *Bulletin*, 17 September 1903; quoted in Wilding, *Wild Bleak Bohemia*, p. 482.

37 Henry Kendall to Nathaniel Swan, 9 July 1880, NLA MS 3227.

38 Hamilton-Grey, *Poet Kendall*, p. 135. That is inconsistent with her own almost immediate admission that Charlotte liked 'Araluen' (p. 141). And in her *Facts and Fancies* she had written that 'He would read his poems (in the course of composition, sometimes) to his wife, who would be called away from her domestic work …' (p. 46).

39 Henry Halloran, 9 August 1869, Parkes Correspondence, ML A923, cited in Ackland, *Henry Kendall*, p. 247. Ackland's footnote to this indicates that Halloran may have been guilty of an omission of duty.

40 Kendall had a letter from Henniker Heaton about Halloran's 'mean reference to your want of classical education is disgraceful to one whom we regard or regarded as a gentleman in instincts' (2 October 1879, cited in Ackland, *Henry Kendall*, p. 317, n. 7). Kendall in turn referred to him as 'an ill-conditioned cat … His blood is turned to spleen with envy' (14 October 1879). Yet they maintained a nominal civility towards each other. Such is life.

41 'Mr Peter Fagan enlisted the influence of the late Rt. Hon. W.B. Dalley, and interviewed the late Sir Henry Parkes (then Premier) on his behalf, and the latter appointed him Forest Inspector' ('Obituary for Michael Fagan, J.P.', *Port Macquarie News and Hastings River Advocate*, 21 December 1912, p. 4). It may also be pertinent

that, according to A.G. Stephens ('Henry Kendall', *Bookfellow*, 15 December 1919), P.J. Holdsworth was Under-Secretary to the newly established Forestry Department.

42 Sir Henry Parkes to James Watson, 7 October 1880, cited in Wilding, *Wild Bleak Bohemia*, p. 500.

43 Henry Kendall to William Maddock, 12 December 1880; cited in Wilding, *Wild Bleak Bohemia*, p. 510.

44 Cited in Donovan Clarke, 'Kendall's views on contemporary writers: a survey of his correspondence', *Australian Literary Studies*, vol. 3, 1964, p. 171.

45 Harry Edwards, quoted in Ackland, *Henry Kendall*, p. 275.

46 W.B.D., 'Review', *Sydney Morning Herald*, 12 January 1881, p. 6.

47 Charlotte Kendall to Peter Fagan, ML 3775/9–11, quoted in Ackland, *Henry Kendall*, p. 276.

48 Hamilton-Grey, *Kendall, our 'God-made Chief'*, p. 143.

49 Frederick Kendall, 'Henry Kendall at Cundletown, 1881', *Manning River Times and Advocate*, 27 May 1939, p. 10.

50 Charlotte Kendall, January 1882, quoted in Ackland, *Wild Bleak Bohemia*, p. 282.

51 A.G. Stephens, *Bulletin* diary, 20 May 1896, quoted in Wilding, *Wild Bleak Bohemia*, p. 468.

52 ibid.

53 Hamilton-Grey, *Kendall, our 'God-made Chief'*, p. 146.

54 Ackland, *Henry Kendall*, p. 283. Ackland has also analysed Kendall's field notes, remarking how unusual it was for him to have revised the entries to improve the record, so as to conceal any mention of time spent at a 'roadside inn' (p. 285).

55 Frederick Kendall, 'Henry Kendall at Cundletown, 1881', p. 10.

56 At no. 137 Bourke St, where, according to Sands Directory for 1884, three of the brothers lived; see Fenton, *The Fagans*, p. 32.

57 Charlotte Kendall to Thomas Surfleet Kendall, 9 August 1882, NLA MS 3227.

58 Frederick Kendall, *Henry Kendall, His Later Years*, p. 19.

59 Charles Tovey, *Champagne: Its history, properties, and manufactures* (London, 1870) cited in Tilar Mazzeo, *The Widow Clicquot* (Collins, New York, 2008), p. 64.

60 Frederick Kendall, 'Henry Kendall at Cundletown, 1881', p. 10.

Chapter 11 ~ The After Life

1 Charlotte Kendall to Thomas Surfleet Kendall, 9 August 1882, NLA MS 3227.

2 'The Late Mr Henry Kendall', *Sydney Morning Herald*, 2 August 1882, p. 3.

3 Stephens, 'Kendalliana IV', p. 2.

4 Philip J. Holdsworth, 'Prefatory note', *Poems of Henry Kendall*, G. Robertson & Co., Melbourne, 1886, p. xvi.

5 Hamilton-Grey, *Kendall, our 'God-made Chief'*, p. 151.

6 ibid., p. 148.

7 Stephens, 'Kendalliana IV', p. 2.

8 'A poet's mother', *Sun*, 9 May 1915, p. 16; 'In Kendall's grave', *Daily Telegraph*, 4 September 1922, p. 6; 'Henry Lawson's mother', *Northern Champion* (Taree), 25 August 1920, p. 2.

9 'Kendall, the poet', *Evening News*, 18 December 1883, p. 6; copied from the Melbourne *Telegraph*.

10 'Kendall's monument', *Queanbeyan Age*, 11 December 1886, p. 2.

11 'Henry Kendall', *Australian Town and Country Journal*, 6 December 1884, p. 14.

12 Jill Dimond, '"From the lips of a lady": Mrs A.M. Hamilton-Grey's first biography of Henry Kendall', *Australian Literary Studies*, May 2004, p. 344.

13 See Alexandra Roginski, *The Hanged Man and the Body Thief*, Monash University Press, Clayton, Vic., 2015, pp. 74–5.
14 'Sparks', *Hawkesbury Chronicle and Farmers Advocate* (Windsor), 13 December 1884, p. 2.
15 Marcus Clarke, Preface to Gordon's *Sea Spray and Smoke Drift* (1867): 'What is the dominant note of Australian scenery? That which is the dominant note of Edgar Allan Poe's poetry – Weird Melancholy ... The Australian mountain forests are funereal, secret, stern. Their solitude is desolation. They seem to stifle, in their black gorges, a story of sullen despair ... In Australia alone is to be found the Grotesque, the Weird, the strange scribblings of nature learning how to write'.
16 'Miscellaneous Items', *Evening Standard*, 29 September 1883, p. 13.
17 Marjorie Kendall, 'Melinda Kendall: mother of Henry Kendall, poet', p. 64.
18 Peter Knox, in his extensive website on Melinda Kendall, speculates that she may have found her way to the recently established Central Methodist Mission, or at least to the Wesleyan Church; see 'Remembering Peter Knox', https://ninglundecember.files.wordpress.com/2008/02/knox-article.pdf
19 'Unveiling of the monument to Henry Kendall,' *Sydney Morning Herald*, 22 November 1886, p. 3.
20 Stephens, 'Kendalliana IV', p. 2.
21 'Henry Lawson's mother', *Northern Champion* (Taree), 25 August 1920, p. 2.
22 P.J. Holdsworth, 'Henry Kendall', *Burra Record*, 20 October 1882, p. 2. The publication in a rural South Australian newspaper is somewhat of a surprise. The article is not identified as copied from a more likely interstate source
23 Hamilton-Grey, *Kendall, our 'God-made Chief'*, p. 146.
24 Melinda Kendall, 'Henry Kendall (by his mother)', p. 4.
25 Ackland, *Henry Kendall*, pp. 283, 285–6. The detail about the champagne is in Charlotte's letter to Thomas Surfleet Kendall in the week following Kendall's death.
26 Brian Matthews, *Louisa*, McPhee Gribble, Melbourne, 1987, p. 149.
27 Lorna Oliff, *Louisa Lawson: Henry Lawson's crusading mother*, Rigby, Adelaide, 1978, p. 48.
28 Hamilton-Grey, *Kendall, our 'God-made Chief'*, p. 151.
29 Frederick Kendall, *Henry Kendall, His Later Years*, p. 6.
30 See Roginski, *The Hanged Man and the Body Thief*. He was an absconder (debts unpaid in Adelaide), a bigamist and a body thief – or at least he had the head of a hanged Aboriginal in his collection. He encouraged the public to think of him as a professor. And phrenology itself was no longer entirely respectable, though Prince Albert had had each of his children 'read'. The Hamiltons' lectures were advertised as 'Amusements'.
31 See Dimond, 'From the Lips of a Lady', pp. 337–49. Additionally, the two men were both Scottish-born, both had strangely sad eyes, both had enormous foreheads and both sported a walrus moustache. Hamilton though had a substantial Victorian beard. See the photograph in Roginski, opposite p. 34.
32 For example, Hamilton-Grey, *Poet Kendall*, pp. 149–50.
33 Reed, 'The life and poetical works of Henry Kendall', p. 27.

Index

A

Ackland, Michael 6–7, 22, 59, 66, 147, 199

Active 32–5

Aitken, James 78–9

Allan, John 95

Athenaeum 100–2

Australian Home Companion and Band of Hope Magazine 92–3, 95

Australian Journal 143

Australian Town and Country Journal 143, 178

B

Badham, Prof. Charles 96, 193–5

Banks, Sir Joseph 32, 42

Barker, Thomas 51, 56, 58–62, 66–7, 70; James 67–8

Barton, G.B. 101–2

Bass, George 32

Bay of Islands 3, 7, 10, 32, 34–6, 41, 43, 46–7, 49–51, 55, 57, 59, 108

Bellambi 62

Bennett, Rose 112–7, 119, 143, 179; Samuel 95, 112, 143, 179; Mrs 193–4

Bent, Judge Jeffrey Hart 15

Bentinck Chapel 27–9, 43

Béranger, Pierre-Jean 99

Biddell Brothers 90

Binney, Judith 3, 6, 29–30, 44–5, 57

Birkinshaw, Jim 71

Blackmore, Richard and *Lorna Doone* 74

Blaxland, John 82

Bowden, Thomas Wheaton 76, 90, 93, 114

Boyd 34

Brampton 45, 47, 50

Brereton, Dr John Le Gay 127–8

Brickfield Hill 89

Brisbane 100, 111, 151

Brisbane 58, 60–2

Brisbane Mills 67

Brisbane Water 153–4, 169

Bristol 28, 31

Brock, General Isaac 13, 15

Broker's Nose 83–4

Brooklyn 154

Browning, Elizabeth Barrett 99

Broxbornebury 15–6, 58, 202

Bulletin 134, 176, 185, 192–3

Bunyan, John, 29, 197; *The Pilgrim's Progress* 20, 85

Burns, Robert 194

Bury/Berry, Wilson 66–9

Bushy Park 78–9

Butler, Rev. John Gare 38–40, 42

Butler, Thomas 179–80

C
Calvinism 7, 29
Cambridge University 39
Camden Haven 3–4, 159, 167–72, 177–8, 184–5
Campbelltown 20, 82
Camperdown 90–1, 118
Canada 10, 12–5, 17, 52
Carrington, Lord and Lady 198
Castlereagh 17–8
Castlereagh Street (Sydney) 19–20, 63, 121
Cervantes, Miguel 185; Knight of the Woeful Countenance 131, 175
Chambly 13
Chile 46–7, 57–8, 74
Chisholm, Caroline 105–7
Church Missionary Society 3, 7, 10, [illegible]
Clarence River 75–7, 85, 97–8, 103–4, 110, 118, 149, 173, 185
Clarke, Donovan 153, 172
Clarke, Marcus 129, 132, 134, 141, 143, 196
Cochrane, Lord Thomas, Earl of Dundonald 57–8
Cockle Bay (Darling Harbour) 18, 51, 59
Conrad, Joseph 44
Cook, Captain James 31, 42
Cooks River 105–7, 116
Cooper, James Fenimore 14
Cooper, Robert 56
Cooranbean Creek 154
Cornhill Magazine 97, 100
Corrimal 88
Courier (Brisbane) 100, 190
Cowper, Charles 127
Cowper, Rev. William 66
Cox, Dr George 81
Crockett, Davy 15
Cromwell, Oliver 11
Cundletown 184–5
Currumbene Creek 61

D
Daley, Victor 130, 191
Dalley, William Bede 142, 147, 179–80, 183–5, 198–9
Darlinghurst Receiving House for Lunatics 143
Detroit 14
Dickens, Charles 27, 76, 79; *Nicholas Nickleby* 27, 29
Dimond, Jill 201–2
Dobie, John 76–7, 168
Donohue, Francis J. 1
Dublin 11, 14, 22, 24
Dunbar 91–2, 94–5
Dungog 104–5

E
[illegible]
Eliot, George (and 'Felix Holt') 194
Emerson, Ralph Waldo 2, 173; 'The Poet' 173
Emmet, Robert 22–4
Empire 94–5, 106, 112, 146
Enmore 105, 115
Esmeralda 58
Evans, Henry 114, 116–8, 120–1, 140, 172–3, 199
Evening News 193, 196–8, 202
Ewin, Joanne 71

F
Fagan, Charles 152–3, 156, 158–60, 164
Fagan, Edward 161
Fagan George 156, 160, 164–6, 168, 187–8
Fagan, Joe 156, 158, 160, 162, 165–6, 176
Fagan, Mary 160, 199
Fagan, Michael 159–60, 168–9, 176, 184
Fagan, Peter Sr 152–5, 159–60; Peter (son) 159–60, 162, 168, 183, 186–8, 200
Fagan, William 159–60, 162, 168
Fairy Meadow 9, 62, 81, 83, 88

Fitzgerald, Lord Edward 22, 24
Flinders, Matthew 32
Florance, Captain Richard 46–8
Florance, Thomas 48, 51–4, 60
Flower, Charlotte 82–3
Forester, C. S. 57
Franklin, Sir John 32
Freeman's Journal 1, 96, 147, 178–9, 192
Fulton, Rev. Henry 18

G
George III 23
George IV 40, 48
Gilmore, Mary 200
Gladesville Hospital for the Insane 127, 145, 147, 149–50, 168
Glebe 96, 117–8, 121, 202
Gordon, Adam Lindsay 129, 132, 134–7, 141, 144, 158, 178, 193; 'Ye Wearie Wayfarer' 91; *Bush Ballads and Galloping Rhymes* 135; suicide 135–6, 141
Gordon Brook 77
Gosford 9, 139, 152–4, 156, 160, 162, 167, 177
Grafton 4, 77–9, 97–100, 102–4, 106–10, 124, 149–51, 168–9: School of Arts 103–4
Green, H.M. 86
Greenway, Francis 15, 17; Mary 15
Grimsby 27

H
Hall, William 31–3, 35–6, 41, 43
Hallen, Ambrose 67
Halloran, Henry 102–3, 105–7, 112, 122, 128, 142, 179, 182–3
Hamilton, Archibald Sillars 201
Hamilton-Grey, Mrs Agnes 12–3, 20, 57, 74, 82, 85–6, 89, 94–5, 104, 114, 117–8, 122–3, 125–6, 135–6, 157–8, 160, 165, 170, 174, 176, 182, 187, 192, 195, 198, 200–1, 203
Hanmer, Thomas 157
Hanson, William 112, 114
Hardy, Thomas (*Return of the Native*) 201
Harpur, Charles 4, 102–3, 106, 124–6, 136, 159; 'A Midsummer Noon in the Australian Forest' 165
Harpur, Joseph 142
Harris, John 18
Hauraki Gulf 38
Heaton, Henniker 18, 178, 193–4, 200
Herd, Captain James 44, 50
Hibernia 20
Hill, Rev. Richard 19–22, 28, 48, 63–6, 75, 85, 93, 99, 154, 197; Mrs Phoebe (nee Kerrison) 20
Hindmarsh, Michael 83
Hogarth, William 29
Hokianga 44, 49
Holdsworth, P.J. 3, 130, 145, 161, 171–2, 176, 179, 187, 191, 194, 199, 202
Homer 91, 197
Hongi Hika 33, 37–43, 45, 49
Hordern's, Anthony 89
Horne, Richard 'Orion' 125–6, 129, 137
Horsley, Charles 137
Hugo, Victor 99
Humbug 134, 141
Hunt, Leigh 91
Hunter Valley 18, 77, 168; River 54, 66

I
Illawarra 3, 51–2, 55, 66, 83, 95, 101, 104, 149, 156, 177, 197–8
Illawarra Mercury 84, 94, 197

J
Jamberoo 95, 97
James Watt 69
Jamison, Sir John 15
Jerry's Wharf 169
Jervis Bay 53, 60

Jimbour 111, 127
Jordens, Ann-Mari 124

K

Keith, Jan 95
Kempsey 168
Kendall, Athol 178, 192
Kendall, Basil Edward 71–2, 84, 86–90, 93–5, 100, 105, 107–8, 111–2, 115, 119–20, 123, 127, 131, 141, 151, 157–8, 163
Kendall, Basil O. 3–4, 29, 51, 56–8, 60, 62, 64–79, 81–2, 85, 90, 93–4, 115, 125, 189, 196
Kendall, Caroline (nee Rutter) 54, 83, 115–6
Kendall, Charlotte (nee Rutter)
1. Sister of Caroline and Cecilia 83
2. Henry Kendall's wife 7, 8, 85, 116–20, 124, 128, 132–5, 138, 140, 144, 148, 151, 167, 169, 170–2, 174–8, 181–2, 184–92, 195, 198–203
Kendall, Edith Emily 76, 82, 94, 105, 114, 116–8, 140, 149, 172–3, 177, 184, 202–3
Kendall, Edward
1. Brother to Thomas, 26
2. Son of Thomas 72–4
Kendall, Elizabeth 48, 51–2
Kendall, Frank 147
Kendall, Frederick 22, 89, 101, 113, 118, 140, 143, 156, 158, 171–2, 175–6, 186–9, 191, 200, 203
Kendall, Henry 2, 75, 77; whaling voyage 86–8; in Newtown 88–97; begins submitting poems 92 ff.; taken up by Sheridan Moore and the Stenhouse circle 95–7; to Grafton with Lionel Michael 98–104; Cook's River 105–7; with Halloran in the public service 105–112; with Parkes in Colonial Secretary's office 112–126; Rose Bennett 112–114; money problems 112, 114–7, 119–21; return to Sydney 139 and erratic behaviour 140–2; after release from Gladesville walks from Newcastle to Gosford and stays with the Fagans 152–67; Camden Haven 169–84, reunited with Charlotte 172; Sydney Exhibition prize poem 180–2; Cundletown 184–6, Inspector of Forests 185
birth and baptism 71–2, 75
education 3, 78, 81, 84–6, 97, 137, 183
reading 3–4, 86, 91, 99
Melbourne 5, 7, 128–38
committal and the Shadow of 1872 5, 141–3, 145–9
wedding 117–8
death 188–90
obituaries 1, 190
poems – 'Araluen' 8, 133–4, 'Bell Birds' 5, 117, 162, 'Beyond Kerguelen' 87–8, 'Black Lizzie' 178, 'Christmas Creek' 184, 'A death in the bush' 79, 120, 'Dedication' 7–8, 133, 'Dungog' 125, 'Elijah' 143–4, 'Euterpe' 137, 141, 'The far future' 93, 'The glen of Arrawatta' 126, 'Keira' 94, 'The merchant ship' 91–2, 94, 'The muse of Australia' 9, 'Names upon a stone' 165–6, 'Orara – a tale' 126, 'Rose Lorraine' 114, 'The voice in the wild oak' 161
Poems and Songs (1862) 101–2, *Leaves from Australian Forests* (1869) 4, 8, 132, *Songs from the Mountains* (1880) 181, 183, 185
Kendall, (Christina) Jane 72, 82, 88, 105, 140, 177, 184, 197, 202
Kendall, Jane (nee Quickfall) 27, 36, 41, 43–5, 47–8, 54, 60–1, 92, 112
Kendall, John 47, 53, 58, 67–70, 72–4, 92
Kendall, Joseph 46, 51, 57, 59–60, 62, 81, 86–8
Kendall, Lizzie (Violet) Araluen 8, 127, 133–4, 143, 145, 164, 169, 187
Kendall, (Mary) Josephine 72, 82–3, 91, 105–7, 112, 119, 140, 177
Kendall, Lawrence 58, 67, 69–70, 82

Kendall, Marjorie 19–20, 66, 73, 75
Kendall, Matilda or Melinda (nee McNally) 3, 17–21, 28, 63–6, 68, 70–3, 75–7, 79–85, 88, 90–1, 94–5, 97, 105–6, 109, 111, 115–8, 120–3, 126, 129, 131, 154, 158, 164, 177, 192, 196–9, 202–3; 'McAllan' 64, 72
Kendall, Orara 187–9
Kendall, Persia 192, 198
Kendall, Roma 180, 198
Kendall, Samuel 36, 48
Kendall, Susanna 48, 51, 76, 92–3
Kendall, Rev. Thomas 3, 6–7, 10, 16, 26–57, 59–62, 66, 72, 99, 111, 194
Kendall, Thomas Surfleet 45, 49–51, 54, 59, 62, 70, 72, 74, 82–3, 93, 114–5, 188; Happy Villa 54
Kendall's Cottage 153, 160
Kendall Dale 54, 61, 70, 75
Kennilworth Lodge 92
Kent Street (Sydney) 18, 20–1, 59, 62
Kerguelen 87
Kerikeri 38–9, 44, 49
Kiama 54, 61, 70, 74, 82–3, 95, 97, 112
King, John 31–2, 35
Kirmington (UK) 27; (Ullladulla) 60, 70–1, 74
Kitchen, Henry 17
Kororareka (Russell) 37, 45

L

Lautaro 58
Lawson, Henry 3, 90, 200
Lawson, Louisa 90, 113, 192–6, 198, 200
Leatherstocking 14
Lee, Prof. Samuel 39–40, 56
Lee, Captain William 88
Leichhardt, Ludwig 111, 127
Lincolnshire 10, 26, 60
Liverpool 16, 19, 58, 70, 145
Logan's wine shop 176, 184
London 20–1, 23, 27–9, 40, 43, 58, 97–8, 101, 108
London Missionary Society 30
Longfellow, Henry 86

M

Maddock, William 191
Madison, President James 15
Maitland 77, 108, 151, 153
Mandnal 70, 90
Maori 3, 6, 30–5, 37–47, 49, 55–6, 59, 74
Maranoa 112, 158
Marryat, Frederick 57
Manning, Dr Frederick 149
Marsden, Rev Samuel 10, 18, 21, 30–4, 36, 38–42, 45–6, 50, 55–7, 59–60, 62; Mamre 18
Martens, Conrad 108
Marylebone 21, 27–9
Massey, Gerald 193–6
Matauwhi 45, 49
Matthews, Brian 200
Mauritius 87
McArthur, Rev G. F. 191
McCrae, George Gordon 125–6, 130–1, 135, 156, 159, 179, 184
McNally, Eliza 15, 17
McNally, John 18
McNally (nee Kilfroy, or McDermott), Judith 13–8, 20–1, 81
McNally, Leonard 22–5
McNally, Matilda (Melinda) see Kendall, Matilda
McNally, Mary 12–3, 17, 62–3, 83–4, 88; and James Martin 62–3, 84
McNally, Patrick 10–22, 24–6, 47, 51–2, 59, 62, 81, 83–5, 88, 95, 131, 149, 156, 192, ('James') 203
McNally, Sarah 18
McNally, William 13, 17, 62, 83
Macquarie, Governor Lachlan 17, 21, 34–5

Melbourne 88, 118, 125, 127–32, 134, 136–42, 144–5, 151, 155, 158, 160–1, 169, 178, 193
Melville, Ninian 183–4
Michael, James Lionel 4, 96–106, 110, 112, 124–5, 136, 150, 163–4, 171, 181; wife 98–9, 106, 110, 164; son Jemmy 106, 109–10, 164
Millard, George 86
Milton, John (*Paradise Lost*) 75
Minerva 16
Mitchell, Thomas 52–3
Mollymook 52
Moore, Sir John 12
Moore, J. Sheridan 92, 95–8, 101, 124, 141–2, 147, 162–4, 167, 170–1, 179, 192
Moore, T. Inglis 99
Mutch, T.D. 66

N

Napoleon 10–2, 26, 57
Narara Creek 152–4
Narrawallee 52–3
Neild, Dr J.E. 118, 129, 133
Newcastle 4, 150–3, 156
Newfoundland 12
New South Wales 3, 10, 16–7, 20, 31, 37, 48, 51–2, 98, 101, 147, 153, 195, 202
Newtown 3, 88, 90, 95, 97–8, 104–6, 112, 118
New York 10, 13, 15
New Zealand 3, 10, 30–5, 37–8, 40–1, 45–7, 49–50, 52, 56–7, 59–60, 62, 84, 87, 107–8, 170
Ngatiwhatua 38
Niagara Falls 15
Nicholas, John Lidiard 33
Nightingale, Florence 13
North Somercotes 27
North Thoresby 26, 27, 29
Norwich, Bishop of 40
Nova Scotia 12
Nugent, Christopher 48

O

O'Brian, Patrick 57
Orara Creek 77–9, 173, 185
Osgathorpe 127–8

P

Parkes, (Sir) Henry 8, 102, 112, 114, 117, 125–6, 129, 142, 145, 182–3, 192
Parramatta 50, 76, 191; Road 67, 139
Paterson, 'Banjo' 3
Pigeon House Mountain 60, 71
Pitt Town 10, 17
Plumstead 86–8
Polding, Archbishop John Bede 96
Pope, Alexander 91
Port Macquarie 110, 176
Portland, Dukes of 28–9
Portsmouth Harbour 16
Powell, John 50 ; John Vittoria Powell 50, 54
Pratt, Rev. Josiah 29
Prince Alfred 182
Prince Regent's County of Dublin Regiment of Foot (100th) 11, 14
Providence 44, 50
Punch 103, 124, 126, 141, 146–7, 180

Q

Quebec 10, 13, 15
Queenston Heights 15
Quickfall, Jane – *see* Jane Kendall

R

Rakau 41, 43
Ramornie 77
Rangihoua 34, 42, 44
Reed, Bishop T.T. 5–7, 19, 81, 92
Reid, George Houston 202
Remenyi, Edouard 194

Retreat Farm 54, 82
Richmond (Melbourne) 131–2
Richmond Hill 23–4
Ridd, Mary Jane and John 74
Robertson, George 132
Roscommon 10–1, 13–4, 26
Rouse, Henry William 48
Ruatara 34–5
Rutter, Charlotte – *see* Charlotte Kendall
Rutter, Frank 117, 140, 171
Rutter, William 82–3

S
Sackets Harbour 13
Santiago 48
Savage, John 31
Schumann, Robert 4
Selwyn, Rev. Augustus 107, 114; Mrs Rose Selwyn 107–11, 149
Shelley, Percy Bysshe 99, 104, 199
Shoalhaven 16, 74, 89
Smith, Vivian 4–5
Society of United Irishmen 11–2, 22, 24
St James' Church 48, 75
St Matthews, Windsor 17
St Patrick 46–7
St Peters 3, 94, 116
Stenhouse, Nicol D. 96, 101–3, 124, 142; Mrs Stenhouse 163
Stephens, A.G. 22, 112, 115, 123, 129–30, 176, 191–3, 196
Stephens, James Brunton 184
Stevens, Bertram 22, 57, 65, 95, 111
Stockwell, Richard 31, 36–7, 39
Surrey 10, 15–6
Sutherland, Alexander 22, 72, 74, 78–80, 86, 116, 121, 123, 131–3, 150, 169, 174–5, 189, 191
Swancott, Charles 160
Sydney Gazette 56, 66, 69
Sydney Mail 178, 193
Sydney Morning Herald 95, 105, 107, 117, 143, 177, 179–80, 190
Sydney School of Arts 96, 116, 194

T
Tahiti 30–1, 56
Talgai 157–8
Tasman Sea 33, 44–5
Tecumseh 14
Telegraph (Melbourne) 193
Tennyson, Alfred Lord 86, 102, 126, 131, 158
Thatcher, Richmond 191
Tindale, William 139–40, 142, 144
Tone, Wolfe 14, 22–3
Tower of London 40
Trafalgar 12
Tungaroa 43–4, 48, 50
Turner, H.G. 136

U
Ulladulla 52–3, 55–6, 70, 75, 82, 90, 105, 157
Ultimo 202
United Empire Loyalists 14

V
Valparaiso 46–7, 49–51, 56–8
Vauxhall Gardens 23
Verde, Cape 15

W
Wagga Wagga 187
Waikato (chief) 39–41, 44
Waitangi 34–5
Washington 14
Waterwitch 86–8
Waverley Cemetery 191–2, 196, 198–9
Wentworth, William 41, 56
Wesley, Charles 21, 28, 32, 62; John 28
Whangaroa 44

White, Patrick 111
Wilde, W.H. 153
Wilding, Michael 7
William III 11
Williams's Illustrated Australian Annual competition 125
Windham 58
Wollongong 62, 81, 83, 85, 88
Woodd, Rev. Basil 28–30, 36
Woollahra 92
Woolley, Prof. John 96, 99, 102
Woolloomooloo 126
Woolwich, Royal Arsenal 40
Wooster, Commander Charles 57–8
Wordsworth, William 2, 81, 99, 105

Y

Yatte Yatta 71
Yorick Club 129–30, 135, 137

Also by Adrian Mitchell, from Wakefield Press

Drawing the Crow

A South Australian point of view, or a set of South Australian eyes, recalling growing up through the fifties, in a perfectly ordinary home, in a perfectly ordinary suburb, and rediscovering the richness of it

Dampier's Monkey

The late-17th century ways of comprehending an expanding world are re-evaluated from the travel narratives of the buccaneer William Dampier. Included in this book is Dampier's journal of his voyage in the South Seas from 1681 to 1691, published here for the first time.

Plein Airs and Graces

This biography examines the extraordinary life of George Collingridge de Tourcey, a landscape painter of the late nineteenth century, just ahead of the Australian impressionists. When migrated to Australia he grew passionate about his new country, and worked tirelessly to contribute to it.

The Profilist

Adrian Mitchell paints a compelling picture of the early years of the Australian colonies, in the imagined voice of the artist Samuel Thomas Gill – or someone very like him.

From Corner to Corner

Henry Colless was one of the old pioneers. In his mid-teens he set out as a carrier across the Blue Mountains and then further to the northwest. He was one of the early settlers in Bourke, and later became one of its leading lights. This is his story.

The Beachcomber's Wife

The Beachcomber's Wife draws upon the published writings of E.J. Banfield, who lived an isolated life with his wife Bertha on Dunk Island. He made very little reference to her in his work. This account imagines what it might have been like from her point of view.

Peat Island

For just over 100 years an institution for the mentally ill has stood on little Peat Island, in the lower Hawkesbury. It was decommissioned in 2010; quite empty now, it remains a locked facility just as it had always been. And eerie.

Printed in Australia
AUHW010323301020
336397AU00002B/2

9 781743 057483